AN INTRODUCTION TO

THE LAW RELATING TO THE HEALTH CARE PROFESSIONS

Studies in Law and Practice for Health Service Management
(ISSN 0263–8630)

AN INTRODUCTION TO

THE LAW RELATING TO THE HEALTH CARE PROFESSIONS

P F C BAYLISS
LL.B., M.B., Ch.B., M.R.C.P.(Lond)

RAVENSWOOD PUBLICATIONS
P.O. Box No. 24, Beckenham, Kent BR3 3AL, England

Published by
Ravenswood Publications Ltd.

P.O. Box No. 24,
Beckenham, Kent BR3 3AL, England

Published 1987

Printed in Great Britain by
Biddles Ltd., Guildford, Surrey

British Library Cataloguing in Publication Data
Bayliss, P. F. C.
An introduction to the law relating to the health care professions.
— (Studies in law and practice for health service management,
ISSN 0263–8630)
1. Medical laws and legislation — England
I. Title II. Series
344.204'41 KD2945

ISBN 0-901812-63-3 – hard cover
ISBN 0-901812-64-1 – soft cover

Contents

Preface

Doctors, dentists, nurses and all the thousands of members of other health care professions are subject not only to the ordinary laws of the land but to additional laws which, if broken, can be devastating in their repercussions.

These additional laws are those of their professions. Disciplinary tribunals can sit in judgement on an individual's conduct and, by removing his name from a professional register, strip him of his livelihood and possibly the last vestige of personal and professional self-respect. Such are the laws which necessarily safeguard the interests of the professions and the people they serve.

Members of the armed forces, accountants, estate agents, clergymen and lawyers are also subject to particular laws drawn up by statutory bodies entrusted by Parliament with the government of their respective occupations.

This book deals with the health care professions which, in addition to doctors, dentists, nurses and midwives, cover pharmacists, opticians, hearing aid dispensers, chiropodists, dieticians, medical laboratory technicians, occupational therapists, physiotherapists, radiographers, orthoptists and auxiliary dental workers. Because the veterinary profession is regulated in a similar manner, a chapter on this group is also included.

There are about 700,000 people in this country who come into the category of these health care professions. The table below shows the number of individuals registered in the various professions using information available at the beginning of 1987.

Nurses	441,079
Doctors	126,448
Midwives	90,590
Pharmacists	35,581

Dentists	24,592
Medical Laboratory Scientific Officers	19,400
Physiotherapists	18,900
Radiographers	14,209
Health Visitors	11,570
Veterinary Surgeons	11,500
Occupational Therapists	8,559
Ophthalmic Opticians	6,531
Chiropodists	5,789
Dispensing Opticians	3,208
Dieticians	2,352
Orthoptists	948
Hearing Aid Dispensers	612

Control of the health care professions is by no means a modern phenomenon at least not in principle. The code of Hammurabi, for instance, written in Mesopotamia 4,000 years ago, included strict laws governing physicians. They left him little room for error if he was to continue his career. He was to be paid ten shekels of silver if he cured a nobleman's wound but have *his* hand cut off if his treatment caused the nobleman's death. Since then single-handed practice has, happily, taken on a different meaning.

The laws under which members of the health care professions work are concerned not only with their professional conduct but also with the extent to which a certain profession may be practised only by individuals on a register and with the nature and quality of the training and experience required for registration.

The existence of such a separate and additional body of law raises some important general issues. For example, what powers should be entrusted to any professional tribunal outside the ordinary system of law courts? To what extent is it acceptable for bodies outside Parliament to make rules which have the full force of law? Such issues are discussed in this book, and the controls that exist to prevent the excessive use of such powers are described.

The book is divided into two parts. Part I deals with the main aspects of the legislation, topic by topic, and draws on examples from all of the professions dealt with. Part II gives a more detailed presentation of the law, profession by profession. It is suggested that all readers should read Part I together with the chapter in Part II relevant to their profession.

Although this is a book about the law it is not written primarily for lawyers but for the professionals who are directly affected by it. It is essentially a full introduction to the subject rather than a legal practitioner's reference book. Any health care professional who finds himself at variance with this body of law would be well advised to seek expert help and advice.

There is no good time to write a legal text, and during the period this book was being researched and written major new law was enacted dealing with the medical profession (the Medical Act 1983), with dentists (The Dentists Act 1984) and with nurses and midwives (the Nurses, Midwives and Health Visitors Act 1979). The law in this professional area does change fairly frequently and this may be seen as a healthy sign. The law stated in this book represents the sources to hand at the beginning of 1987.

It is hoped the book will be of interest and value to all members of the professions covered, anyone training for one of these professions, lawyers seeking an introduction to the subject, and anyone else with an interest in the control of the health care professions.

P. F. C. Bayliss

July 1987

Acknowledgements

I should like to thank Dr. W. A. J. Farndale, general editor of this series for his help and encouragement in writing this book and, as always, my wife for her constant support.

P. F. C. Bayliss

July 1987

Table of Statutes and Bills

List of Statutory Instruments

Table of EEC Directives

List of Cases

List of Reports

PART I

Chapter One

Review of Legal, Historical and Social Aspects

Historical Background

Most of the ancient civilisations had a variety of codes controlling professional practice, but in this country the development of our modern system of control can be dated from the appearance of the ancient guilds.

The City of London guilds first appeared almost 1,000 years ago, the earliest written charter being granted by Edward the Confessor who died in 1066. They were essentially brotherhoods of members of a trade, usually governed by a Council of 12 men elected from their numbers. The main privileges of each guild were to enjoy a monopoly over its particular trade in the city, to hold property and to exercise a power of discipline and punishment over its members, and over non-members who infringed its rights. The guilds controlled entry to their trades by use of apprenticeships, and they guarded their trade secrets closely. As their influences and privileges grew disputes broke out between them over certain areas which each claimed as its own. For instance, in 1226 the goldsmiths and the tailors decided to settle a dispute by a battle with 500 members on each side; the ringleaders, however, were arrested and 13 were executed.

Many of the principles of the guilds will be found in the modern-day legislation which controls the health care professions. There is an attempt to delineate each profession one from another, to regulate admission to it by means of a common standard of training, to exercise a disciplinary power over its members in their professional practice and to punish unauthorised practice. Problems of overlap between professions still cause occasional difficulties, although resort to massed battle with 500 aside has been replaced by less militant means of solution. An apparent difference between the form of control exercised by the guilds and that used today is that the guilds regulated their activities from within the brotherhood and now it is Parliament which creates the framework of controls. The professional bodies, however, still have great powers to make specific rules which have the force of law and to exert disciplinary powers.

Later Developments

As will be seen later in this chapter, the present-day legal controls over the health care professions have developed over the last 100 to 140 years. This has been associated partly with a more rapid evolution of these professions over that period and partly with the growth of a more systematic approach to public health from the early nineteenth century, culminating in the modern-day health services. However, a brief account needs to be given of the long gap in time from the days of medieval guilds to the nineteenth century.

This time gap may be thought of in two overlapping phases. In the first phase, from the Norman Conquest to the sixteenth or seventeenth centuries, there was relatively little scientific or technical development in the various health care professions which then existed. The guild system controlled the practice of medicine, surgery and dentistry, the monasteries acted as hospitals and provided a nursing service to the sick and the poor, and midwifery was essentially a domestic art passed from mother to daughter. Such development as did occur over this period really amounted to no more than the consolidation of existing practices.

The second phase, however, was a period of rapid scientific and technical growth dating from the Renaissance. The disciplines of anatomy, physiology, medicine, surgery and pharmacy developed rapidly in parallel with the sciences of chemistry, physics and botany (the sole source of materia medica at the time). This period was followed in the nineteenth century by many improvements in public health as the infective nature of much disease (the germ theory) became increasingly recognised. It was this nineteenth century phase that set the scene for the development of today's legislation.

Later in this chapter a brief historical introduction will be given to each of the professions dealt with. The bibliography at the end of this book suggests sources where the reader can obtain fuller accounts of these historical aspects.

Legal and Social Problems

The ways in which the present controls over the health care professions are exercised give rise to certain problems or potential problems. These can be divided mainly into legal and social or sociological problems.

Legal Problems

There are two broad legal problems. One relates to the power which the controlling bodies have been given to make rules carrying the full force of law. The other concerns their disciplinary powers.

Rule-making powers English history, and in particular English legal history, has seen the law-making process become the prime function of a democratically elected Parliament. This contrasts with earlier days when the Sovereign had an arbitrary and total power to make laws, sometimes complicated by the delegation of such powers to his barons in return for payment. The concept of Parliament supremacy in legislative matters requires not only that Parliament may make and change laws but that no-one else has such a power. It was this latter aspect which led to the struggle in the seventeenth century with the King's claim to make laws by order and proclamation in addition to Parliament's legislative powers. Finally, Parliament was successful and today the Crown's legislative powers are very limited.

However, an important power of the controlling bodies of the health care professions we are considering is to make rules which have the full force of law over members. Such power may seem to be contrary to Parliamentary supremacy, but only Parliament can give this power and a wide variety of controls and checks ensures that the power is not abused. This type of non-Parliamentary law-making is called delegated legislation and will be considered in more detail later.

Disciplinary power Just as legal history has seen the centralisation of the law-making process to a democratically elected Parliament, it has also seen the development of a single system of law courts. This contrasts with the ancient system in which every lord had his own court where he dispensed his own version of justice. A single judicial system is part of the concept called the rule of law. There are many aspects to this idea, but one of the meanings as defined by A. V. Dicey, Professor of Law at Oxford University in the late nineteenth century, is: "The absolute supremacy or predominance of regular law as opposed to the influence of arbitrary power, and excludes the existence of arbitrariness or prerogative or even of wide discretionary authority on the part of the government. (A man may be punished for a breach of law, but he can be punished for nothing else.)"

The bodies which control the professions we are considering have wide disciplinary powers. They require all members to conduct themselves in a professional manner, although nowhere do they, or can they, supply a precise and all-encompassing definition of what such conduct is or is not. They enable the controlling bodies to punish someone found guilty of professional misconduct by striking his name off the register, thus depriving him of his livelihood. It is a situation in which a person is subject to some degree of arbitrary judicial power as no clear "offence" is defined. He is punished by a loss of livelihood, not for a breach of the ordinary law but for breaking a special type of professional law relating to conduct. The way in which this disciplinary power is exercised and the controls and checks on it are the subject of Chapter Six.

Natural Justice

While considering professional discipline and the rule of law another relevant legal concept may be introduced, and that is natural justice. Natural justice is seen to be a basic requirement for any judicial process if it is to be fair, equitable and just. The High Court will intervene in the activities of any disciplinary body which acts contrary to the rules of natural justice. There are two basic rules: firstly, that no man may be a judge in his own cause (nemo judex in parte sua) and, secondly, that no man may be condemned without a proper hearing (audi alteram partem). The objective is always to ensure that proceedings before the disciplinary tribunals are as just as they would be in the ordinary courts of law.

Social and Sociological Problems

Because of the very special relationship that the health care professions must have with the public, and vice versa, there are many social and sociological aspects to this subject. The aim of this book is to outline the law in this area rather than take a sociological approach, but this aspect cannot be entirely ignored. The following is a brief introduction to some of the more important social and sociological aspects.

Public vs Professional Interests

The controls which the old guild system operated over the trades were very much directed to the protection of their own interests. The basic concept of modern legislation in health care professions is the protection of the general public as patients or as the owners of sick animals. The requirements for high standards of professional training and professional conduct and the limitation of practice in some instances to fully qualified individuals are all evidence of this concept of public protection. However, this leads to the problem that, although Parliament has imposed controls, the management and execution of such controls are very much the responsibility of the professions themselves rather than of any independent consumer-type body. This has been justified on the grounds that in highly technical areas, such as professional training or conduct, only members of that profession are competent to reach opinions and make recommendations. It is also claimed that members of a profession tend to be more rather than less critical and discerning in such matters than lay people, and clearly control from one's peers is more acceptable to any professional person. The actual direct influence that lay people have in professional control is limited to the occasional representation on some professional councils, such as the General Medical Council, and the important ability to submit a complaint of professional misconduct directly to the professional disciplinary machinery. The paradox still remains, however, that while the interests of the public are the main objective of the controls the public have very little direct part to play.

Professional Conduct

An example of the potential clash between public and professional interests received wide debate in 1984. A doctor was charged before the General Medical Council with three counts of failing to treat, examine and recommend hospital treatment for an eight-year old boy who subsequently died of meningitis. Although the facts were proven the GMC found the doctor not guilty of serious professional misconduct. There was a public outcry and the GMC was criticised for being too ready to see cases of dishonesty or sexual lapses on the part of doctors as serious misconduct yet unwilling to punish negligent medical practice. The member of Parliament for the constituency in which the dead boy lived (Mr Nigel Spearing MP) introduced a Private Member's Bill – the Medical Act 1983 (Amendment) Bill, which proposed to modify section 36 of the 1983 Medical Act so that where a doctor has "behaved in a manner which cannot be regarded as acceptable professional conduct", the Committee may make that doctor's registration subject to conditions (see Chapter Seven for conditional registration).

The Department of Health wrote to the GMC seeking its views on Mr Spearing's Bill. The president, Sir John Walton, replied that he believed the existing Medical Act was fully adequate to protect the public, and that the Spearing Amendment would mean that a doctor guilty of unacceptable professional conduct would automatically be subject to conditional registration, whereas a doctor guilty of serious professional misconduct might be subject to a lesser penalty such as an admonition. The Council set up its own working party which recommended additional guidelines in a pamphlet on professional conduct which it issues to all doctors. These additional guidelines (Professional Conduct and Discipline: Fitness to Practise, GMC April 1987) emphasise a doctor's professional medical responsibility to his patient and therefore, where breached, will make the doctor liable to disciplinary action under the existing legislation.

The effect of these changes remains to be seen but a lay member of the GMC, Mrs Jean Robinson, emphasised that the medical profession could only be allowed to continue to judge itself if the public saw that it did it properly.

Restrictive Practices

The old guild system was clearly a restrictive practice creating a monopoly for a certain trade within a certain geographical area. This feature is certainly found in some of the health care professions which are "closed" professions, that is, professions restricted to properly qualified and registered individuals. Not all the professions we are dealing with are "closed" and surprisingly, while midwifery and veterinary surgery are limited to registered professionals, the practice of medicine is not. The original Victorian legislation relating to the medical profession had the stated objective of permitting the public to determine by reference to a register whether a doctor had achieved a certain level of training so that they were then free to choose whether to consult him or not. The situation is still basically the same today.

While it might be argued that a monopoly of medical and surgical practice by properly qualified and registered doctors would be a very desirable thing socially, monopolies in some other health care areas have come under criticism. The legislation controlling the opticians' profession, introduced in 1958, limited among other things the sale of spectacles to registered practitioners only. This monopoly, unique to this country, was often blamed, among other things, for the increasing price of non-NHS spectacles which made up about half of those sold. The situation, it was claimed, was made worse by a professional ban on advertising to the public which restricted competition and thus kept prices high. However, the rules about advertising were somewhat relaxed in 1981 to permit prices to be displayed in opticians' windows.

A Bill to end the opticians' monopoly of selling spectacles was introduced in 1981 by Lord Rugby (the Opticians Act 1958 (Amendment) Bill) and appeared to have considerable support. However, when it became clear that the Government was determined to keep the existing law and place its hopes for reform on a review by the Director of Fair Trading, Lord Rugby withdrew his Bill. In addition, the Government was trying to extend the range of spectacles available on the NHS. The main argument for the monopoly is to provide some sort of expert screening for eye disease as and when spectacles are sold. However, medical opinion about the value of this is divided, one expert medical ophthalmologist being quoted in 1980 commenting: "It's like saying that only chiropodists can fit shoes." The opticians' monopoly on selling spectacles was eventually dismantled (with exceptions and conditions) in December 1984 (See Chapter Two).

Personal Freedoms and Fringe Areas

The limitation of aspects of professional practice to qualified and registered individuals may be seen as a restriction of the freedom of others to act. Whereas carrying out surgical operations on animals may reasonably be restricted to veterinary surgeons in a modern society, many might pause to think about a law which convicts a father who delivers his own child where his wife was unwilling to go into hospital and her general practitioner refused to attend a home delivery (see page 56). Consideration of this aspect is further complicated by the fact that the practice of human medicine and surgery is not limited to registered, or even qualified, practitioners.

Alternative systems of medicine, such as acupuncture, naturopathy, herbalism, hakims and so on, may be practised freely by all, whatever their training and qualifications, provided they do not claim to have qualifications they do not have and provided they do not handle dangerous drugs, restricted medicinal products or poisons. Such alternative medical systems appear presently to be on the increase.

The problem is essentially twofold. Firstly, there needs to be a sensible and flexible boundary between any profession and the public's freedom to act so that account may be taken on the one hand of the evolution of new approaches to health care (for example, the shift from home confinements to hospital deliveries) and on the other the appearance of new alternative systems. Secondly, there is the obvious problem that making a closed profession of something like selling spectacles will always look inconsistent while no restriction is placed on the practice of human medicine itself.

Future Trends and the EEC

The law covering the health care professions is not static. There has recently been major new legislation concerning the medical and dental professions and also nursing and midwifery. Such things are inevitable and indeed desirable as the science and technology which underpin the various practices develops and as attitudes to the social aspects of health care change. Certain possible future trends have already been suggested above. They include a possible restriction of medical practice to qualified doctors, a tendency to de-restrict certain trading aspects of practice, such as has happened with the selling of spectacles, and possibly a move towards more lay involvement in professional control.

However, one trend which has already begun and is likely to continue is that towards internationalism, at least within the European Economic Community. The basis of the Treaty of Rome, which established the EEC, is the concept of freedom of trade within the Community. In the context of the health care professions this means a freedom for any professional to practise in any member state. While this position has not yet been reached, arrangements already exist whereby doctors, dentists, nurses and veterinary surgeons qualified in one member state may practise in another. This trend to a more international or European approach to professional control is likely to continue, although it inevitably brings problems with it, such as the basic and historical differences between approaches to health care in the member states and indeed the simple problem of language.

Another possible future trend, of which there is already some evidence, is that of specialist registration. Generally, the United Kingdom legislation recognises a basic professional qualification but does not single out further specialisation in that profession. In Europe the concept of specialist registration is stronger, and with the trend towards the harmonisation of these laws in Europe this concept may well develop in this country.

General Organisation of the Modern Legislation

The modern legislation controlling the health care professions is all constructed on similar lines, although some variations exist which are important in certain instances. In all cases a body is created with the function of controlling and governing the profession within the frameworks provided by the parent Act of Parliament. Membership of each profession is defined by a system of registration of names, and the process of registration is based on the acquisition of a basic standard of training and a recognised qualification. The governing body therefore has an important controlling function in connection with professional education. The legislation will prescribe whatever limitation on professional practice is enacted, and disciplinary machinery will be created. Each of these five functions is dealt with in Chapters Two to Six, but summaries of them are given here.

The Controlling Bodies

The various controlling or governing bodies for the health care professions were either created specifically for the purpose or inherited their functions from a previous professional body. Either way, the controlling bodies are usually elected by the membership of the profession, although they do have members nominated to represent other interests such as the educational institutions, the general public or other related professions. They have wide functions. They are responsible for the registration process, for standards of professional education and for the disciplinary process, and, under their parent Act of Parliament, have the power to make rules which carry the force of law. To do all of this they clearly have important management and executive roles. Generally speaking, they are self-financing from fees charged for registration or retention of a name on the register. Because of their extensive powers they are watched over by the Privy Council (see page 35) which may intervene if it finds the controlling body to be in default.

Registration

Because membership of a certain profession will confer privileges and impose responsibilities it is necessary to have an unequivocal system of definition. The one that is used is registration. Each professional group maintains a register or a set of registers which are kept fully up to date. The presence of a name on a register is legal evidence that that person is a member of the said profession and attracts the appropriate privileges and responsibilities of that profession. Because of the important evidential value of the registers, steps are taken to ensure that the contents of the registers are fully available to the public, and generally they are accepted without question by courts of law. It is a criminal offence to obtain a fraudulent registration. As indicated above, the registration system is the main source of income to finance all aspects of professional control.

Registration is normally obtained by undergoing a recognised course of training at a training institution in the United Kingdom and passing the prescribed examination. Sometimes a period of additional practical experience is required. Professionals who have qualified overseas may be able to obtain registration in the United Kingdom if the controlling body has recognised their overseas qualification. Otherwise, further training and/or examination may have to be completed in this country. As far as the European Community is concerned, any national of a member state who has obtained certain qualifications in an EEC country is entitled to be registered in the United Kingdom in the professions of medicine, dentistry, nursing, midwifery or veterinary surgery.

Professional Education

An important function of the controlling bodies is setting and maintaining high standards of professional training. This is clearly of great significance as far as their role of protecting the public is concerned. Although, as noted above, the system of registration is, generally speaking, based on the completion of an approved course of training, the controlling bodies have, in fact, considerable powers either to approve training institutions, courses and examinations or to recommend their approval. Refusal to approve, or removal of an approval, is a powerful sanction to bring about improvements in any training system which is sub-standard. A professional training school whose qualifications no longer entitled a holder to registration would soon find itself without students. To monitor standards the controlling bodies are empowered to visit and inspect the training courses and the examinations.

Controls on Practice

As mentioned earlier, a major control on the practice of some of the health care professions is that they are "closed" – that is to say, practice is limited to registered individuals only. This is the case for dentists, pharmacists, midwives, opticians (partially), hearing aid dispensers and veterinary surgeons, and it is a criminal offence for a non-registered person to practise. Exceptions are usually made for students and in the event of emergencies.

Another form of control is the limiting of certain important appointments to registered staff only. Although medicine is not a "closed" profession the fact that all public medical appointments are limited by the Medical Act to registered staff means that non-registered individuals can work only in the private sector. There are other limitations which also tend to restrict practice to registered professionals even where the profession is not "closed". An important one is the legislation which prohibits the availability of drugs, medicines and poisons to the public but allows them to be supplied to properly qualified individuals for professional use. There are also restrictions on the use of titles that imply registration. Only qualified people can use them, and this applies to all the professions discussed in this book.

Professional Discipline

All the governing bodies of these professions have the duty to maintain high standards of professional conduct and are given wide disciplinary powers to achieve this objective. Most bodies issue guidelines on what standards are or are not acceptable, but they can only be guidelines and can never be comprehensive. Broadly speaking, a professional person may be liable for disciplinary action where he has been convicted of a crime which brings into question his fitness to practise, or has been found guilty of professional misconduct. The governing bodies usually adopt a two-stage process in disciplinary cases. The first is an investigation of the case, collecting all of the facts. The second is the hearing and determination. Proceedings at the disciplinary hearings are like those in a court of law and the legislation has a variety of mechanisms to ensure fairness. The most severe sanction available to the disciplinary committee is the erasure of a name, although in some cases suspension or just a warning may ensue. In almost all cases an appeal procedure to a higher court against a disciplinary decision is available. The concept of disciplinary procedure is based on the belief that a professional may be unfit to practise because of unacceptable behaviour which is wilful on his part. However, his fitness to practise may be brought into question because of his health, and in recent years in the medical, dental and nursing and midwifery professions powers have been introduced to take action in such cases.

Review of Present Legislation

Here now is a brief introduction to each of the professional groups dealt with in later chapters.

The Medical Profession

The first Medical Act which introduced a system of registration for doctors was introduced in 1858. The present law is found in the Medical Act 1983 and in the various statutory instruments made under it. This legislation covers the whole of the United Kingdom. The governing body for the profession is the General Medical Council which was reconstituted in 1978 and is an elected body with a number of members being nominated by key interest groups. The Council is responsible for medical registration and publishes the Medical Register – the "principal list" of fully and provisionally registered medical practitioners. In addition, an overseas register, a register of visiting overseas and visiting EEC doctors and a register of doctors with limited registration are kept. In January 1986 there were 126,448 fully or provisionally registered medical practitioners on the principal list. A provisionally registered practitioner is one who has completed his training and passed the final examinations and is undergoing the required one-year period of experience.

The Education Committee of the Council is responsible for all matters relating to professional training and the inspection and approval of medical schools. Two other committees of the Council, the Preliminary Proceedings Committee and the Professional Conduct Committee, are responsible for investigating alleged disciplinary offences and for adjudicating on them. The Health Committee, a new committee introduced in 1978, is empowered to investigate a doctor's fitness to practise in the light of his physical or mental health. Appeals against decisions of the Professional Conduct Committee or the Health Committee are taken to the Judicial Committee of the Privy Council. Although medicine is not a closed profession, the Medical Act limits the use of titles, such as physician, doctor of medicine, general practitioner and so on, to registered medical practitioners. Only registered medical practitioners are permitted to sue in a court of law for recovery of professional fees, and a wide range of public medical officer appointments is limited to registered individuals.

Dentistry

Dentistry is an ancient art which probably emerged separately from that of surgery, although by the fifteenth century the barber's guild was teaching tooth extraction, and the guild formed in 1540 by the barbers and the surgeons continued such training. In 1745, however, the guild broke up and training in dentistry fell into private hands. By the first half of the nineteenth century the state of dentistry had deteriorated with a proportion of practice in the hands of "mechancial dentists" whose training was obtained often by apprenticeship to watchmakers and jewellers. In 1841 a member of the Royal College of Surgeons, George Waite, urged Parliament, the medical profession and the public to empower the College to examine the fitness of those intending to practise dentistry. It was not until 1859, however, that the Royal College was given this power by charter and not until the Dentists Act of 1878 that a register of qualified dentists was created and the use of the term dentist was restricted to registered dentists or registered medical practitioners. The British Dental Association, headed by Sir John Tomes, was also established in 1878, partly to help support the Act. But dental practice was not restricted to dentists and, while an unregistered person could not style himself dentist, an office labelled, "Dental Surgery", was a legal loophole through which many unqualified "mechanical" dentists and others continued to practise. Under the Dentists Act of 1921 the practice was limited to registered dentists or registered medical practitioners, and the Act also established a Dental Board which, working in conjunction with the General Medical Council, controlled the profession.

The present law is contained in the Dentists Act 1984 and its associated statutory instruments. The legislation covers the whole of the United Kingdom. The old Dental Board has been dissolved and the governing body is now the General Dental Council which acts quite independently of the General Medical Council. The General Dental Council is predominantly an elected body with representation of other interested parties such as the dental schools. The Council is responsible for maintaining the dental register. In January 1986 there were 24,592 dentists registered in the United Kingdom list. The Council maintains standards of professional education by the systematic inspection of dental schools.

Committees of the Council are responsible for professional discipline. The Preliminary Proceedings Committee considers cases of alleged misconduct and, if satisfied there is a case to answer, refers it to the Professional Conduct Committee. This Committee must hear the case and reach a decision. Appeals against its decisions are to the Judicial Committee of the Privy Council. The Council also has the power to restore a name it has erased. As already stated, the practice of dentistry is restricted to registered dentists or registered medical practitioners, although exceptions are made for bona fide students in training. Use of titles, such as dentist, is restricted to registered individuals and it is an offence to do anything which implies by any means that one is registered if that is untrue. The practice of dentistry by a business is also limited to registered dentists or registered medical practitioners.

The 1984 Act also controls practice by auxiliary dental workers. These are individuals who are trained and registered under the Act to perform certain aspects of dentistry under the supervision of a qualified dentist. But for their recognition by the Act their practice would be illegal. Two types of auxiliary workers are presently recognised – dental therapists and dental hygienists.

Pharmacy Profession

The governing body for pharmacists is the Council of the Pharmaceutical Society of Great Britain. The Society was founded in 1841 and incorporated by Royal Charter in 1843. The Pharmacy Act of 1852 confirmed the charter and empowered the Society to maintain a register of members, and only qualified pharmaceutical chemists could become members. The Pharmacy Act 1868 established two classes on the Society's register, – the pharmaceutical chemist and the chemist and druggist. Up to the time of the Pharmacy and Poisons Act 1933 membership of the Society was voluntary but from that date all registered pharmacist's automatically became members. This now allowed the Society to exercise control over the whole profession. Although the major part of the pharmacist's job today involves modern medicines, the legal control of the profession evolved in parallel with the legal controls imposed on poisons and their availability. Indeed, before 1954 the same act of Parliament controlled both poisons and the profession.

The present legislation controlling the profession of pharmacy is the Pharmacy Act 1954 and the bye-laws of the Pharmaceutical Society of Great Britain made under its powers. This legislation does not extend to Northern Ireland where there is an analogous system of legal control. However, pharmacists registered in Northern Ireland may also be registered on the register kept in Great Britain. The Society keeps the register of pharmaceutical chemists. Eligibility for registration and thus membership of the Society comes either from obtaining a degree in pharmacy at a United Kingdom University or because of a reciprocal recognition agreement with an overseas school of pharmacy. The Council of the Society is predominantly an elected body responsible for the control of the profession and the management of the Society's affairs.

Professional discipline is the responsibility of the Statutory Committee – a committee of the Society and not of the Council of which it is independent. It's chairman must be an experienced practical lawyer. The investigatory phase of any alleged disciplinary case is handled by the chairman of the Statutory Committee who must gather together all relevant details and decide whether to refer the case to the whole Committee for consideration. Appeals against Statutory Committee decisions go to the High Court, and the Council has the power to restore names. The practice of retail pharmacy is limited to registered pharmacists and it is an offence to use a variety of titles falsely indicating or implying that one is registered. Pharmacy is both a trade and a profession, and the legislation also provides controls over carrying on a pharmacy business by corporate bodies.

Nursing Profession

The practice of nursing is ancient in the history of mankind. One thousand years BC in India the physician Charaka wrote that nurses who attended the sick must be "of good behaviour, distinguished for purity, possessed of cleverness and skill, endued with kindness, skilled in every service a patient may require, competent to cook food, skilled in bathing and washing the patient, rubbing and massaging the limbs, lifting and assisting him to walk about, well skilled in the making and cleaning of beds, ready, patient and skilfull in waiting upon one that is ailing, and never unwilling to do anything that may be needed". In early Christian times deacons and deaconesses cared for the sick, often in their own homes, and, later, hospitals developed as part of the new religious houses. Military nursing orders, such as the Order of St John of Jerusalem – the hospitallers, appeared at the times of the Crusades and this association of nursing and the religious orders continued until the dissolution of the monasteries in 1536–1540.

From the dissolution of the monasteries to the mid-nineteenth century standards declined. Nursing was carried out by uneducated women with low morals who were often found guilty of drunkeness and dishonesty. However, in the nineteenth century the profession underwent a renaissance in this country related in part to the rapid development of new ideas of social medicine, and of medical and surgical techniques. In the Crimean War public opinion was outraged to learn that while the French soldiers had the Sisters of Charity to nurse them (the continental religious orders had continued an unbroken tradition of nursing) the British soldiers had none. The improvements brought about by Florence Nightingale are well known, and in 1861 she established a nurse training school at St Thomas' Hospital in London. Many others followed. For the first 20 years after the Nightingale school was set up the profession extended its influence to hospitals across the country. In the 1880's however, the profession split into two factions of opinion, one seeking state registration after passing a standard examination and one which violently disagreed. However, after years of sometimes bitter debate, the Nurses Registration Act was passed in 1919 and thus established the General Nursing Council for England and Wales which was to set educational standards and organise the qualifying examinations. It was also to maintain the register which was to be divided into several parts. The Nurses Act 1943 introduced provision for the training and enrolment of assistant nurses, while the 1949 Act reconstituted the General Nursing Council and strengthened the training process.

The present law controlling the nursing profession is contained in the Nurses, Midwives and Health Visitors Act 1979, which, as its name suggests, deals with three related professions which were previously dealt with by separate bodies of legislation. The Act extends to the whole of the United Kingdom, unlike the situation before it came into effect when separate, albeit very similar, bodies of legislation existed for England and Wales, for Scotland, and for Northern Ireland.

The controlling body for nursing is the United Kingdom Central Council for Nursing, Midwifery and Health Visiting , which is primarily an elected body. Additionally, there are four National Boards – one each for England, Wales, Scotland and Northern Ireland – which are also elected bodies.

The Central Council is responsible for the registration of nurses, midwives and health visitors in the appropriate section of the register. The name of a nurse, midwife or health visitor may be struck from the register for misconduct. Initially, alleged misconduct cases are investigated by the appropriate National Board and if they think there is a case to answer it is heard and determined by the Professional Conduct Committee – a committee of the United Kingdom Central Council. In addition, the legislation introduced by the 1979 Act also introduced a procedure for taking action where the fitness of a nurse, midwife or health visitor to practise is seriously impaired for health reasons.

Midwifery

Midwifery is obviously an ancient art which tended to be passed on from mother to daughter. This sort of apprenticeship produced a wide range of levels of competence. During the sixteenth century the English bishops began to license the midwives in their dioceses, more to control their moral background than to standardise their skills. However, this system did not survive into the seventeenth century. Early in that century the obstetrician, Peter Chamberlain, unsuccessfully petitioned James I for a Parliamentary Bill for the control of midwives, but it was not until the Midwives Act 1902 that such legal control appeared. The Act set up the basis of the modern law, introducing a controlling body, the registration of midwives, standardisation of training and disciplinary powers over midwives. Local supervision of midwives by the local authorities as well as more central control was introduced, and it became illegal for anyone other than a midwife to attend a woman in childbirth. The term midwife could only be used by a qualified woman.

As was outlined above when discussing the nursing profession, midwifery is now controlled by the provision of the Nurses, Midwives and Health Visitors Act 1979, a single Act for the whole of the United Kingdom. However, certain special provisions were made for midwives. Firstly, the 1979 Act ensures significant representation of the profession on all bodies that it creates (Council, Boards, Committees etc.). Secondly, the Act continues the separate existence of a set of special rules controlling the practice of midwifery. Thirdly, the Act continues the system of local supervision of midwives in addition to their more central control. Finally, it should be noted that it was not until 1984 that men were free to train and practise as midwives on fully equal terms with women.

Opticians

The magnifying properties of lenses have been known for centuries and it is believed that the medieval monks used magnifying glasses while illuminating manuscripts. Meissner (1260–80) stated that old people benefited from the use of spectacles, and it is recorded that in 1282 a priest named Nicholas Bullet used spectacles while signing a document. In spite of these early origins the opticians' profession did not come under legal control until the Opticians Act of 1958 was enacted.

The 1958 Act extends to the whole of the United Kingdom and created the General Optical Council as the governing body for the profession. Although there are elected members on the Council it is predominantly an appointed body. The Council is responsible for professional education, registration and discipline and has the power to make rules which have the force of law in these matters. Five registration categories exist – one of opticians undertaking sight testing; one of opticians undertaking sight testing and sale of spectacles (both categories being called ophthalmic opticians); one of opticians selling optical appliances (called dispensing opticians); one of businesses carrying on the practice of ophthalmic opticians; and one of businesses carrying on the practice of dispensing opticians. Registration is based on undertaking an approved course of training and taking certain qualifying examinations. The Council is empowered to inspect training establishments to satisfy themselves of the standards.

Two committees of the Council are responsible for disciplinary matters. The Investigating Committee must consider all cases referred to it where it is alleged that an optician is liable to disciplinary proceedings. If it is satisfied there is a case to answer, it will refer the matter to the Disciplinary Committee which must hear the case and reach a decision. Appeals against the decisions of the Disciplinary Committee go to the Judicial Committee of the Privy Council. The opticians' profession is a closed one, the testing of sight being limited to appropriately qualified opticians or to registered medical practitioners, although exceptions are made for students and in certain other circumstances. As has already been discussed, the opticians' monopoly of selling spectacles has recently been abolished. The use of a variety of titles containing the word "optician" is limited to properly registered individuals and it is a criminal offence to use any title or do anything that falsely implies that one is registered.

Hearing Aid Dispensers

The inventions of Alexander Graham Bell relating to the telephone began the development of the modern hearing aid. However, the amplification of early devices was limited by the noise inherent in the then available microphones. They were also very bulky because of their use of valves. Great improvements occurred after the Second World War with the introduction of low-noise crystal microphones and miniature valves giving rise to higher amplification, and by the early 1950's devices weighing only a few ounces were available. With the appearance of transistors and, later, microcircuitry, aids weighing only a fraction of an ounce were developed. It was at this stage of technical development that legal controls on the sale of such devices first appeared.

The Hearing Aid Council Act was passed in 1968 and controls the selling of hearing aids. Since an Act of 1975 which extended the 1968 Act to Northern Ireland this legislation has covered the whole of the United Kingdom. The Act created the Hearing Aid Council which is the governing body for the profession. The Council is essentially an appointed rather than an elected body. It is responsible for keeping two registers – one of the dispensers of hearing aids and one of their employers. To be registered as a dispenser an individual must satisfy the Council that he or she reaches the standard of competence required by its rules. The dispensing of hearing aids is a closed profession and only duly registered individuals may act as such. Similarly, only a registered employer may employ hearing aid dispensers.

The Council is responsible for professional discipline and this is dealt with in two committees. The Investigating Committee must consider any case reported to it where it appears that a registered dispenser is liable to proceedings against him. If the Committee is satisfied that there is a case to answer it must refer the case to the Disciplinary Committee. The Disciplinary Committee also has the power to restore to the register a name it has ordered to be erased.

Professions Supplementary to Medicine

With the development of modern medical practice there has grown a variety of new supporting disciplines such as physiotherapy, radiography and laboratory science. As early as 1936 a Board of Registration of Medical Auxiliaries was set up. This body registered medical auxiliaries, advised on their training and offered guidance to prospective employers on the background and training of individuals. However, registration was voluntary and was stronger in some professions than others. With the advent of the National Health Service after the Second World War the view emerged that a more formal approach was required. In 1957 the report of a series of committees set up by the Government to investigate the issue (The Cope Report Cmnd 8188) argued strongly in favour of a system of state registration. However, there was a divergence of opinions about the precise nature of this new system and it was not until 1960 that the Professions Supplementary to Medicine Act was passed.

The 1960 Act covers the whole of the United Kingdom and created a Council for Professions Supplementary to Medicine. In addition it created seven Boards to govern the seven professional groups covered by the Act – chiropodists, dieticians, medical laboratory technicians, occupational therapists, physiotherapists, radiographers and remedial gymnasts. The Act permits the creation of new Boards up to a total of 12, and since 1960 orthoptists have been added as an extra professional group and remedial gymnasts removed. The Boards are responsible for registration in their own discipline, which is based on the satisfactory completion of the required training course. The Boards have the power to inspect training establishments and recommend or otherwise approval of courses and qualifications. Each Board is also responsible for discipline within its own professional area. An Investigating Committee considers all cases where it is alleged that a member is liable for disciplinary proceedings and, if satisfied that there is a case to answer, it must refer the case to its Disciplinary Committee. The Disciplinary Committee must hear the evidence and reach a decision. Appeals from such decisions go to the Judicial Committee of the Privy Council.

The function of the Council is to supervise the activities of the Boards, to comment on any Board recommendation concerning the approval or disapproval of a training institute or qualification and to consider any proposals to extend the Act to cover new professions. The professions the 1960 Act deals with are not closed, although National Health Service regulations restrict employment in the Service to registered individuals. Nonetheless, unregistered individuals may practise in the private sector and also in the non-NHS public area – for example, local authorities. The term "state registered" in connection with one of these professional titles is restricted to registered people but the use of a title of the profession itself is not so limited. Proposals have been made to close these professions but the Government has so far rejected such moves on the ground that the definition of the boundaries of such professions is difficult. What precisely is the work of a physiotherapist that separates it from others? However, the suggestion that the common titles of these professions as well as the term "state registered" be limited to a registered individual appears to be more favourably viewed by the Government at the present time.

Veterinary Surgeons

The governing body for veterinary surgeons is the Council of the Royal College of Veterinary Surgeons. The College was founded by Royal Charter in 1844 granted to the graduates of the veterinary colleges of London and Edinburgh. The first Veterinary Surgeons Act was passed in 1881 and, besides confirming the charter, established a register of qualified veterinary surgeons so the public could distinguish between qualified and unqualfied practitioners. Registration in veterinary surgery came from passing the College's examinations but the Veterinary Surgeons Act 1948 permitted the holders of recognised degrees of university veterinary schools to be registered. Up to this time veterinary surgery was not a closed profession but the 1948 Act limited its practice to qualified people. However, unqualified practitioners who had latterly practised were, if they satisfied certain conditions, permitted to continue subject to some restrictions and their names were entered on a Supplementary Veterinary Register. They are described as "veterinary practitioners".

The present law is contained in the Veterinary Surgeons Act 1966. The governing body – the Council of the Royal College of Veterinary Surgeons – is essentially an elected body but has a variety of nominated members, including two from each veterinary school. The register is kept by the Council and consists of four parts: the general list which contains the names and people registered on the basis of a United Kingdom qualification, a Commonwealth list, a foreign list and a list of temporarily registered practitioners. In addition, as indicated above, there is the Supplementary Veterinary Register. In 1985 there were 11,500 veterinary surgeons on the general list. The Council sets educational standards for the profession and recommends or otherwise the issue of a recognition order for training schools.

Two committees of the Council are responsible for discipline. The Preliminary Investigating Committee investigates cases referred to it where it is alleged that a veterinarian is liable to disciplinary action. If satisfied, it will refer the case to the Disciplinary Committee to adjudicate and reach a decision. Appeal from these disciplinary decisions is to the Judicial Committee of the Privy Council, although before the 1948 Act it was to the High Court. The Council has the power to restore a name to the register. Except for a variety of minor procedures and supervised students, veterinary surgery is limited to practice by registered individuals only. Further, the title "veterinary surgeon" is limited to use by registered individuals and it is a criminal offence for an unregistered person to imply by whatever means that he is so registered.

Chapter Two

The Controlling Bodies

Each profession dealt with in this book is governed and controlled by a separate body created for that purpose. The fact that the controlling bodies are independent of one another and also separate from any pre-existing body, such as the courts of law, local authorities or government departments, that might have been chosen to exercise control arises from a variety of factors. The numerous functions these bodies have to serve and the large number of people belonging to each profession generate an administrative burden too great for any single pre-existing body to absorb. Moreover, the desire by a trade or profession to govern its own members is ancient and understandable. Much of the value that comes from having legal controls over these professions is, however, in the protection of the general public who must rely on their services. It is therefore important that the controlling bodies are composed and constituted in such a way that the interests of members do not outweigh those of the public, or vice versa. Although the governing bodies have very similar functions, there is very little sharing of administrative resources. This is mainly because the legal control of each profession has evolved at a separate pace. The Nurses, Midwives and Health Visitors Act 1979 brings together under one Act of Parliament the control of nursing, midwifery and health visiting, and has brought a degree of rationalisation of the resources needed to govern these professions, and it is possible in the future we may see more rationalisation.

The functions of the various controlling bodies are wide and will be dealt with later in this chapter. However, two functions call for particular attention because of their special legal and, indeed, sociological importance. The first is the power to make rules which, at least for members of the particular profession, have the full power of law. The second is the power to sit as a court of law in disciplinary cases and to deprive a member of the profession of his professional privileges. The power to make laws belongs predominantly to Parliament. It is a power won only after many hundreds of years of battle mainly with the Crown and the Executive. The power to sit in judgement on a man and impose a penalty on him has, since Magna Carta, been exercised mainly by the ordinary courts of law. (The judicial and punitive powers of the controlling bodies will be dealt with in Chapter Six.)

Corporate Bodies

The bodies discussed in this book were all created as corporate bodies (bodies corporate). Much of the general law has evolved in relationship to natural human beings and their rights, duties and status. However, two problems have led in legal history to the recognition of artificial persons or corporations for a variety of purposes.

The first problem is the fact that natural persons are mortal and their death may lead to problems of legal continuity. The law has therefore long recognised certain posts or positions to be "corporations sole", and has endowed them with perpetual succession, whatever happens to their mortal holder. The best known example is, of course, the Crown which, in spite of the natural death of the Sovereign, is deemed never to die – hence the adage, "The King never dies" and "The King is dead, long live the King". Other examples include bishops, parsons and the Public Trustee.

The second problem with natural persons arises when they join together for some enterprise or other. We tend to recognise that a commercial company should have, and indeed has, an existence beyond the sum of its members, but the value of having separate recognition becomes obvious when an outsider wishes to have dealings with such a group of people. If he enters into a contract with the group, is it with each member or certain individuals? If things go wrong, whom or what does he sue? If the group wishes to buy land, in whose name is it to be held? These and other such problems are overcome by the concept of a corporation aggregate as a separate legal person to those making up its members. Generally speaking, the powers and responsibilities of a corporation are the same as those of any natural person but with the important addition that it has perpetual succession.

Corporations or corporate bodies may be created in three different ways (although in the history of a corporation more than one may have been involved). They may be created by Royal Charter under the prerogative of the

Crown, by specific Act of Parliament or, in the case of commercial enterprises, by the process laid down generally in the Companies Act 1985. As far as professional bodies are concerned, all have been created by charter or Act of Parliament or a combination of both, and in every instance their powers and responsibilities will be described in detail in the charter or Act creating them. Any act outside these powers is described as being "ultra vires" (beyond the power) and a court of law can take steps to prevent or nullify it. This can be illustrated by two examples relating to the governing body for pharmacists, the Pharmaceutical Society of Great Britain, incorporated by Royal Charter in 1843.

In 1921 the Society proposed to form an industrial council to regulate wages, hours and working conditions for the pharmacy profession. The relevant objective in the 1843 charter was the "protection of those who carry on the business of chemists and druggists". In Jenkins v Pharmaceutical Society of Great Britain (1921) 1 Ch 392 the High Court held that this clause did not empower the Society to regulate members' hours of business, wages or conditions of employment, regulate prices or provide insurance for its members.

In 1953 the Society received a new charter in which the objective "to maintain the honour and safeguard and promote the interest of members in the exercise of the profession of pharmacy" appeared. The Society proposed that it should control the nature of premises in which all new pharmacies were to be situated. Mr Dickson, a member of the Society and a director of the Boots Pure Drug Co. Ltd., sought an injunction in the courts to prevent the Society's proposed action on the grounds that it was outside its powers and was also in restraint of trade. The House of Lords considered the case in Pharmaceutical Society of Great Britain v Dickson (1968) 2 A11 ER 686 and held that the Society could not control selling activities which did not interfere with the performance of professional pharmacy duties.

The general power of the courts to declare an action by a corporate body ultra vires and void is a most important factor in ensuring that the professional bodies do not go beyond their statutory or chartered powers.

The advantages of creating the professional controlling bodies as corporate bodies will be apparent. Perpetual succession avoids problems arising from changing membership, and the corporate identity allows it to fulfil its extensive administrative functions by holding land, entering into contracts, employing staff, receiving and paying out money, all without any of the complications inherent in an unincorporated group of people.

Origins of the Controlling Bodies

The Medical Profession

The first statutory governing body for the medical profession was the General Council of Medical Education and Registration in the United Kingdom, established by the Medical Act in 1858. Now known as the General Medical Council, its continuing existence is confirmed by Section 1 of the Medical Act 1983. The first president of the original Council was the famous surgeon, Sir Bejamin Brodie (1783–1862).

The Dental Profession

The controlling body for dentists is the General Dental Council which was originally set up by the Dentists Act 1956. However, since an Act of 1878 there had been a register of dentists which was maintained by the General Medical Council and the 1956 Act transferred this responsibility to the new Dental Council. The Act of 1878 had laid down the requirements for registration, but it was not until an Act of 1921 that all who practised dentistry had to be registered. The Council's continuing existence is confirmed by Section 1 of the Dentists Act 1984.

The Pharmacy Profession

The Pharmaceutical Society of Great Britain is the governing body for pharmacists. It was founded in 1841 and received its charter of incorporation in 1843. When legal controls on pharmacy were introduced by the Pharmacy Act 1852 this recognised and confirmed the existence of the Society. Most of the original charter and later supplemental charters were consolidated in a new Royal Charter of 1953. The ruling body of the Society is the Council and much of its powers and duties in respect of professional control are determined by the Pharmacy Act 1954.

The Nursing Profession

The controlling body for nurses was the General Nursing Council for England and Wales and its equivalent in Scotland and in Northern Ireland, until all of these bodies were replaced by a single Central Council for Nursing, Midwifery and Health Visiting, introduced by the Nurses, Midwives and Health Visitors Act 1979.

Registration was originally introduced by the Nurses Registration Act 1919, and the existence of the General Nursing Council was confirmed by the Nurses Act 1957. The registration of nurses in 1919 was achieved only after a long and bitter battle which lasted over 30 years. The concept of registration based on achieving a certain standard of training and examination was strongly rejected by many an eminent nurse of the period, including Florence Nightingale, who believed that such a move would lower standards rather than elevate them. She stated: "You cannot select the good from the inferior by any test or system of examination . . . Indeed, those who come off best in such examinations would probably be the ready and the forward, not the best nurses." The British Nurses' Association was formed in 1887 by Mrs Bedford Fenwick with a view to carrying forward a scheme for registration. Princess Christian became its president and persuaded her mother, Queen Victoria, to grant it a Royal Charter. In 1891 the Royal British Nurses' Association established its own register of nurses. In 1895 the British Medical Association and in 1889 the General Medical Council passed resolutions in favour of state registration. Many abortive Bills were introduced into Parliament, the first being in 1903. In 1916 the College of Nursing was founded and a Bill drafted by it was introduced in 1918. It was withdrawn on the assurance given by the newly formed Ministry of Health that it would introduce its own Bill, although this turned out in fact to be based on the College's draft. It became law in 1919. For administrative reasons separate Acts were required for Scotland and for (as it was then) Ireland.

Midwifery Profession

The controlling body for midwives was the Central Midwives Board, the constitution of which was determined by the Midwives Act 1951. However, the present controlling body is the United Kingdom Central Council for Nursing, Midwifery and Health Visiting introduced by the Nurses, Midwives and Health Visitors Act 1979.

As early as in the seventeenth century a petition had been presented to James I by the obstetrician, Peter Chamberlain, for a Parliamentry Bill to "settle some order and civil government for midwives". However, it was not until 1881 that the Midwives Institute was founded and began the standardisation of training and practice. The Central Midwives Board was set up by the Midwives Act 1902 as the statutory governing body for the profession.

Opticians Profession

The governing body for opticians is the General Optical Council which was established by the Opticians Act 1958. For many years there had been some pressure from among opticians for a system of registration and control based on agreed training standards. However, there was also opposition to the idea from inside the profession and from doctors. A working party, under the chairmanship of Lord Crook, was set up to consider the problem and in 1952, in the "Report of the Interdepartmental Committee on the Statutory Registration of Opticians" (Cmnd 8531), it came out in favour of such a scheme. There was little Government action on the report, although in answer to specific questions in July 1954 a spokesman indicated that the Government had legislation in mind but could not say when. The Opticians Bill was in fact introduced into Parliament in 1957 as a private Member's Bill by Mr Roland Russel (MP Wembley South, Con.) and received the Royal Assent in 1958.

Hearing Aid Dispensers

The controlling body for hearing aid dispensers is the Hearing Aid Council. This is the most recently created of the professional bodies dealt with in this book, being created by the Hearing Aid Council Act 1968.

Professions Supplementary to Medicine

The Professions Supplementary to Medicine Act 1960 controls a wide variety of professions, and within the Act there is the power to add new professional groups. At present, chiropodists, dieticians, medical laboratory technicians, occupational therapists, physiotherapists, radiographers and orthoptists are included. Each profession is controlled by a Board and there is an overall Council for Professions Supplementary to Medicine. The Boards and the Council are corporate bodies. As early as 1936 the Board of Registration of Medical Auxiliaries was incorporated. This was a voluntary organisation with which medical auxiliaries could register and which provided guidance to hospitals and other employers on the credentials of auxiliaries.

However, the extent of voluntary registration depended on the attitude of the professional associations and, with the advent of the National Health Service, the question of statutory registration was raised. The Government set up eight small committees, each chaired by Mr Zachary Cope, to consider the registration of almoners, chiropodists, dieticians, laboratory technicians, occupational therapists, physiotherapists and remedial gymnasts, radiographers and speech therapists. The Cope report – Report of the Committees on Medical Auxiliaries (Cmnd 8188) – appeared in 1951 and, broadly speaking, recommended a system of state registration (although inevitably with such a wide range of professions there were dissenting views on precisely who should be included and how). After two years the Government announced that it had been decided not to implement the recommendations because it believed there was insufficient agreement on fundamental issues. Discussions continued in an attempt to find common ground and in 1959 the Government introduced the Professions Supplementary to Medicine Bill which covered chiropodists, dieticians, medical laboratory technicians, occupational therapists, physiotherapists, radiographers, remedial gymnasts and speech therapists. Speech therapists were later removed from the scope of the Bill. A new argument then broke out over the medical profession's insistence on a predominance of doctors on the registering body, although the Government did not finally agree to this.

The Veterinary Profession

The controlling body for the veterinary profession is the Council of the Royal College of Veterinary Surgeons. The College was created in 1844 by Royal Charter which gave it power to govern the profession. A charter of 1965 consolidated the previous charters and the present constitution, functions and powers of the Council are determined by the Veterinary Surgeons Act 1966.

Membership of Governing Bodies

The detailed composition and membership of each of the bodies dealt with in this book are set out in Chapters 7–13. This section considers the general issues concerned with composition.

Two broad questions arise: who should be a member of the controlling body, and how should that person be chosen? In answering the first question, three groups need to be considered in particular – members of the profession itself over whom the controlling body exerts its influence, the various educational institutions whose activities are controlled, and members of the public who may be considered as the ultimate "consumers" of the service provided by the profession in question. As far as the mechanics of selection are concerned, the balance between elected members and nominated or appointed members needs to be considered, as does the power of nomination or appointment itself.

Elected Professional Members

Over the years there has been a natural pressure from within various professions to have the controlling bodies composed of a majority of elected professional members. Although the governing bodies are created to put into effect a variety of statutory professional controls rather than to be a representative organisation, the impact which their activities can have on any profession has stimulated this pressure.

The events leading up the 1978 Medical Act, which, among other things, reconstituted the General Medical Council to give elected members a majority, illustrate some aspects of this pressure. In 1965, at a time when the elected membership of the General Medical Council did not constitute a majority, the Council proposed an annual retention fee for all doctors in addition to the fee payable on initial registration. This produced a furore within the profession, particularly among the junior hospital doctors, and stimulated a demand for an independent inquiry into the structure and functioning of the Council. The negative role the Council was forced to play in medical ethics and its unrepresentative image through lack of accountability to rank-and-file doctors were criticised. The demand for an inquiry was hotly debated over the next seven years both within the profession and between the General Medical Council and the British Medical Association. To bring pressure to bear, a large number of doctors (some 5,300) decided to withhold their registration fees and the Council voted in favour of striking their names off the register. Faced with the prospect of hospitals being closed due to lack of registered doctors the Department of Health and Social Security had no choice but to act. On 23rd March 1972 Sir Keith Joseph, the then Secretary of State for Social Services, set up an independent committee of inquiry into the registration of medical practitioners under the chairmanship of Sir (then Dr.) Alex Merrison. It reported in 1975 (Committee of Inquiry into the Regulation of the Medical Profession, Report Cmnd 6018), and among a wide variety of recommendations for reform was a strong proposal for the General Medical Council to have a majority of elected members. Most of the recommendations of the Merrison Committee were finally enacted in the Medical Act 1978, and continued by the present 1983 Act.

As with the General Medical Council there is a majority of elected professional members on the Council of the Royal College of Veterinary Surgeons, the General Dental Council, the Council of the Pharmaceutical Society of Great Britain and the United Kingdom Central Council for Nursing, Midwifery and Health Visiting.

There are no elected members on the General Optical Council, the Council for Professions Supplementary to Medicine or the Hearing Aid Council.

Representations of the Educational Bodies

One of the major general functions of the controlling bodies is to set standards of professional education. In most cases the bodies have the power to inspect educational institutions and approve or disapprove them, their courses of instruction and their examinations. It is therefore not surprising that the constitution of most of the controlling bodies includes a significant representation of the appropriate educational bodies.

Thirty-four members of the General Medical Council are appointed by those universities and other bodies in England, Wales, Scotland and Northern Ireland which have the power to grant a registerable medical qualification. Such members must be registered medical practitioners. Each recognised veterinary school has the power to appoint two members each to the Council of the Royal College of Veterinary Surgeons, while any medical authority with the power to grant dental diplomas and choose members of the GMC has the right to nominate one member each (two from the University of London) to the General

Dental Council. The General Optical Council has six members nominated by specified examining bodies while the Council for Professions Supplementary to Medicine includes members nominated by the various medical Royal Colleges. The main exception to the general statement that each controlling body has significant educational representation is the Council of the Pharmaceutical Society of Great Britain which consists of 21 elected members of the Society and three appointed by the Privy Council who need not be members of the Society.

Representation of the General Public

Considering that the major consumers of the services provided by the professions dealt with in this book are members of the general public, whether as patients or as animal owners, they have surprisingly little formal representation on the controlling bodies. The constitution of the Hearing Aid Council does require the Council to include a proportion of members who are not registered hearing aid dispensers but either have specialised knowledge of deafness or are otherwise capable of representing the interests of people with impaired hearing; even in that case, however, the representation is more of a technical or medical nature than a consumer one. Of the ten nominated members on the General Medical Council a majority must be non-medical and include people directly representing patients' interests.

Involvement of other Professions

The governing bodies for the medical, pharmaceutical and veterinary professions are not required to include members of any other profession in their composition. However, the medical profession has fairly extensive membership of the General Dental Council, the General Optical Council, the Council for Professions Supplementary to Medicine and the Hearing Aid Council. The Central Council for Nursing, Midwifery and Health Visiting also has medical membership appointed by the Secretary of State.

Powers and Functions of the Governing Bodies

The primary function of the bodies considered in this book is the control and government of their particular professions as directed by the relevant Acts of Parliament. As they are not bodies designed to represent the interests of the profession per se and are therefore not trade unions, they do not generally become directly involved with matters such as terms and conditions of employment and service in the profession. Thus, the "trade union" for the medical profession is the British Medical Association and not the General Medical Council, and it is the Association which negotiates remuneration for its members.

The actual powers given to these bodies are very wide indeed. For example, the first schedule to the 1957 Nurses Act, which dealt with the powers of the old General Nursing Council, stated that it could "do such things which in its opinion may be necessary for the exercise or performance of any of the powers and duties conferred on it under the Nurses Act". It is perhaps noteworthy that the section of the Nurses, Midwives and Health Visitors Act 1979 that lays down the function of the central council is more specific than the old Nurses Act was.

Similarly, the Dentists Act 1984 empowers the General Dental Council to "do anything which in its opinion is calculated to facilitate the proper discharge of its functions". Because of this breadth of powers a variety of checks and controls (described more fully later in the book) exists to prevent these bodies acting in abuse of these powers. The main functions of the controlling bodies may now be summarised.

Registration

As has already been seen, registration is the system adopted to define membership of a particular profession and to attract the various privileges and duties which membership entails. Registration of members is a prime function of all the bodies, and the power to grant or withhold registration effectively controls who may practise a particular profession. While clear rules are laid down for registration there is nevertheless considerable freedom to act or not in a variety of cases where an individual's training and experience are somewhat atypical, as for example in the case of people trained outside the United Kingdom. Because of Britain's membership of the European Economic Community special arrangements are necessary in certain instances for professions from other EEC countries. The question of professional registration is dealt with in detail in Chapter Three.

Education

The prescribed programme of professional education, on which the system of registration in the United Kingdom is mainly based, usually includes a particular course of training and instruction, the satisfactory completion of certain examinations and possibly the acquisition of a certain period of additional practical experience. It is the function of the governing bodies to determine what programme of training and experience is required and in the process they are required to promote a high standard of professional education and competence. In order to do so they are given considerable powers to approve and recognise training institutions, their courses of instruction and their examinations. The power of control over professional education is a significant one: it determines both the type of person successfully entering a profession and also the technical competence of the profession itself. This is dealt with in detail in Chapter Four.

Professional Discipline

The governing bodies are not only responsible for setting and maintaining a high standard of professional training for registration. They are also empowered to maintain high standards of professional conduct among those who are registered. To do this they have very significant disciplinary powers. The main one is the ability to remove an individual's name from the register in cases of professional misconduct and certain other specific cases. In addition, the General Medical Council, the General Dental Council and the UK Central Council for Nursing, Midwifery and Health Visiting has the power to consider an individual's fitness to practise on the grounds of health. The effect of a professional person being struck off a register is to deprive him of his livelihood. It is therefore a particularly far-reaching power. It also involves the governing body, or usually in ad hoc committee of it, acting as a court to consider cases put before it – a court which is outside the normal system of courts of law and one that could be seen as judge and jury in its own cause, as it is responsible for determining what amounts to professional misconduct. This important area is dealt with in detail in Chapter Six.

Law-making Function and Delegated Legislation

One particularly significant power of the governing bodies is the ability to make rules which bind all members of that profession and have the full force of law. This is particularly significant for two reasons: firstly, because it is a basic principle of the British constitution that only Parliament may make laws – a legal principle called the supremacy of Parliament which was hard-won only after many years' battle with the Crown – and, secondly, because the law-making powers of these professional bodies concern the very important functions of registration, education and discipline.

The law-making powers of the governing bodies are called delegated legislation – a fairly widely used process in modern Parliamentary procedure. Basically, Acts of Parliament may be classified into two types – constituent Acts, which introduce new laws and are complete in themselves, and enabling Acts which give another body (usually a Minister of the Crown but here the controlling body) power to make detailed regulations carrying the force of law. The enabling Act may give reasonably clear directions as to the nature and scope of the regulations to be made but delegate the drafting of the detailed definitions. This body of delegated legislation is contained in documents known as statutory instruments. These are published by Her Majesty's Stationery Office and listed in its Daily List. The value of delegated legislation is that it reduces the heavy demand on Parliamentary time, and also permits more direct specialist input into the drafting of regulations. The problem perceived with delegated legislation is that it may be seen as a derogation of Parliamentary supremacy for, although Parliament has given the power in the first place and may at any time withdraw it, it does nevertheless mean that a legislative power is given to perhaps a Government Minister rather than to the representatives of the electorate. For this reason a variety of controls and checks on delegated legislation has evolved. While the position with the governing bodies is a little different, insofar as they are for the most part bodies with an elected majority, such controls and checks still apply.

The first level of control on the law-making functions of the governing bodies is that imposed by the enabling Act itself. It may – although it is not always the case – require some level of consultation before the body makes its rules. Thus, the Nurses, Midwives and Health Visitors Act 1979 (section 22) empowers the Central Council to make rules to give effect to the Act and requires that before doing so it consults with representatives of any group which appears likely to be affected by the proposed rules and also with the National Boards for those parts of the United Kingdom to which the rules are to apply. The enabling Acts invariably require some level of approval outside the governing body before the rules can become effective. For example, rules made by the General Medical Council, the General Dental Council and the Council of the Royal College of Veterinary Surgeons need approval by order of the Privy Council while rules made by the General Optical Council require the approval of the appropriate Secretary of State. Rules relating to quasi-judicial matters may require approval by order of the Lord Chancellor or, in Scotland, the Lord Advocate. This is the case with rules relating to disciplinary procedure under the Nurses, Midwives and Health Visitors Act 1979 (sections 12 and 22). Most enabling Acts in this area indicate that even when approved and effective the rules are subject to anulment by resolution of either House of Parliament, and in order to permit this the rules in the form of statutory instruments or orders of the Privy Council are laid down before each House. Parliamentary control is further effected by means of the Scrutinising Committee of the House of Commons which has the task of reviewing all statutory instruments presented to Parliament.

Not only are there Parliamentary controls on delegated legislation but there are also judicial controls exercised by the courts of law. It is now well established that the courts may challenge the validity of delegated legislation, either on the grounds that the legislation is outside the powers given by the parent Act or because it has been made without observance of some important procedural point required by the enabling Act, such as a requirement for consultation. In either case, the court may declare the legislation to be ultra vires – that is, outside the power conferred by the Act and therefore null and void.

Finance and Management

Maintenance of the governing bodies is an expensive exercise. The 1986 report of the General Medical Council shows for instance that its annual expenditure was more than £3.4m. Such costs include the payment of salaries to employees, expenses paid to members and all the usual costs of running any administrative office (rates, heating, lighting, stationery, postage etc.). The major source of income for all the controlling bodies is the fees they are empowered to levy for a variety of activities related to registration or the retention of a name on the register. Central government is not a major source of funds, although when setting up any new system the responsible Minister may have to finance it; section 19(3) of the Nurse, Midwives and Health Visitors Act 1979, for example, empowers the Secretary of State to make grants to the Central Council and to the Boards in connection with their initial establishment.

The Acts establishing the various governing bodies gives them specific power to pay staff salaries and pensions, and also to reimburse the expense of their members. Scales of payment are approved either by the Privy Council or the responsible Minister of the Crown. The bodies are required to keep proper accounts, which must be audited, and annual financial reports must be published. The bodies controlling the veterinary profession and the pharmaceutical profession also have the general role of managing the affairs of the Royal College of Veterinary Surgeons and of the Pharmaceutical Society of Great Britain.

Advisory

The governing bodies have, to a greater or lesser degree, an advisory function, although this is not always clearly defined by their parent Act. Section 35 of the Medical Act 1983 specifically requires the General Medical Council to advise members of the profession on matters of conduct and ethics – a requirement which arose from earlier criticisms of the Council. The advice given may not always be to the profession. Thus the Council of the Royal College of Veterinary Surgeons is to advise the Privy Council on the recognition of any new veterinary school.

Procedural Aspects of the Governing Bodies

The governing bodies dealt with in this book are complex organisations with many functions to fulfil. Predictably they require a considerable body of procedural rules in order to be able to function properly. The parent Acts of Parliament or delegated legislation made under them lay down these rules of procedure. The second part of this book and the actual instruments themselves should be read for the full details, but what follows is a summary.

Membership

The actual composition of the bodies has been dealt with earlier. However, procedures are laid down for matters such as the duration of office of members, their resignation and the replacement of casual vacancies. Where a member of a body is required to be registered he ceases to be a member if he ceases to be registered (see GMC v Waring 1932 2 Ch 115).

Officers

The bodies will elect senior officers such as a president, a chairman, a treasurer and perhaps some deputies. Provision will be made for the duration of these offices.

All the bodies dealt with are required to appoint a registrar who is responsible on a full-time basis for managing the day-to-day affairs of the body and in particular that of registration. A variety of permanent support staff will also be appointed and, as has already been stated, the bodies are empowered to pay their employees salaries and pensions.

General Procedures

Detailed rules of procedure at meetings are laid down. For each body there will be a quorum. For example, as far as the General Medical Council is concerned this is 22 of whom not fewer than 12 must be elected members (General Medical Council (Quorum Rules) Order in Council 1979 SI 1979 No. 1358). Matters are decided by a simple majority vote of members present at a meeting. Rules are usually laid down about the frequency of meetings.

Committees

The vast majority of the work is done by the bodies in committee. This is more practical than operating by means of plenary meetings, and it also allows a degree of specialisation to be developed. Usually the parent Act of Parliament not only gives a general power to the body to form committees but also specifically requires certain named ones to be constituted. Matters commonly dealt with by committees include discipline, education and finance.

Reporting

To a greater or lesser extent all of the bodies produce some sort of regular, mainly annual, report of their activities and finances.

Default Powers

It has already been indicated in this chapter that the various professional councils have very considerable powers. Possible abuse of these powers is dealt with by means of a variety of controls and checks. Some of these have already been described and later chapters will expand on them. However, an opposite problem could occur, namely the failure of a body to discharge its statutory functions. In order to deal with this possibility the professional councils for the medical, veterinary and optical professions, as well as the professions supplementary to medicine, are subject to a degree of control by the Privy Council if they fail to carry out their functions. As an example, section 22 of the Veterinary Surgeons Act 1966 provides that if it appears to the Privy Council that the Council of the College has failed but ought to discharge any of its functions under the Act, then the Privy Council may notify the Council of its opinion and direct it to act in a specified time period to discharge those functions. If the Council of the College fails to do so, the Privy Council is empowered by the Act to discharge those functions itself.

The Privy Council

The origin of the Privy Council may be traced back to the select body of officials which the Sovereign gathered about him to exercise his powers. For the Saxon kings this was the Witenagemot, and for the Norman kings, the Curia Regis. Originally, the Curia had judicial, legislative and executive powers, but gradually over a period from the thirteenth to the seventeenth centuries these powers were reduced with the development of Parliament, the courts and the modern form of executive government. The Court of Star Chamber, which had developed from the Kings Council, was abolished in 1641, but there remained a jurisdiction to deal with appeals from places beyond the jurisdiction of the ordinary courts, particularly from the newly-formed colonies.

Today, the Privy Council numbers about 300 Councillors who are appointed by the Sovereign from among people who hold, or have held, high political, legal or ecclesiastical office in the United Kingdom or the Commonwealth. Cabinet Ministers are invariably members. Privy Councillors hold office during the life of the Sovereign, may be dismissed by the Sovereign or may be removed at their own request. The present-day powers of the Privy Council are small compared with those of its antecedents, but they are still important. The two main areas of activity are executive and judicial.

Executive

The Privy Council provides an important method of giving force of law to delegated legislation made by the Government or a professional body. As already stated, while legislation gives the governing bodies wide powers to make rules having the force of law they all need some sort of formal approval to be effective, and approval by Order of the Privy Council is one such mechanism. The approval is given by the Sovereign at a meeting of the Privy Council, usually with three or four members present.

Judicial

The remaining judicial power of the Privy Council is exercised by the Judicial Committee, composed of Privy Councillors who hold, or have held, high judicial office in the United Kingdom or the Commonwealth. The Committee is an appeal court and hears appeals from courts in British colonies, dependencies and trust territories and those Commonwealth countries which have chosen to retain this right of appeal. It is the final court of appeal for the Channel Islands and the Isle of Man and the Prize Courts (courts concerned with captured ships or goods in time of war). As far as the subject of this book is concerned, the Judicial Committee of the Privy Council is the final court of appeal against disciplinary decisions of the General Medical Council, the General Dental Council, the General Optical Council, the Council for Professions Supplementary to Medicine and the Council of the Royal College of Veterinary Surgeons.

Other Functions

A wide variety of other functions may be placed on the Privy Council from time to time. These range from ad hoc requests to consider certain topics – for example, in 1957 the issue of legality of telephone tapping was referred to a committee of the Privy Council (see Cmnd 283 (1959)) – to specific statutory requirements, such as the power to nominate members of some of the governing bodies, as it does for example in the case of the General Medical Council. The important power to act when the Privy Council considers a governing body to be in default of its duties has been mentioned earlier.

Chapter Three

Professional Registration

The body of law dealt with in this book gives members of designated professions a variety of important privileges so they may practise their skills fully. It also imposes on them a variety of duties and responsibilities and makes them subject to a strict code of discipline. To do this it is first necessary to define who at any one time is, or is not, a member of a particular profession, and a system of professional registration has been adopted for this purpose. If an individual's name is on a particular register he enjoys the privileges and bears the responsibilities, duties and discipline of that profession; he does not if he is not registered.

The normal route of registration is by means of a recognised course of training and examination, possibly followed by a period of mandatory practical experience. The controlling bodies are therefore charged to determine what are registerable qualifications. Although we are dealing with English law it must make provision for overseas professional qualifications. Historically, this particularly concerned Commonwealth countries, but now provisions for professionals qualified in the European Economic Community must also be made. The process of registration attracts the payment of a fee, as may the retention of a name on the register, and this is the major source of income to defray the costs of the controlling bodies.

The existence of a system of professional registration also leads to the main disciplinary sanction to which professional people are liable – erasure from the register, which in most cases effectively deprives an individual of his livelihood.

The whole topic of professional discipline is discussed in Chapter Six, but there is a variety of criminal offences related to registration itself which will be summarised in this chapter.

Because the presence of a name on a register determines whether someone is registered, it has great importance in terms of evidence in a legal sense. The register needs to be an open document easily available to the general public who may wish to determine the professional status of someone they may intend to have dealings with.

It might be thought there is a single register for each profession, but in fact within each profession there may be a wide variety of categories of people, from trainees to fully qualified. There may also be people whose registration is in some way limited to certain purposes or for certain periods of time. Therefore the register also represents some degree of internal classification of their profession.

Eligibility for Registration

United Kingdom Trained Professionals

For individuals who have received their professional training in the United Kingdom eligibility for registration comes from the satisfactory completion of a period of training and the passing of the prescribed examinations at a recognised training institution. The control of professional education is dealt with in Chapter Four, but, in summary, the controlling body is empowered formally to recognise courses of instruction and educational institutions for this purpose. It may also inspect these institutions. Depending on the profession, the course of training may also lead to a formal qualification at degree or diploma level, and it is often this specific qualification which leads to entitlement to registration.

In addition to a period of training and the passing of the prescribed examinations an element of experience will also be prescribed before registration. In most cases this experience will be an integral part of the period of training, but in the case of the medical and pharmaceutical professions it is an additional requirement to be fulfilled after the acquisition of a professional qualification. This may lead to the need for a special category of registration to permit a doctor for instance, to gain such experience.

Where a set of registration regulations has been introduced to control a profession for the first time, or where the registration rules are changed so that a higher standard is demanded, a variety of rules is usually introduced preserving the rights of individuals who have practised before the introduction of the new controls. There are various registers or parts of registers which deal with what are often called "grandfather clauses".

Professionals Trained Overseas

Because of Britain's imperial history there has always been a demand for professional registration in the United Kingdom based on qualifications gained overseas. Most of the professions dealt with in this book have evolved regulations whereby they recognise some overseas qualifications as being equivalent to ones in the United Kingdom and therefore a basis for registration. There are problems in doing this on a large scale for two main reasons. Firstly, the nature of British professional training reflects a certain historical tradition which may well be different in other countries, and therefore courses of training differ in significant detail. Secondly, even if there is a similar course, it is operationally impossible for the professional council concerned to inspect overseas courses and institutions in the way they can in this country. Nevertheless, in the case of most of the professions covered in this book certain overseas qualifications are recognised as a basis for registration in the United Kingdom.

In addition to having a suitable overseas qualification a candidate may also have to show he has gained a certain level of experience, be of good character and be competent in the English language.

To offset the difficulties of approving many overseas qualifications the professional bodies exercise a reasonable degree of freedom in recognising individual candidates for registration. They may, for instance, require them to sit ad hoc examinations to demonstrate their knowledge and competence, undergo a limited period of extra training in the United Kingdom or acquire a specific period of additional experience.

Position of Professionals from the European Economic Community

As far as the medical, dental, nursing, midwifery and veterinary professions are concerned, specific provisions have been made to permit the registration in the United Kingdom of people who have qualified in a member state of the European Economic Community. Similar provisions are planned in pharmacy. The system works in a similar way for all professions and is based on the mutual recognition of certain qualifications which are listed in the appropriate statutory instruments (see Part II for details). The legislation which controls the registration of EEC qualified individuals is made, not by the specific professional legislation, but under the European Communities Act 1972 by means of which the United Kingdom ratified the Treaty of Rome which founded the Common Market. In the 1980 annual report of the General Medical Council the chairman of the Education Committee expressed some concern about the standards of medical education in some member states and about the lack of ability on the part of the Council to control European standards. He pointed out that of 68 European qualified doctors who in 1979 took a test set by the Council to examine proficiency in the English language and professional medical knowledge, 55 failed – eight of them on the language component only and the rest on the medical component or both.

As far as the medical, dental and nursing professions are concerned, the legislation originally dealing with mutual recognition of EEC qualifications also required an applicant for registration in the United Kingdom to show he had that knowledge of the English language necessary in the interests of the patients and the doctor, dentist or nurse to render professional services in the United Kingdom. This requirement was particularly concerned with the need to have a good understanding of colloquial English. The Common Market challenged the British Government, claiming that making a linguistic test a requirement of registration was illegal under EEC law because it contravened a basic principle of the Treaty of Rome – free movement of labour. The Government has now withdrawn this linguistic requirement as a pre-requisite of registration (see European Communities (Medical, Dental and Nursing Professions) (Linguistic Knowledge) Order 1981 SI No. 432). However, the Government now requires all National Health Service employers or contracting authorities to make linguistic proficiency a condition of employment – a requirement which is not considered to offend EEC law. This applies to staff employed in NHS hospitals and to general practitioners but not to professionals practising in the private sector, which remains an anomaly. The language pre-requisite for registration of overseas but non-EEC professionals remains unchanged, thus creating another anomaly.

Categories of Registration

The professional registers are not only statements of who is legally recognised in these professions. They may also provide some degree of categorisation of individuals into sub-groups. There is no general pattern across the professions dealt with in this book as each has used this facility in a somewhat different manner. Full details are given in Part II but here is a summary of the divisions of the registers, profession by profession.

Doctors

There are two registers – the Register of Medical Practitioners and the Register of Medical Practitioners with Limited Registration. The former is divided into four lists – the principal list, which is the familiar Medical Register as published and contains the names of fully and provisionally registered doctors; the overseas list which covers fully and provisionally registered doctors who reside outside the United Kingdom or the European Community; the visiting overseas doctors list and the visiting EEC practitioners list. Provisional registration is appropriate to a qualified doctor who is in the process of obtaining the mandatory 12 months' experience for full registration. Visiting practitioners are those, whether from the EEC or elsewhere, who intend to visit the United Kingdom to provide medical services of a specialist nature. The Register of Medical Practitioners with Limited Registration includes overseas doctors who are in the United Kingdom for further training. The registration is limited to a particular employment for a particular period of time and will always provide for specified supervision by a fully registered medical practitioner.

Dentists

The dentists' register contains three separate alphabetical lists – one of dentists registered as United Kingdom or EEC graduates; the Commonwealth list of dentists registered on the basis of a Commonwealth diploma, and the foreign list of dentists registered on the basis of some other overseas qualification. The Commonwealth and foreign lists contain sub-divisions for overseas dentists who are temporarily registered to permit them to practise dentistry for a limited period of time in a hospital or other institution in this country.

Pharmacists

There is a single register of pharmacists. However, the Pharmaceutical Society of Great Britain is also required to keep a register of premises.

Nurses and Midwives

Before the Nurses, Midwives and Health Visitors Act 1979 the General Nursing Council kept three registers, although only one was called the register; the other two were called the roll and the list. Nurses on the register – State Registered Nurses (SRNs) – have completed a somewhat more advanced course of training than nurses on the roll – State Enrolled Nurses (SENs). The register was divided into a general part; a part listing nurses trained in the care of mental disorders (but excluding sub-normality and severe subnormality); a list of nurses trained in the care of the subnormal and the severely subnormal, and a list of nurses trained in the care of sick children. The roll was divided into a general part; a list of enrolled nurses trained in the care of mental disorders (excluding subnormality and severe subnormality), and a list of those trained in the care of subnormality and severe subnormality. The list, which is now closed, included nurses who, while not registered or enrolled, applied within two years of the passing of the 1943 Nurses Act on the grounds that they had completed a course of training before 1st July 1925 and met certain other requirements. The midwives register – called the roll – was kept by the Central Midwives Board. Because there were separate bodies of legislation for England and Wales, Scotland, and Northern Ireland, there were nine separate registers prior to the implementation of the 1979 Nurses, Midwives and Health Visitors Act. The 1979 Act introduced (from 1983) a single register which is divided into eleven parts:

Part 1 – First-level nurses trained in general nursing.
Part 2 – Second-level nurses trained in general nursing (England and Wales).
Part 3 – First-level nurses trained in the nursing of persons suffering from mental illness.
Part 4 – Second-level nurses trained in the nursing of persons suffering from mental illness (England and Wales).
Part 5 – First-level nurses trained in the nursing of persons suffering from mental handicap.
Part 6 – Second-level nurses trained in the nursing of persons suffering from mental handicap (England and Wales).
Part 7 – Second-level nurses (Scotland and Wales).
Part 8 – Nurses trained in the nursing of sick children.
Part 9 – Nurses trained in the nursing of persons suffering from fever.
Part 10 – Midwives.
Part 11 – Health visitors.

First-level nurses are the registered nurses while second level nurses are the enrolled nurses.

Opticians

Three registers and two lists are kept. There is a register of opticians engaged in both the testing of sight and supply of spectacles; a register of opticians engaged only in the testing of sight, and a register of dispensing opticians (i.e. those engaged only in the supply of optical appliances). There is a list of corporate bodies carrying on business as ophthalmic opticians and one of corporate bodies carrying on business as dispensing opticians.

Professions Supplementary to Medicine

Each Board keeps a register of the individuals registered in that particular profession. There are therefore separate registers for chiropodists, dieticians, medical laboratory technicians, occupational therapists, physiotherapists, radiographers, and orthoptists.

Hearing Aid Dispensers

Two registers are kept – one of hearing aid dispensers and one of their employers.

Veterinary Surgeons

Two registers are kept by the Royal College of Veterinary Surgeons – the main register and the supplementary register. The main register is divided into four parts – the general list of United Kingdom and EEC qualified persons; the Commonwealth list of people registered on the basis of a Commonwealth qualification; the foreign list where the registration is based on an overseas but non-Commonwealth and non-EEC qualification, and the temporary list. The temporary list includes overseas veterinary surgeons who wish to gain experience in the United Kingdom, and the Royal College issues registration subject to a variety of specified restrictions. The supplementary register includes individuals who before the introduction of veterinary registration had been earning a livelihood as veterinary practitioners for seven out of ten years up to 30th July 1949 – an example of a "grandfather clause". No new names may now be added to this list.

Publicity and Evidence

Because registration in a profession represents a certain standard of attainment as far as training is concerned and is also associated with a variety of privileges and liabilities, there is a wide variety of occasions when it may be important to confirm that a particular person is registered in his profession. Members of the public who may wish to approach someone for professional advice and care for themselves or their animals may want to confirm that that person is registered, and will wish to do so in a fairly straightforward manner. On the other hand a professional person may himself need to demonstrate his registration – when, for example, he applies for employment where registration is a requirement.

It may be necessary occasionally to prove to a court of law that an individual is registered. For example, it is generally a criminal offence, under the Misuse of Drugs Act 1971, to possess certain controlled drugs, but in some circumstances exceptions are made for (inter alia) registered medical practitioners. In such a case, therefore, it may be necessary to prove that an individual was indeed registered at the time in question. This problem involves the law of evidence – a complex area which is outside the scope of this book. However, as a general rule, if a document is to be used as proof in a court of law the original rather than a copy must be produced. Certain exceptions exist to this rule and generally any public document may be proved by an authenticated copy. Many of the registers are put into this category by the enactments which created them.

This need for publicity and formal proof in connection with registration is met in the professions in one of four ways, or more usually a combination of them. They are: publication and selling of copies of the register, making certified copies of entries on the register, issuing certificates of registration to people who are registered, and making the original register open for public inspection.

Publication of Registers

The registers of doctors, veterinarians, dentists, pharmacists and opticians and the registers for the professions supplementary to medicine are all printed, published and offered for sale to the general public by the respective controlling bodies. Some are published on a strictly annual basis. A degree of discretion is given to the controlling bodies in other cases, although, if they do not publish a copy in any one year, they must publish a list of alterations to the last edition. Publication of these registers serves to bring to the public's attention the professional status of individuals, and the registers are readily available at local libraries. They are also deemed by the particular enactment controlling the profession to be evidence of whether or not an individual is registered.

Certified Copies of Entries

Clearly, a published copy of a register is correct only at the time it is sent to the printers and even an annual publication will not be totally adequate to present the exact picture on registration. One solution is to empower the appropriate registrar to issue an authenticated copy of any particular entry in the register, and the enactments dealing with the medical, veterinary, dental, nursing, midwifery and optical professions provide for this. The authentication normally required is the registrar's signature.

Certification of Registration

Another solution to the problem is to issue a certificate of registration to an individual. For instance, the General Medical Council and the Pharmaceutical Society of Great Britain issue certificates of registration to individuals when they first register, and these may be used as proof of registration. Because of the permanence of such certificates provision must be made for their return if and when an individual becomes unregistered; it would be a criminal offence on the part of a non-registered person to use the certificate to represent himself as being registered. Where a retention fee is charged an annual certificate may be issued.

Public Inspection

The final mechanism used to ensure the free availability of up-to-date information on registration is to make the register itself open for inspection by the general public free of charge. This would be at the offices of the controlling body and during normal business hours. For instance, such provision is made for inspection of the register kept by the Hearing Aid Council and the one kept by the Council for Professions Supplementary to Medicine.

Procedural Aspects of Registration

The process of registration and the maintenance of the registers are major administrative exercises in view of the complexity of the arrangements and the large numbers of people belonging to the various professions. Responsibility for this administrative burden usually falls to the registrar who is a full-time official appointed by the governing body and is in effect the chief executive officer. The procedural aspects of registration for any profession are determined partly by the parent Act of Parliament and partly by detailed regulations made under it, usually by the governing body. As with delegated legislation, such regulations require some degree of outside approval before becoming effective. Generally, the regulations deal with the procedures for entry of a name onto the register and the procedure for removing names. Details of both aspects are given in Part II, but here is a general summary.

Entries to the Register

As stated earlier, the basis of registration will be the satisfactory completion of a prescribed training programme. An essential prerequisite must be to demonstrate to the registrar that such training has indeed been completed. This may be done either by the individual concerned supplying documentary evidence or by an arrangement between the training institution and the governing body whereby examination results may be supplied directly. In all cases registration is dependent on making application in the prescribed manner, and in some cases the applicant will be required to furnish evidence of good character. Registration will also be provisional on payment of the appropriate fee.

Removal from the Register

Removal of a name from the register is the major disciplinary sanction available to the governing bodies. This is dealt with fully in Chapter Six. However, in order to keep the register up-to-date as far as possible, and for certain other reasons, the registrars have power to remove names in a variety of different circumstances:

Death The registrar needs to remove the name of a professional person who has died. In many circumstances there is a statutory arrangement whereby the registrar of births and deaths involved will send a copy of the death certificate free of charge to the registrar of the appropriate professional body.

Non-payment of Fees When a professional person fails to pay the stipulated annual fee for registration, the registrar can remove his name after the prescribed reminders. However, a simple procedure will exist to restore his name when the fee has been paid, although the process may be subject to a further fee for restoration.

Not in Practice An individual who is not in practice may request the registrar to remove his name. If the registrar enquires by post whether a professional has changed his address or has ceased to practise and fails to receive a reply within six months, he may remove the person's name.

Incorrect or Fraudulent Entries The registrar is bound to correct any entry which is incorrect and remove any entry which appears to the governing body to be fraudulent.

Offences Relating to Registration

A variety of offences exist in relation to certain aspects of the registration.

Offences by the Registrar

The post of registrar to a governing body is clearly a very responsible one, and holders of the post are likely to have had impeccable training in some branch of public administration. Nevertheless, some of the parent enactments (for example, the Pharmacy Act 1954) have made it a criminal offence for the registrar wilfully to falsify the register.

False Claims of Registration

As a general rule it is a criminal offence for any unregistered person to claim or imply that he is registered. This subject is covered fully in Chapter Five.

Fraudulent Entries

Again as a general rule it is an offence to obtain registration fraudulently. This is usually dealt with by the disciplinary process in the particular profession so that any fraudulently entered name may be removed speedily, as described in Chapter Six.

Chapter Four

Control of Professional Education

As stated in Chapter Three, the process of professional registration is, by and large, based on the attainment of some recognised professional qualification awarded after a period of training. This is so that people who obtain professional status have a common and, it is hoped, high standard of training. However, this can only be ensured if there is some control over the whole area of professional training. This chapter considers the functions of the professional governing bodies in respect of training, the training institutions themselves, the examination process, practical experience requirements and the control of the whole process by means of a system of inspection.

Role of the Professional Councils

All the professional bodies dealt with in this book have a general role and a series of specific roles in respect of professional education. These were referred to briefly in Chapter Two. The general role is the promotion and maintenance of high standards of professional training and attainment. This may be stated as a function for the appropriate council itself, or the legislation may, as in the cases of the medical, dental and opticians' professions, require the creation of specific committees of the Council to deal with education. Even where this is not a legislative requirement many governing bodies deal with educational matters in ad hoc committees. In the nursing profession the Nurses, Midwives and Health Visitors Act 1979 (section 9) empowers the Secretary of State to constitute training committees of the four National Boards. The committees' functions are to assist their Board in the exercise of its training function.

Of the various specific powers over professional education possessed by the Councils perhaps that of approval is the most important. The power of approval may relate to training institutions, to courses of instruction, to the teaching of staff, or to the professional examinations. Approval is given on the basis of a minimum prescribed standard being achieved. Withdrawal or withholding of approval is a stringent control over standards. To exercise control the governing bodies are given various powers of inspection over the training process. Where an approval is to be withheld or withdrawn some sort of appeal process may be provided for by the legislation.

In some instances the governing bodies will make rules which prescribe the precise course of training to be completed successfully before registration is possible; in other examples the body itself may have the right to set a qualifying examination. None of these bodies, however, is a training institution. In the nursing and midwifery professions qualifications in professional teaching are granted to those who have undergone the appropriate training and examinations. Although participation in refresher courses for existing professionals may be encouraged in certain professions only in the case of midwifery is this a legal requirement.

Training Institutions

Training for entry to the professions covered by this book is at universities or their specialist schools (for example, medical, dental, veterinary), at the polytechnics and similar bodies, or in the specialist nursing and midwifery schools attached to National Health Service hospitals. As mentioned above, none of the professional governing bodies is itself a training institution. In many instances (for example, nursing, midwifery, optics, professions supplementary to medicine) the governing body must approve the training institution itself before successful training there will be considered to confer eligibility for registration. Such approval will usually be given on the basis of the number and quality of the teaching staff, the availability of appropriate equipment, the provisions of practical experience (for example, the size of a catchment area for a midwifery school), and the institution's general organisation. Approvals may in some cases be limited – in midwifery, for instance, to a maximum number of students, or, in the case of optics, perhaps to dispensing optics or to ophthalmic optics.

If a governing body refuses to approve a training institution, or decides to withdraw approval, it must in all cases inform the institution of its intention and give reasons for its views. The institution must be given an opportunity to present its case and the profession's governing body must consider this before finalising its decision. Nurse training schools may appeal to the Lord Chancellor against any such decision while a school of optics may in a similar situation appeal to the Privy Council. Although the Council for Professions Supplementary to Medicine in effect decides whether or not to approve an institution (on the recommendation of the appropriate Board), the final approval is given by the Privy Council, and so any aggrieved institution may appeal directly to the Privy Council.

In a recent consultation paper on training called 'Project 2000' prepared by the United Kingdom Council for Nursing, Midwifery and Health Visiting, wide ranging proposals have been made for changes in training and thus in the nature of respective professions.

Courses of Training

The degree of direct control exercised over training courses varies from profession to profession. In only one instance is there a power actually to approve training courses and this is given to the various Boards under the Professions Supplementary to Medicine Act 1960. In two professions, nursing and midwifery, the appropriate legislation requires the respective controlling bodies to determine by rules what the nature of the training courses should be. In other professions the training institutions themselves determine the nature of the courses, but the controlling bodies exert a strong influence through other constraining factors, such as the approval of qualifications and the process of inspection of institutions. For instance, while a veterinary school's courses of training do not require specific approval to obtain a recognition order and so make its degrees a basis for registration, the school must satisfy the Privy Council, in consultation with the Council of the Royal College of Veterinary Surgeons, that the course of training and examination will guarantee that the holder of a degree has acquired the skills and knowledge needed to practise veterinary surgery efficiently.

Registration of Students

Generally the legislation controlling the professions does not provide any system for the registration of students. That function is usually left to the training institution's internal administrative procedures. However, as far as nurses, midwives and health visitors are concerned the Rules (SI 1983 No. 873 and SI 1986 No. 786) provide for an index of all students in these disciplines.

Examination and Experience

Three of the controlling bodies dealt with in this book are examining bodies in their own right. They are the Royal College of Veterinary Surgeons, the Pharmaceutical Society of Great Britain and the United Kingdom Central Council for Nursing, Midwifery and Health Visiting. The power to hold examinations in veterinary surgery and in pharmacy is little used today; the examinations are now an integral part of the various approved university courses. However, in nursing and midwifery the controlling body is the sole examining authority in their disciplines in this country.

No general system of approval of professional examinations as such has been developed. As explained in Chapter Three, professional registration is usually based on, among other things, the acquisition of an approved qualification. However, in approving a particular qualification, consideration will be given to the level of knowledge and skill which that qualification must represent. In doing so it is necessary to determine whether the examination on the basis of which the qualification is awarded actually represents the attainment of such standards.

In all of these professions where the governing councils are not primarily the examining bodies the appropriate legislation provides for a system whereby examinations may be inspected. The governing bodies have the power to appoint inspectors to attend the professional examinations although they may not in any way interfere with them. The inspectors must issue a report of their findings and this may be the basis for further action by the governing body. The subject of inspection is considered more fully below.

All the courses of professional training and examination involve the acquisition of, and testing of, some degree of experience. The nature of this experience is usually defined in the various approved courses and syllabuses. Some subjects, such as nursing and midwifery, are by their nature highly practical, and practical experience is therefore an integral part of their teaching. However, as noted in Chapter Three, inclusion in the medical or pharmaceutical registers requires a period of practical experience in addition to the prescribed qualification, the period at present being 12 months.

Control by Inspection, Sanctions and Appeals

One of the general functions imposed on the governing bodies by the legislation we are considering is that of keeping themselves informed of the standards of training and examination actually provided at the various training institutions.

They are required to do this to ensure that the standard of knowledge and skill possessed by successful students is of the required level. To fulfil this function the controlling bodies have certain powers to demand information from, and to inspect, training institutions. Where it appears that the standards are inadequate they have certain sanctionary powers.

Right to Demand Information

Clearly, it is in the general interests of the professional educational institutions to co-operate with the controlling bodies and supply them with whatever information they may request. However, in some instances the legislation imposes a duty on the training school to supply information on demand to the controlling body. For example, dental schools must supply information on demand to the General Dental Council about any aspects of training.

Control by Inspection

In virtually all the professions dealt with in this book the appropriate legislation empowers the controlling council for that profession to inspect part or all of the educational process. The exception to this is the nursing profession where this power is given to special Local Training Committees which have a duty to advise their Boards in all matters relating to training in their geographical areas. In all instances the training institutions themselves and their courses of training are subject to inspection and where the controlling body is not the primary examining body, examinations will be attended by visitors. These "visitors" or "attendees", as they are also variously known, may not interfere with the instruction or examination in any way but must report back to their appropriate controlling body about the adequacy of the institution, its training and examinations. The controlling body must decide on the basis of such reports whether to issue new approvals or withdraw existing ones. The appropriate legislation may provide rules for appointing such inspectors and establishing their duties and will empower the controlling bodies to pay the inspectors' expenses.

Sanctions and Appeals

It has been shown above that various aspects of professional training are subject to some sort of approval process if they are to be recognised as a basis for registration. Approval is given on the basis of a certain required standard being met, and in order to set and maintain this standard, a refusal to approve or the withdrawing of an approval is a major sanction. The systems of inspection, outlined above, represent the major source of information on which a decision to pursue sanctions is based. The sanction may be available to the controlling body, in which case there may be an appeal process, or it may be available to the Privy Council on the advice of the appropriate controlling body.

Sanction by the Controlling Body In the nursing, midwifery and opticians' professions it is the controlling body which has the power to withhold or withdraw a prescribed approval. In nursing, the Local Training Committee must report to their Board on its inspections of new or existing nursing schools. If its report shows standards to be inadequate the Council may decide to withhold or withdraw its approval. In such a case it must inform the management of the nursing school and hear the management's objections before finalising its decision. The nursing legislation provides for an appeal against such a decision to be made to the Lord Chancellor. In midwifery the Central Council inspects midwifery schools and has the power to withhold or withdraw its approval. If it decides to do so it must give the school 28 days in which to object and must consider such representations before finalising its decision. However, there is no appeal process against such a decision laid down by the legislation.

In the opticians' profession where the General Optical Council, after considering an adverse report of a training institution, decides to withdraw or withhold an approval, the institution must be given 28 days in which to object and the Council must consider the objections before making its final decision. A further 28 days is allowed for an appeal against the decision to the Privy Council.

Sanctions by the Privy Council An account of the history and functions of the Privy Council was given on page 35. The Privy Council has an important role to play in professional education, and in the case of the medical, veterinary and dentistry professions and professions supplementary to medicine it has the power to withhold or withdraw approvals. In all these cases the visitors to the training institutions must make their reports to the professional body which appointed them. That body must send a copy of the report, together with any comments it cares to make, to the training institution for comments or representations, and then sends all the papers to the Privy Council with its overall recommendations. The Privy Council must decide whether to withhold or withdraw approval and it may need to do this by order i.e. by statutory instrument. It also has the power to revoke an order it has made withholding or withdrawing an approval. One general point that needs to be made about the withdrawal of an approval is that it does not have retrospective effect. Therefore, unless and until an approval is withdrawn, anyone qualifying from the institution is entitled to be registered. Similarly, the revocation of such a decision is not retrospective, and so individuals who might have passed examinations while the approval was withdrawn do not become registerable when it is restored but must re-sit the examinations or undergo further training.

Overseas Training

The legislation relating to professional education discussed above covers only this country and in no way permits any direct control of overseas professional training. Certain overseas qualifications are recognised for the purposes of registration. This was considered more fully in Chapter Three. There are two approaches to such recognition. One involves recognition proper following formal consideration by the professional council in the United Kingdom. The other is the approach taken to the EEC countries in certain professions as a result of which the United Kingdom recognises qualifications for registration in any member country as the basis for registration in the United Kingdom. Thus the controlling bodies in the United Kingdom have no influence over standards because they do not have the power to approve or reject a specific qualification. As was discussed in the last chapter, the chairman of the Education Committee of the General Medical Council expressed concern in the Council's 1980 report about the standards of medical education in some member states of the EEC and about the Council's lack of powers to influence them. This may become an important issue for the future.

Chapter Five

Controls and Limitations on Professional Practice

The effect of the professional legislation dealt with in this book is to define membership of a profession by means of some registration procedure. The educational standards of that profession are controlled by making registration dependent on the satisfactory completion of a recognised programme of training. Having defined a professional group with certain standards of training, a large part of the legislation has the effect of limiting the practice of a particular discipline to members of the appropriate profession. This limitation may be achieved in a variety of ways. In some cases the actual practice of a discipline is limited by law to registered individuals, while in others the limitation is placed on business aspects of practice. Appointments to certain posts may be limited to registered professionals either by law or by practice, and, in the various professions dealt with, by extensive restrictions on the actual titles describing them.

In the first half of this chapter these and other limitations to professional practice will be considered in general, while in the second half a brief account will be given of some of the more major professions. Full details will be found in Part II.

Limitation of Practice to Registered Individuals

The body of law dealt with in this book makes it a criminal offence for individuals not registered as belonging to the particular profession to practise, or hold themselves out as practising, veterinary medicine, dentistry, pharmacy, midwifery, sight-testing or the selling of hearing aids. In order to create such offences the particular enactment must first prepare a definition of what a particular practice comprises.

Not every discipline dealt with in this book is restricted in this way to practice by registered professionals only. For example, there is nothing to stop an unqualified layman from practising medicine or surgery provided he does not offend against some of the further limitations discussed below. There was a case reported in 1980 of a person who, wanting his tonsils removed, persuaded an unqualified friend to perform the operation. Surgery took place on the kitchen table without anaesthetic. Massive bleeding resulted and the patient had to be given urgent orthodox medical treatment. Because the patient gave consent for the operation no question of battery or criminal damage arose, and, in so far as an amateur surgeon can hardly be expected to have the skill of a trained and qualified person, a case for negligence would be difficult. The basic objective of the 1858 Medical Act – which in many ways was the cornerstone of all subsequent professional legislation in the field of health care – was not to control who may practise medicine but to ensure that the public could identify who had received basic medical training and who was registered. It was then up to the patient to decide whom he approached for diagnosis and treatment.

Where the practice of a profession is limited to registered individuals, two important aspects of the limitation need to be considered: firstly, what exceptions need to be provided to the limitation, and, secondly and more specifically, how the limitations affect the boundaries between different but related professions.

Exceptions

When the legislature has determined to limit practice to a recognised body of people there is a desire to keep the number of exceptions to a minimum. Three categories of exception tend to be found: students, emergencies and minor procedures.

Students In training to become registered a student obviously needs some degree of practical experience in his chosen discipline. For this reason exceptions are made to enable students to complete their training. However, some control over these exceptions is exercised either by requiring students' names to be notified to the controlling body so they achieve a degree of recognition or by requiring some degree of supervision over students' practice by a fully qualified individual, or both.

Emergencies Exceptions will be made, where relevant, when an unqualified person has done something in an emergency situation which would otherwise be an offence. Thus, the ambulanceman or policeman who delivers a baby in such circumstance does not commit an offence. However, in a recent case in Scotland, a father was convicted of delivering his own child in circumstances where the mother refused to go into hospital and the general practitioner refused to agree to a home delivery. This was not considered by the court as an emergency (defined by the then Midwives Act 1951 and its Scottish equivalent as "a sudden and urgent necessity"). Nor was a defence, available only in Scotland, namely that reasonable efforts to gain the services of a qualified medical practitioner or a certified midwife had been made and failed, accepted by the court.

Minor Procedures The main profession in which a variety of exceptions is made for minor procedures is the veterinary profession. This is because a significant proportion of what might otherwise be veterinary practice is also included in other activities, such as farm management and animal husbandry. The details are given in Chapter 13.

Boundaries Between the Professions

Because all the professions dealt with in this book are concerned with some aspect of health care, either of human beings or animals, there is inevitably some degree of overlap between them. Where appropriate the legislation needs to recognise the overlap and ensure that any limitation on practice is tailored accordingly. On the other hand, although the legislation we are dealing with is not designed primarily to create restrictive practices, it does in effect tend to do that. Therefore, any overlap between two or more professions may be a potential area for friction, especially where such an overlap could adversely affect another's business or financial position. The main areas of overlap are listed below.

Veterinary Medicine A registered medical practitioner may operate on an animal to remove an organ or tissue for the treatment of human beings. A registered veterinarian may request a registered medical practitioner or dentist to carry out any treatment, test or operation on an animal.

Dentistry A registered medical practitioner may practise dentistry even though the routine undergraduate course includes little training in dentistry.

Pharmacy The practice of a retail pharmacy business – that is, a business consisting of the retail sale of medicinal products (those controlled by the Medicines Act 1968) other than those on the General Sale List – is limited to registered pharmacists. The definition of a retail pharmacy business excludes a professional practice carried on by a doctor, dentist or veterinarian, any of whom may therefore supply medicinal products as part of his practice, but general practitioners working for the National Health Service are covered by the National Health Service Regulations which limit a doctor's dispensing to rural areas and then only where there is no chemist's shop within one mile of any particular patient. Even this relatively small overlap between medicine and pharmacy has been a source of friction between the two professions. A report into the problem (the Clothier Report) recommended a preservation of the status quo of existing rural dispensing arrangements and new NHS regulations to control any change in the status quo. It was seven years before such regulations were introduced in 1983. Under the regulations a doctor wanting to set up or extend rural dispensing or a pharmacy wanting to set up in a rural area must, as well as satisfying the guidelines on rural areas, also obtain the approval of the local Family Practitioner Committee. That Committee may, if it wishes, refer the issue to a permanent Rural Dispensing Committee, comprising three doctors, three pharmacists and three laymen. The Clothier Report recommended the creation of a state scheme to compensate either doctors or pharmacists who were financially disadvantaged by any changes in the balance of rural dispensing. This was not accepted by the Government and both professions have created voluntary funds for this purpose.

Midwifery None of the restrictions which limit the practice of midwifery to a certified midwife applies to registered medical practitioners. Indeed, the Midwives Rules (SI 1986 No 786) require a midwife to call in a registered medical practitioner in any case of emergency.

Opticians The testing of sight is restricted to registered opticians or registered medical practitioners. The Opticians Act 1958 imposes a duty on an optician to refer to a registered medical practitioner any patient consulting him who appears to be suffering from an injury or disease of the eye.

Business and Financial Controls

Business Control

Some of the professions we are considering are practised primarily as businesses, and certain of the enactments limit such business practice to registered individuals. Thus, a dentistry business (which is defined by the Dentists Act 1984) may be conducted only by a registered dentist or a registered medical practitioner, and a retail pharmacy business (which is defined by the Medicines Act 1968) may be conducted only by a registered pharmacist. It is a criminal offence for anyone not on the register of employers of hearing aid dispensers to employ anyone to dispense hearing aids. Various exceptions are made to these general prohibitions (details of which will be found in Part II).

Where a professional businessman either dies or becomes bankrupt in dentistry or retail pharmacy, provision is made by the relevant legislation for the business to be carried on for certain periods of time either by the personal representatives of the deceased or the trustee in bankruptcy. Both arrangements, however, are subject to various specific controls.

Fees

In medical practice a somewhat different business control is adopted, and this relates to fees. The Medical Act 1983 provides that only a fully registered medical practitioner may recover in any court of law any fee or charge for any medical or surgical advice or attendance or the performance of any operation or supply of medicines.

Appointments

Another control which can be applied in some of the health care professions is to limit certain appointments to individuals who are duly registered. Considering that the National Health Service is the major employer of most of the professional groups dealt with in this book, this can be a potent controlling factor, most importantly perhaps in the medical area where practice is not limited by law to registered doctors. The legislation which restricts appointments to registered professionals only may be in the main controlling Act, may be part of the statutory instruments controlling the Health Service, or may be only a matter of practice. Section 47 of the Medical Act 1983 is an example of the main controlling Act also dealing with appointments. It provides that only fully registered medical practitioners may be appointed as medical officers in the armed services, in any mental hospital or other hospital or infirmary or dispensary not controlled wholly by voluntary contributions, in any prison, or in any public establishment, or to any society providing mutal relief in sickness, infirmity or old age. The effect of this is that where a doctor's name is struck off the register (see Chapter Six) any appointments he holds in any of the above categories will automatically cease. In Tarnesby v Kensington, Chelsea and Westminster Area Health Authority (Teaching) QBD Dec. 14 1978 (Lancet Dec. 23/30 pg. 1388) it was held that a year's suspension from the register would also frustrate any contract of employment.

An example of Health Service legislation limiting certain appointments in the service to registered individuals is the National Health Service (Professions Supplementary to Medicine) Regulations 1974 SI 1974 No. 494, which (as amended) prohibit the employment for the purpose of providing services under the National Health Service of chiropodists, dieticians, medical laboratory technicians, occupational therapists, orthoptists, physiotherapists or radiographers who are not registered under the Professions Supplementary to Medicine Act 1960 (or so employed immediately before 1st April 1974).
In spite of such legislation, anomalies still occur. For example, X-rays may still be taken by unqualified staff in prisons because the NHS regulations do not extend to that area, and unqualified doctors may still hold appointments in private practice – provided in each instance that no other offence is committed.
An obvious problem with the restriction that only registered medical practitioners may hold NHS appointments is that of the bogus doctor who embarks on a course of wilful deception. In spite of procedures aimed at preventing this, it still happens every year or two. For example, in one case (The Guardian, 17th July 1979) an unqualified man named Murphy assumed the identity of a real doctor of that name and obtained a post as an orthopaedic surgeon at a hospital in Surrey. It was not until he had completed 17 operations that his deception was discovered. He was gaoled for two years at the Central Criminal Court for criminal deception. A very similar case was reported in 1983.

Use of Titles

As noted above, the philosophy behind the 1858 Medical Act was that the public should be able to distinguish between qualified and unqualified doctors, and this concept applies to all the professions we are considering. One important aspect of this is the use of titles to describe individuals. Nearly all the legislation we are primarily concerned with restricts the use of certain specific titles to registered people and makes their use by unregistered people a criminal offence. Details will be found in Part II, but the following are some of the titles that may be used only by the appropriately registered professional: physician, doctor of medicine, licentiate in medicine or surgery, bachelor of medicine, surgeon, general practitioner, apothecary, veterinary surgeon, veterinary practitioner, dentist, dental surgeon, dental practitioner, chemist and druggist, druggist, dispensing chemist, dispensing druggist, pharmaceutical chemist, pharmaceutist, pharmacist, nurse, midwife, ophthalmic optician, dispensing optician.

Having made it an offence for unregistered persons to use these and other titles, most of the legislation also makes it a criminal offence to do anything which implies registration. This would include use of any title, name, addition, description, uniform or badge or anything else implying registration.

Supervision

Generally, the degree of supervision under which a fully registered professional is required to work is relatively small. In the structure of any practice or hospital there will be some sort of hierarchy under which professionals work. In many ways they can be regarded as undergoing training with a view to becoming a senior partner, a consultant or whatever post represents the apex of the hierarchy. In only one of the professions dealt with in this book does the law enforce any system of supervision of fully qualified people, and that is in midwifery. This is largely because of the considerable degree of professional independence enjoyed by midwives practising under the traditional home delivery system. Provided a pregnancy was expected to be normal a pregnant woman would book her expected confinement with her local midwife who would look after her during pregnancy, delivery at home and the lying-in period – all with little involvement of the general practitioner and no involvement of a hospital. Modern midwifery now centres on hospital deliveries with a consequent change in the midwives' practice, but the system of local supervision continues.

Section 16 of the Nurses, Midwives and Health Visitors Act 1978 continues the system of local supervision. The supervising authorities used to be the local authorities but since the re-organisation of the National Health Service in 1974 the supervising authorities are the regional health authorities in England, the area health authorities in Wales, in Scotland the Health Boards and in Northern Ireland the Health and Social Services Boards. The health authority must appoint people to exercise supervision over midwives in its area, and the minimum qualifications of such people are laid down by statutory instrument (Nurses, Midwives and Health Visitors (Midwives Amendment) Rules 1986 SI 1986 No 786).

Before a certified midwife may practise in an area she must notify her intention to do so to her local supervising authority. She must give such notice annually as long as she continues to practise, and failure to do so is a criminal offence. She must also notify her authority of any change in her address or name. In order to supervise midwives' practice the health authority has wide powers and duties. It must investigate any charge of malpractice or negligence and, if the charge is proved, must report it to the Central Council. It may suspend any midwife from practice for the purpose of preventing the spread of infection. It must report to the Council the names of any midwives convicted of criminal offences and must send an annual list of all midwives who have notified their names. It must provide refresher courses for midwives, may suspend from practice any midwife against whom a charge of malpractice or misconduct has been made, and may prosecute any offence under the Act. The expenses of such prosecutions may be defrayed by the authority.

Sex

Since the enactment of the Sex Discrimination Act 1975 it is generally an offence to discriminate against anyone on grounds of sex as far as training, employment or promotion are concerned. Any control on professional practice which offended against this would therefore be void. However, a degree of legal discrimination against men in midwifery was retained. Before the 1975 Act, the Midwives Act 1951 defined a certified midwife as "a *woman* who for the time being is certified under the Act" (section 32). The Sex Discrimination Act initially permitted men to train as, and become, certified midwives. However, courses of training for men needed special approval by the Secretary of State, and it remained lawful to discriminate against a man on grounds of his sex as far as training, employment or promotion in midwifery was concerned. A certified male midwife could attend a woman in childbirth only in a place specially approved by the Secretary of State for Social Services. The 1979 Nurses, Midwives and Health Visitors Act continued this state of affairs until a day appointed by the Secretary of State. That date was 1st January 1984, since when men have been on an equal footing to women in midwifery.

Use Drugs and Medicines

A major element of any health care practice is the use of various drugs and medicines for therapeutic and other purposes. A considerable body of law, contained mainly in the Medicines Act 1968, the Misuse of Drugs Act 1971 and the Poisons Act 1972 and in the many statutory instruments made under these three statutes, imposes strict limitations on the availability and use of many such substances. This law also imposes controls on professional practice because as a general rule only fully registered professionals have access to drugs and medicines, and even then perhaps only on a limited basis. This topic is outside the scope of this book, but a fuller account is given in "Law on Poisons, Medicines and Related Substances", by P. F. C. Bayliss, (Ravenswood Publications, 2nd Edition 1986).

Negligence

What have been outlined so far in this chapter are the major limitations imposed on practice by the main body of statutory law controlling the health care professions. However, the professional groups dealt with in this book are also subject to the ordinary civil law. One particular aspect of that law – negligence – also has a bearing on professional practice in that it enables individuals who in some way have been wrongly harmed by a professional to make a claim on him.

Although no direct "before the event" controls arise, the very existence of the law of negligence tends to modify how any practice operates. The law of professional negligence is a wide-ranging subject, discussed in other books in the law series for health service management, published by Ravenswood Publications. However, here is a brief summary.

Negligence is a branch of the law of torts which deals with the rights and duties individuals owe to one another and which also includes such actions as trespass, defamation and nuisance. It is part of the civil rather than criminal law. The basis of negligence is the concept that the plaintiff (the person who believes himself wronged) was owed a duty of care by the defendant (the wrongdoer). There needs to have been a breach of that duty of care which has resulted in the plaintiff suffering some harm. The test of whether a duty of care exists or not in a particular situation was laid down in the famous case of Donoghue v Stevenson (1932 AC 562 HL (LC)), in which the plaintiff drank ginger beer from an opaque bottle which was found to contain a decomposed snail in consequence of which she fell ill. In this case Lord Atkin said: "You must take reasonable care to avoid acts or omissions which you can reasonably foresee would be likely to injure your neighbour. Who then is my neighbour? The answer seems to be – persons who are so closely and directly affected by my act that I ought reasonably to have them in contemplation as being so affected when I am directing my mind to the acts or omissions which are called in question."

While there are exceptions to this test it certainly applies to cases of alleged negligence in the health care professions.

An important question is: what is the standard of care required? Generally, it is the standard of care an ordinary prudent man would adopt taking into account all the circumstances such as the likelihood of harm occurring, the seriousness of any possible consequences, the importance of the defendant's objective, and the practicality of taking precautions. As far as any of the professions dealt with in this book are concerned, the standard of care required is that usually found in such persons and not that actually possessed by the defendant.

Controls Profession by Profession

Here are brief summaries of controls in some of the major professional groups.

Medical Profession

The actual practice of medicine and surgery is not limited to registered medical practitioners but use of the titles of physician, doctor of medicine, licentiate in medicine and surgery, bachelor of medicine, surgeon, general practitioner or apothecary or any other title implying registration under the Medical Act is so limited. Only registered medical practitioners may recover practice fees in a court of law or hold a wide variety of public medical officer appointments. Duly qualified medical practitioners may also practise dentistry, retail pharmacy, midwifery and sight-testing.

Dental Profession

The practice of dentistry is, with some minor exceptions, limited to registered dentists or medical practitioners. The main exception is the one made for students. The titles of dentist, dental surgeon and dental practitioner may lawfully be used only by registered dentists or medical practitioners and it is a criminal offence falsely to imply that one is so registered. Only registered dentists or registered medical practitioners may carry on a dentistry business, although special exceptions are made in cases of death or bankruptcy of the dentist. Auxiliary dental workers may carry out certain aspects of dental practice.

Pharmaceutical Profession

The practice of retail pharmacy is limited to registered pharmacists. However, because a professional practice carried on by a registered medical practitioner, a registered dentist or a registered veterinarian is outside the statutory definition of retail pharmacy, these professions are excluded in such circumstances. While a corporate body may carry on the business of retail pharmacy, the keeping, preparing and dispensing of medicinal products must be under the management of a superintendent pharmacist who is registered.

The premises at which a retail pharmacy business is carried on must also be registered under the Medicines Act 1968 and the retail sale of medicinal products must be under the personal control of a registered pharmacist at those premises. The meaning of personal control was considered in the case of Hygienic Stores Ltd v Coombs 1937 1 All ER 63. Here a company had 16 shops but only three pharmacists. It was held that to effect control one pharmacist had to be allocated to each shop and to be in personal control he had to be present there at all times. Statutory arrangements are made for a pharmacy business to be carried on in the event of the death or bankruptcy of the pharmacist. The titles of chemist and druggist, druggist, dispensing chemist or druggist, or the title of the chemist in connection with the retail sale of goods, are restricted by law to registered pharmacists, as are the titles of pharmaceutical chemist, pharmacist, pharmaceutist or member or fellow of the Pharmaceutical Society.

Nursing Profession
The practice of nursing the sick is not limited by law to registered nurses, although all senior nursing posts in the National Health Service are so restricted. However, subject to certain exceptions, it is an offence for anyone who is not duly registered to use the title of nurse, either alone or in combination. Exceptions are made for the use of such titles as children's nurse, maternity nurse, pupil nurse and student nurse. It is also an offence for anyone who is not registered in the appropriate part of the register to use any title addition, description, uniform or badge implying he or she is so registered.

Midwifery Profession
Only a registered midwife or a registered medical practitioner may attend a woman in childbirth. However, exceptions are made for midwifery and medical students and someone acting under the direction and personal supervision of a registered medical practitioner. The title of midwife may be used only by a registered midwife and it is an offence for an unqualified person to use any title, addition, description, uniform or badge implying certification. Men may now train and practise as midwives on the same conditions as women.

Midwives are subject to a system of local supervision exercised by the local health authorities.

Veterinary Profession
Only registered veterinary surgeons or veterinary practitioners may lawfully practise this profession. However, exceptions are made for a variety of minor procedures and also for students. Only appropriately qualified individuals may use the titles of veterinary surgeon or veterinary practitioner or indeed any title implying registration.

Chapter Six

Professional Discipline and Fitness to Practise

A major function imposed on controlling bodies by the legislation which created them is that of maintaining high standards of professional conduct (see also Chapter Two). All members of the professions covered by this book are therefore subject to a code of discipline which is in addition to their ordinary responsibilities and liabilities as British citizens. These codes of practice are partly set by the originating legislation and partly by the appropriate controlling body. The controlling bodies are responsible for enforcing professional discipline. In order to do so they are empowered to sit in judgement upon an individual's conduct and decide whether to apply sanctions against him. While these sanctions are primarily designed to protect the public from unacceptable conduct, they are inevitably punitive in nature. Erasure of a name from the professional register, and therefore deprivation of a livelihood is a clear example.

Tribunals

The history of the English legal system has seen a move away from arbitrary powers – be they executive, legislative or judicial – towards a separation of such powers and a much less arbitrary system. The doctrine of "separation of powers" is an important concept of British constitutional law. It signifies that there is an effective separation of the law-making process from the judicial process and from both the executive and governmental process. As explained in Chapter Two, the controlling bodies have law-making powers, as well as a judicial and an executive function. This is contrary to the doctrine of separation of powers, but there are various checks and controls to prevent abuse of the powers, particularly in the legislative and judicial functions. In fact, the doctrine of separation of powers has a number of exceptions to it even at a national level, although the separation of the judicial from the legislative is almost total.

The other outcome of the historical separation of powers has been the centralisation of the judicial function upon the ordinary courts of law. Thus, from an original position in which every baron had his own court in which he exercised legislative, judicial and executive powers, by the end of the nineteenth century the vast majority of the judicial function was centred on the High Court of Judicature with only a few exceptions, and even then the High Court was – and, importantly, still is – able to exert some influence on such other courts.

Over the past 50 years, however, various judicial procedures, called tribunals, have developed outside the ordinary courts of law. They are usually classified into administrative tribunals (for example, the National Insurance tribunals, Mental Health tribunals, Rent Act tribunals, Employment Appeals tribunals), tribunals of enquiry set up under the Tribunals of Enquiry (Evidence) Act 1971 to investigate matters of urgent public interest (for example, the Aberfan disaster) and domestic tribunals which are concerned with the discipline of members of a particular profession or organisation. In 1957 the Franks Committee (Committee On Administrative Tribunals and Enquiries Cmnd. 218, 1957) estimated there were some 2,000 tribunals in existence.

Benefits and Disadvantages of Tribunals

The use of judicial tribunals has several benefits. They are less costly than the conventional courts and they can operate to a fixed date for a hearing rather than the system used in the courts whereby a case is entered on a list and the parties must wait until the case is called. Tribunals can operate with much more informality than is usual in a court of law, and an appearance before it should be less unpleasant for everyone. Because of the limited nature of its work, a tribunal can develop very considerable expertise in its own field and thus ensure a more uniform approach to similar problems. But perhaps the most important benefit of the tribunal system is that the ordinary courts just could not cope with the volume of work tribunals deal with.

The main reservations about the tribunals arise from the very fact that they are not courts of law with a long history, a tradition of impartiality and a procedure designed to ensure justice. The judicial standard might therefore be lower with a tribunal, which is essentially a lay body, and the risks of injustice, unfairness or partiality greater. This potential problem is dealt with by means of controls and checks which are either found in the statute creating the disciplinary power or are part of the general power of control exercised by the High Court.

Statutory Controls and Checks

The legislation – statutes and statutory instruments – which created the various professional disciplinary tribunals and their procedures provides controls and checks to ensure fairness and impartiality. All of these are designed to ensure that the tribunals act as fairly and reasonably as any court of law. Clear rules of procedure are laid down in all cases, and the tribunals will normally follow the rules of evidence observed in the ordinary courts. The person accused of misconduct is permitted to use a representative, either legally qualified or lay, to present his case to the tribunal. In most cases the rules provide that a legal assessor must be appointed to advise the tribunal on matters of law. The assessor will be a fully qualified and experienced lawyer. Normally, all disciplinary hearings are held in public, although the tribunal may sit in camera if justice demands. However, the decision of the tribunal must always be given publicly. A clear process of appeal against a decision of the tribunal is available in almost every case, either to the High Court or to the Judicial Committee of the Privy Council (see page 36). In all cases a process permitting the restoration of any name erased from the register is also provided.

Control by the High Court

The High Court has always retained the power to oversee the activities of inferior courts and, indeed, to prevent the abuse of executive power (see ultra vires doctrine, page 32). Because this power is part of the common law and based on precedent it is not possible to state precisely in what circumstances and how the High Court might intervene to control a disciplinary tribunal. However, in general the High Court may be willing to intervene when a tribunal acts contrary to the rules of natural justice, where it fails to carry out a statutory duty imposed on it, where it acts in error of the law (called an error on the face of the record), acts in excess of its jurisdiction or acts ultra vires. Most of these abuses of judicial power are self-evident.

The rules of natural justice are in essence unwritten rules of the common law (that is non-statutory or judge-made law), although many have been embodied into statutory provisions. The two main rules of natural justice are the rule against bias (no man may be a judge in his own cause, nemo judex in parte sua) and the right to a hearing (no man to be condemned unheard, audi alteram partem). An example of the rule against bias is the case of The King v Sussex Justices ex parte McCarthy (1942) 1KB 256 in which a conviction for a motoring offence given by magistrates was quashed by the High Court because the clerk to the magistrates was a member of a firm of solicitors acting for a plaintiff in a civil action arising from the same motoring offence. This was in spite of the fact that the clerk did not advise the magistrates about this particular decision. An example of the High Court intervening where the right to a hearing was being denied is the case of Ridge v Baldwin (1964) AC 40 where the Brighton Watch Committee dismissed the Chief Constable following his acquittal by the Old Bailey on a charge of conspiracy. The Committee had formulated no charge against him as a basis for the dismissal, nor had it given him any real opportunity to present his case to the Committee. In all cases the legislation which established the professional disciplinary bodies referred to in this book requires that the accused must be given an opportunity of being heard by the tribunal. It also attempts to avoid bias by ensuring that no member of any disciplinary committee has had any dealings with a specific case at the preliminary investigatory phase.

An example of the High Court intervening to quash a decision of a professional disciplinary body is The General Medical Council v Spackman (1943) AC 627. The Court quashed the Council's decision because, although it was under a statutory duty to hold a "due inquiry", the Council had refused to hear fresh evidence disputing a finding in the Divorce Court of adultery by a doctor with a patient. The Medical Act 1956 later clarified the situation by requiring the General Medical Council to accept the decison of the divorce or other decisions of the High Court. The Divorce Reform Act 1969 (repealed) abolished adultery as a ground for divorce, substituting "irretrievable breakdown" of a marriage as the sole basis for divorce.

The mechanism whereby the High Court will intervene to control an inferior court or tribunal is a somewhat complex issue, but it can be outlined briefly. Normally, an individual who is in some way affected by the action, or inaction, of a disciplinary body will apply to the High Court for one of three possible prerogative orders depending on the circumstances. They are the orders of certiorari, mandamus and prohibition. An order of certiorari is used by the High Court to quash the decision of an inferior court or tribunal for one of the reasons described above. An order of mandamus is used by the court to compel a tribunal to carry out a statutory duty. An order of prohibition is used to prevent a tribunal exceeding its jurisdiction or acting against the rules of natural justice. Failure to observe the rules of natural justice or any of the other reasons given above for the High Court to intervene may also be a basis for an appeal.

Consideration of the disciplinary powers and procedures of the professional bodies should take in five broad areas: the acts or omissions which can lead to disciplinary action (the offences), what action the disciplinary body can take against someone found guilty of an offence (the sanctions), the tribunals themselves and their procedures, the process of appeal, and the process of restoration. In additon, the power to deal with an individual thought to be unfit to practise because of physical or mental illness must also be considered.

The Disciplinary Offences

There are three major categories of offence which may make a professional liable to disciplinary procedure and sanction: criminal conviction, professional misconduct, and fraudulent registration. A variety of other offences can be committed.

Criminal Conviction

A criminal conviction may be the basis for disciplinary action in any of the professions dealt with in this book. In some cases the conviction must be such as to render the individual unfit to practise; in others the disciplinary body is not limited in this way. Section 16 of the Veterinary Surgeons Act 1966, for example, indicates that the Disciplinary Committee may remove a name where a registered veterinarian has been convicted of a criminal offence which in its opinion renders him unfit to practise veterinary surgery. However, section 36 of the Medical Act 1983 indicates that, if it thinks fit to do so, the Professional Conduct Committee of the General Medical Council may, inter alia, erase a name from the register where a doctor has been convicted of any criminal offence. In fact, the disciplinary bodies are only likely to apply sanctions where a conviction does in some way make an individual unfit to practise. The principle is not to punish a criminal twice but to promote high standards of professional practice and so protect the public.

In some cases the crime must have been committed in the United Kingdom but in others a criminal conviction anywhere in the world may be the basis for disciplinary action. In reality, this geographical distinction is not very important because, whereas a conviction has to be in the United Kingdom, the Channel Islands or the Isle of Man, a crime committee elsewhere, whether resulting in a conviction or not, could still amount to serious professional misconduct. The disciplinary bodies are generally not limited to considering convictions which occur only when a professional person is registered, but they can exercise jurisdiction only over people who are registered. A pre-requisite to registration in all professions will be some evidence of good character, and there may be a power to withhold initial registration in some professions where the applicant has been convicted of a criminal offence (as in the pharmaceutical profession).

An impression of the sort of criminal convictions considered by professional disciplinary bodies may be had from the General Medical Council's Annual Report for 1986 (March 1987). Thirty-five convictions relating to the abuse of alcohol were reported to the Council. Eight convictions related to the abuse of drugs. Twenty concerned dishonesty. One conviction concerned violence, while two convictions were for indecency.

Professional Misconduct

Members of all the professions dealt with in this book are liable to sanctions when they are judged by their disciplinary body to be guilty of professional misconduct. Various terms have been used in various professions to describe this unacceptable behaviour – "serious professional misconduct", "disgraceful conduct in a professional matter", "infamous or disgraceful conduct in a professional matter " and so on. The concept throughout, however, is that there is an acceptable code of conduct in any profession and that disciplinary proceedings may be taken against any professional who falls below this standard.

How then is a professional person to know what is the standard of conduct to be expected of him and what constitutes misconduct? Most professions issue written periodic advice and guidance to their members on such matters. One of the complaints against the General Medical Council in the 1970's was that it did not do this adequately, and one recommendation of the Merrison Committee (see page 28) was that the Council should issue positive advice and guidance on standards of conduct for doctors. Thus, section 35 of the 1983 Medical Act empowers the General Medical Council to provide in such a manner as it thinks fit advice for members of the medical profession on standards of professional conduct or medical ethics. In 1979 the Council established the Committee on Standards of Professional Conduct and Medical Ethics. The guidance issued in any profession will never be treated as exclusive or comprehensive and no-one may use the defence that his alleged misconduct was not covered in the guidelines. In addition to any guidelines, the accumulated decisions of the disciplinary bodies are also an important source of what is or is not currently seen as misconduct.

As stated above, various terms are used in legislation to describe misconduct. Sometimes – especially on an appeal against a decision – the precise wording may need to be considered. Where the term "disgraceful" is used (as, for example, in the veterinary profession) the conduct is not limited to that involving moral turpitude; it could include conduct which is reprehensible in anyone but so reprehensible in a professional man as to bring disgrace on his profession (Marten v Disciplinary Committee of the Royal College of Veterinary Surgeons (1966) 1QB 1 (1965) 1 All ER 949 DC). The term "in a professional respect" appears not only to relate to practice itself but also to a judgement on a person's fitness to practise. Thus, in Stocks v Central Midwives Board (1915 3 KB 756 DC), it was held that immorality by a midwife, while not affecting the discharge of her duties per se, might make her unfit to discharge those duties. Again, the annual report of the General Medical Council for 1986 (March 1987) illustrates some of the commoner types of misconduct which a disciplinary body may have to consider. They include disregard of responsibility to patients, abuse of prescribing privileges, breach of professional confidence, emotional or sexual relationships with patients, advertising or canvassing, false certification and false claims to certain qualifications.

Fraudulent Registration

Most of the disciplinary bodies also have the power to erase a name from a register where they are satisfied it has been entered falsely. Cases of this kind may be dealt with by the appropriate disciplinary body or by some other part of the professional council – the registration committee of the General Medical Council, for example.

Other Disciplinary Offences

Medical Practitioners As will be seen later in this chapter, one of the disciplinary powers of the General Medical Council is to make a doctor's registration conditional upon the observance of certain requirements. Failure to comply with these requirements may itself be a basis for further disciplinary action and a further sanction.

Midwives In addition to misconduct generally, a midwife may be subject to disciplinary procedure if she disobeys any of the rules laid down in the Midwives Rules 1986.

Corporate Bodies

As far as retail pharmacists, opticians and hearing aid dispensers are concerned, a significant proportion of practice involves businesses which are corporate bodies (see page 22). These may be liable for disciplinary action in certain instances. For example, the disciplinary jurisdiction of the Pharmaceutical Society of Great Britain extends to where a corporate body has been convicted under the Pharmacy Act, the Medicines Act 1968 or the Misuse of Drugs Act 1971, or where a board member of a corporate body carrying on a retail pharmacy business has been convicted of a criminal offence (even though he is not himself a registered pharmacist). Similarly, the General Optical Council may take action against a corporate body convicted of any offence under the Opticians Act, and the Hearing Aid Council may take action against a registered employer of hearing aid dispensers who has not made the necessary provisions to ensure that the dispensing is under the supervision of a registered dispenser.

Disciplinary Sanctions

The disciplinary sanctions available to some or all of the controlling bodies are removal of registration (erasure), suspension of registration, making registration conditional, or warning, admonishing or advising the alleged wrongdoer. It should be noted that no power exists to impose any direct monetary sanction, except for opticians. As stated above, the philosophy behind these sanctions is to achieve high standards of professional conduct and to protect the public, not primarily to punish the wrongdoer. Inevitably, however, all sanctions have some punitive element about them; even the investigation and hearing of an alleged disciplinary case may be considered to have such an element about it. Underlying any punitive sanction must be an important deterrent effect. It may be argued that a major value of the disciplinary sanctions is their preventative or sobering influence on any professional group.

The problem of "making the punishment fit the crime" was referred to in Chapter One. There, it was pointed out that the General Medical Council had appeared to be lenient in cases of disregard of responsibilities to patients but sterner in the more traditional type of misconduct, such as sexual relationships with patients, advertising, and canvassing patients. Although attempts to modify the Medical Act by a Private Member's Bill were withdrawn, it remains to be seen if the changes made by the General Medical Council to its guidelines on conduct will allay public concern.

Erasure

Erasure of a name from the professional register is the most potent sanction and is available to all professional disciplinary bodies considered in this book. The effect is, of course, to de-register an individual and therefore deprive him of all the privileges that come with registration. As was seen in the last chapter, where the practice of a certain professional is restricted to duly registered individuals, erasure effectively removes their livelihoods as they may no longer lawfully practise. Even in those cases, such as the medical profession, where practice is not restricted to registered doctors, section 47 of the Medical Act 1983 limits all public medical officer appointments to registered personnel. An erasure takes effect from the date when any appeal (see below) is finally determined if there is an appeal, or from the date when any application for an appeal is rejected or, where an individual does not appeal, from the expiry of the period allowed for such appeal.

It is not only individual names that may be struck off a register. If there is a register of businesses (for example, dentistry, pharmacy or optician's) or similar registers (for example, of pharmacy premises or of employers of hearing aid dispensers), then the appropriate disciplinary body may in specific disciplinary cases de-register these. Details are given in Part II of this book.

Suspension and Conditional Registration

In the cases of the medical, veterinary and midwifery professions the appropriate disciplinary body may also suspend a name. The effect is the same as erasure insofar as the person is de-registered, but its effect comes to an automatic end after a pre-determined period of time.

In the case of the medical profession there is also the power to make an individual's registration conditional on such requirements as the Professional Conduct Committee thinks fit. Such requirements may be imposed for any period up to three years. Conditional registration may also be used where impaired health may effect a doctor's fitness to practise (see below). Failure to observe the conditions imposed may itself be the basis for futher disciplinary action, such as suspension or erasure.

Warning and Advice

In many cases where it is alleged that a professional man is liable to disciplinary sanctions the result may be some sort of written warning or advice. The nature of such an outcome will, of course, depend much upon the precise circumstances, but there are two broad types of approach. The outcome may be a caution, warning, admonition or censure, all of which have an element of rebuke in them, or it may be advisory, with an individual given guidance on what conduct is suitable in a given situation. Many outcomes will have both elements in them.

While warning letters are a valid and very reasonable outcome to a disciplinary charge proper, some concern was expressed in late 1980 about their possible misuse. The concern arose from an incident in which an overseas doctor was interviewed for a job with the Sheffield Area Health Authority and was offered the post. When the written offer arrived certain conditions of employment he had stipulated at the interview were not included in the contract and he turned it down. A junior NHS administrator then told the doctor she would report him to the General Medical Council "as is my usual custom in these circumstances". A letter from the deputy registrar of the Council followed which said: "The President has carefully considered your observations and he has asked me to say that the information concerning you has been placed on the records of the Council . . . In all the circumstances no further action by the Council will be taken on this occasion. The President trusts, however, that your conduct will not in future give further cause for concern." Considerable anxiety was expressed in the medical profession that a contract between a health authority and a doctor was seen to be outside the Council's jurisdiction and that the health authority was using the Council to frighten an overseas doctor. The whole issue was debated at a Council meeting on 6th November 1980 and it was agreed that the procedure over warning letters should be reviewed.

The Disciplinary Bodies: Structure and Procedure

Except for the pharmaceutical profession, all the professions dealt with in this book have adopted a two-stage process of disciplinary procedure. The first stage is an investigatory one. The second stage is the disciplinary tribunal proper. In the pharmaceutical profession there is a single, combined stage.

The Investigatory Stage

Except in the pharmaceutical profession, the investigatory stage is dealt with by an ad hoc committee. This is called the Investigating Committee in the cases of opticians, professions supplementary to medicine and hearing aid dispensers, the Preliminary Proceedings Committee in the medical and dental professions, and the Preliminary Investigating Committee in the veterinary profession. In nursing and midwifery the National Board carries out the preliminary investigation. In all of these the committee is a committee of the appropriate controlling body. Membership of the controlling bodies themselves was considered in Chapter Two, and the rules laid down under the parent Act which embodies the constitution of disciplinary committees often specify measures to enure that the ratios of different types of Council member are reflected in the disciplinary committees. Thus the General Medical Council's Preliminary Proceedings Committee consists of a chairman, six elected Council members, two appointed Council members and two lay Council members. The rules which determine the composition of these committees will also determine their procedure and quorum. The quorum is usually relatively small, being between two and five members. As stated above, the function of these committees is to investigate cases referred to them and to decide whether or not to refer them to the disciplinary stage of the procedure. The chairman of the committees may also have an investigatory power as a step before consideration by the full committee. In the pharmaceutical profession, where there is only one disciplinary committee, the chairman of this has an important investigatory role (see below). More details of the investigating committee's work are given in Part II.

The Disciplinary Stage

The disciplinary stage – that is the phase in which the case against someone is heard and a decision is reached – is dealt with by an ad hoc committee. It is called the Disciplinary Committee in the veterinary, opticians' and hearing aid dispensers' professions and in the professions supplementary to medicine, the Professional Conduct Committee in the medical, dental, nursing and midwifery professions, and the Statutory Committee in the pharmaceutical profession.

The constitutions of the disciplinary committees are all determined by rules made under powers given in the parent Act, and it is often required that the committee should have as its chairman the president of the controlling body. Rules usually ensure that elections of members to these committees reflect the proportion of different types of Council member. A quorum for such committees is usually between four and six, and clearly it could be somewhat oppressive, if not impractical, to have a bench of adjudication in excess of these numbers. In all cases steps are taken to separate the investigatory process from the disciplinary process to ensure that the disciplinary phase proper is not in any way biased. In some cases no-one may be a member of both committees either at the same time or dealing with one and the same case; and in the case of the General Medical Council no-one may be elected to the Professional Conduct Committee if in the previous year he was a member of the Preliminary Proceedings Committee. The only exception to this separation is that in some cases – those of hearing aid dispensers and opticians, for example – the chairman of the Disciplinary Committee may also be the chairman of the Investigating Committee.

The Statutory Committee of the Pharmaceutical Society has some differences from the other professional disciplinary committees. As already mentioned, there is no Investigating Committee, and the chairman of the Statutory Committee will carry out what investigations are necessary to decide whether a case shall go to the Statutory Committee. This committee is not a committee of the Council of the Pharmaceutical Society of Great Britain, the controlling body for the profession, but a committee of the whole Society. The chairman is appointed by the Privy Council as someone having practical legal experience and is usually an eminent member of the legal profession. There is no legal requirement that members of the Statutory Committee appointed by the Council need be members of the Council or indeed of the Society, although with the exception of the chairman, they usually will be so.

Procedure

The procedure for dealing with any case in which it is alleged that a professional person may be liable to disciplinary action is in all cases laid down in the form of detailed rules made by the controlling body and approved by whatever machinery is required by the parent Act. In some instances, because of the judicial nature of these rules, approval may be required from the Lord Chancellor – the highest judicial functionary in the United Kingdom. By prescription he is speaker of the House of Lords, always a Privy Councillor and a Cabinet Minister. Because he is a member of the Government of the day, he goes out of office with that Government. He is an example of one person having judicial, executive and legislative powers. He cannot be a Roman Catholic.

The Investigatory Procedure

The procedure will begin when either a complaint is made about a professional's conduct to the controlling body or it receives information about a conviction. In some cases – for example, in the medical and pharmaceutical professions – the chairman of the investigating body may initially investigate the case, obtaining whatever information is deemed necessary. In other cases the investigating committee will do this. Complaints must be obtained in the form of statutory declarations except where the complainant holds a public appointment. A statutory declaration is one made before a magistrate or commissioner for oaths in the form required by the Statutory Declarations Act 1835. Anyone making a false statement is guilty of an offence under the Perjury Act 1911. The accused person is informed of the complaint against him and is invited to make any observations he may have. The investigatory process is carried out in private and the committee is not required to give reasons for its decisions. However, it must announce its decisions publicly and inform the accused and any complainant. The basic decision it must reach is whether or not to refer the case to the disciplinary tribunal for determination. In certain instances where the investigating committee refers a case to the disciplinary committee it may also have the power to suspend the accused from practice until determination of the hearing. This is so in the medical and midwifery professions.

Disciplinary Hearing

The procedure at a disciplinary tribunal is very similar to that in a court of law. The hearing will not normally commence until at least 28 days' notice has been given to all parties concerned. When notice of a hearing is served on the accused a copy of the rules of procedure must also be given. The accused will have the right to be represented at the tribunal by lawyer (a solicitor or barrister) or by a lay person. Hearings are normally held in public, although the committee has the power to sit in camera if it considers it necessary to do so in the best interests of justice. However, its decision must always be given in public. The rules of evidence followed in a normal court of law are observed. The tribunal may administer oaths and the parties may obtain writs of subpoena ad testificandum and subpoena duces tecum. The former writ is designed to secure a witness's attendance and requires him to appear and give evidence under penalty for disobedience. A subpoena duces tecum requires someone to attend and bring with him specified documents as evidence. A transcript of the proceedings will normally be taken.

The hearing will commence with the charge being read out, and the accused or his representative may then claim that there is no case made out. If that view is not accepted by the committee, evidence in support of the charge is then presented unless the accused admits the facts. Where evidence is brought against him the accused or his representative may cross-examine the witnesses against him. Once the case against him has been presented the accused or his representative may submit either that the facts alleged have not been proved or that, if they are proved, they do not constitute misconduct. If the tribunal does not except this view the accused may then present evidence in his defence. His witnesses may be cross-examined.

At the close of the hearing the disciplinary committee has to decide if it finds the alleged facts proved, and, if so, whether that constitutes misconduct and what sanction it needs to impose. Decisions are reached by voting, usually with the chairman having a casting vote. Generally, a committee will give its decision at once although, in some instances, it has the power to postpone the decision. As stated above, that decision must always be made in public. In all instances, except for the pharmaceutical profession, the legislation requires the controlling body or the disciplinary committee to appoint a legal assessor. The assessor must be a solicitor or barrister of at least ten years' standing and his duty is to advise the committee on matters of law. While the committee is not bound to heed his advice it normally does so. Where it does not, this must be recorded and made known to parties to the proceedings. Detailed rules are laid down by the Lord Chancellor dealing with the duties of legal assessors for each profession and these are issued in the form of statutory instruments.

Appeals and Restorations

Appeals

In all of the professions considered in this book a decision of a disciplinary tribunal is not final but may be appealed against to a higher court. For the pharmaceutical, nursing, midwifery and hearing aid dispensing professions appeal is to the High Court (a divisional court of the Queen's Bench Division). For the other professions it is to the Judicial Committee of the Privy Council (see page 36). The time allowed for appeal is three months for the pharmaceutical, nursing and midwifery professions and 28 days for the others. Because of the time allowed for appeals no decision is normally effective until this time has elapsed, unless an interim suspension has been applied. Where the appeal is to the High Court the usual rules of that court apply to hearing appeals. Where the appeal is to the Judicial Committee of the Privy Council specific rules are laid down for each profession in the form of statutory instruments. For the purpose of costs the controlling body of the appropriate profession is always considered a party to any appeal, whether it appears or not.

On appeal, the Privy Council or the High Court will not generally intervene to substitute their own discretion for that of the disciplinary body. Nor will they normally interfere with the disciplinary body's decision on the sentence. They may intervene on points of fact or of law, however, and certainly they may do so where the rules of natural justice have not been observed. An example of an unwillingness to intervene was the case of Laud v General Medical Council 4th March 1980 (Times 8th March 1980). A doctor had been convicted in 1974 of obtaining money from an insurance company by deception, and again in 1978 of obtaining money by deception from the National Health Service. On the latter occasion he asked the court to take into consideration six other offences. He was given a suspended sentence of six months' imprisonment. The Disciplinary Committee (as it was then) of the General Medical Council ordered his name to be suspended from the register for 12 months. He appealed to the Judicial Committee of the Privy Council against the suspension but the appeal was dismissed on the grounds that the Council would not interfere with the decision of any professional disciplinary body as far as the proper sentence to be imposed in cases of misconduct.

Restoration

Machinery exists in all the professions covered by the book for the restoration to the register of a name removed for disciplinary reasons. In many instances there is a minimum time – usually ten months – before a request for restoration may be considered. Where this is the case no request for restoration may be made less than ten months after the last one. The request is normally direct to the disciplinary tribunal which imposed the erasure. Rules made to deal with the disciplinary procedure itself will also deal with applications for restoration. Application must be made in the form prescribed and must be supported by all relevant information. In many instances character evidence will be required. When considering an application for restoration the Disciplinary Committee usually sits in private. However, it may not refuse to restore a name until it has given the applicant an opportunity to appear before the Committee and present his case.

Fitness to Practise

The disciplinary procedures considered so far have all been addressed to the concept that a professional might be unfit to practise because of his criminal behaviour or other unprofessional conduct. In some instances such behaviour may be the result of physical or mental illness (for example, alcoholism, drug abuse or mental illness). In other cases illness might make a person unfit to practise but, provided his behaviour is not criminal and his conduct not unprofessional, he would not be subject to disciplinary procedures. Such cases are particularly difficult to deal with in the medical profession where doctors are unwilling to report their worries about a colleague's health because of professional confidentiality. This was particularly so in the past because the disciplinary procedure proper had to be used in such cases and was clearly inappropriate. This legalistic and juristic approach to illness rather than a more clinical and humane approach had long been criticised, and one recommendation of the Merrison Committee (see page 28) was that an alternative procedure should be introduced. This was brought into being by the Medical Act 1978 and by the rules made under that Act. The dental, nursing and midwifery professions are in the process of introducing similar systems. The procedure in the medical profession will be described as the most developed example. The medical profession's arrangements involve a two-stage process. The first stage is of a less formal nature and is dealt with by the president of the General Medical Council. It is assumed that all but the most recalcitrant of doctors will be dealt with in this way, and only totally non co-operative doctors would be referred to the Health Committee where a more formal, tribunal-like approach is adopted. The formalities of a disciplinary-type procedure may be stressful, and, tragically, two doctors, both involved in disciplinary proceedings, committed suicide in the first half of 1981.

Investigation by the President

Where the Preliminary Proceedings Committee, the Professional Conduct Committee or an outside party refer for consideration a case in which the doctor's health is brought into question, it must initially be dealt with by the president. If the complaint comes from an outside party it must be in the form of a statutory declaration (see above) unless the complainant is acting in a public capacity. The president will inform the doctor of the situation, invite him to undergo medical examination by two doctors chosen by the president and to submit any observations he may have. The doctor is told he may nominate an additional doctor of his own choice to examine him at the Council's expense. The president must send copies of the medical reports to the doctor, although he has the power to exclude any information which is not relevant to the question of fitness to practise and which would not be in the interests of the practitioner to see. This power to withhold some medical information applies only to the fitness to practise procedure and not to the disciplinary procedure. Indeed, in the case of Crompton v General Medical Council 1981 (Lancet 1981 December 5th pg. 1298) the Judicial Committee of the Privy Council quashed a decision to erase the name of the doctor. This was on the grounds that the Professional Conduct Committee had requested Dr. Crompton to supply them with two psychiatrists' reports, which was done, but then refused to let him see these reports or even let him know their tenor. This refusal was considered to be in breach of natural justice.

If a doctor agrees voluntarily to accept the medical recommendations for treatment and the president is satisfied with this undertaking further action is postponed. If he does not or refuses to be examined then the president, after consultation with two Council members appointed for this purpose, must refer the case to the Health Committee. If the president considers that urgent action is required he may refer the case to the Preliminary Proceedings Committee for imposition of an interim suspension or an interim conditional registration.

Health Committee Procedure

The Health Committee consists of a chairman, deputy chairman, six elected Council members, three appointed Council members and one lay member. The president may choose to sit as chairman and members are elected annually. A quorum is five. Rules are laid down in the form of statutory instruments for the procedure of the Committee. When a case is referred to the Health Committee notice of the inquiry is sent to the doctor giving at least 28 days' warning of the hearing. The Committee sits in private, but the doctor, his representative and his medical adviser may attend. One or more medical assessors appointed by the Council, but who are not Council members, must also attend. The Committee hears evidence of the practitioner's fitness to practise and the doctor or his representative may address the Committee. The Committee may adjourn for further medical evidence. It may either suspend the doctor for up to one year or make his registration conditional on some specific requirement – usually medical treatment – for a period of up to three years. It may renew either order but only for periods of up to one year and three years respectively, and it may suspend a doctor whose registration was previously conditional. It does not have the power to erase a name. A legal assessor must be present at all Committee meetings to advise on matters of law, and the doctor may appeal against a Health Committee decision to the Judicial Committee of the Privy Council.

PART II

Chapter Seven

The Medical Profession

The Medical Act 1983

Up to 1983 the practice of medicine was governed by the Medical Act 1956, the Medical Act 1969, the Medical Act 1978 and the various statutory instruments made under their powers. These Acts, collectively known as the Medical Acts 1959–1978, were repealed by, and consolidated into, a single statute, the Medical Act 1983. It extends to the whole of the United Kingdom.

The General Medical Council

The General Medical Council is the body which controls the medical profession. It was originally created as the General Council of Medical Education and Registration in the United Kingdom by the Medical Act 1858. The continued existence of the Council as a corporate body is confirmed by section 1 of 1983 Act. Schedule 1 to the Act lays down the constitution of the Council including its composition, powers, proceedings, officers, finances and committees. Wide powers are given to the Council. For example, paragraph 9 provides that the Council may "do such things and enter into such transactions as are in their opinion incidental or conducive to the performance of their functions under this Act, including the borrowing of money".

Composition

Schedule 1 to the Medical Act 1983 provides that the General Medical Council shall consist of three groups of members: those elected, those appointed and those nominated. The number of elected members must exceed the number of all other members. Members of the Council must be less than 70 years of age. However, schedule 1 permits the Council to make rules lowering this age limit, these rules to be approved by the Privy Council.

Elected Members

Schedule 1 provides for four electoral constituencies – one each for England (including the Channel Islands and the Isle of Man), Wales, Scotland and Northern Ireland. In order to vote in a Council election an individual must be resident at the time of the election in the constituency and must be a medical practitioner who is fully registered, provisionally registered or registered with limited registration. However, in this last case the individual must have been so registered for at least three out of the preceeding four years, either continuously or in the aggregate. Only registered medical practitioners (fully, provisionally or limited with the same proviso as above) may be elected to, or hold office as a member of, the Council. There are 50 elected members. Elections are held under a scheme drawn up and administered by the Council. The scheme needs the approval of the Privy Council.

Appointed Members

Schedule 1 empowers those universities and other bodies in England, Wales, Scotland and Northern Ireland which have the power to grant a registrable medical qualification under the Act to appoint members of the General Medical Council. At present there are 34 appointed members. Appointed members must be fully or provisionally registered as medical practitioners or hold limited registration and have done so for a period of three out of the previous four years.

Nominated Members

These members are nominated by the Queen on the advice of Her Privy Council. A majority must be non-medical and there must be at least one member each for England, Wales, Scotland and Northern Ireland. There are 13 nominated members (SI 1987 No. 457).

Branch Councils

Part IV of schedule 1 to the 1983 Act provides for one branch council each for England, Wales, Scotland and Northern Ireland. A council consists of the General Medical Council members (elected, appointed and nominated) for that particular area. The General Council may delegate to a branch council such functions as it thinks fit except that of erasure from the registers of any entry which has been obtained fraudulently or in error. Each branch council has a registrar, but the registrar of the General Council is the registrar for the branch council for England and may be registrar for any or all of the others. The effect of the 1978 Act was that the pre-existing branch council for England and Wales was split into one for England and one for Wales and the branch council for Ireland ceased to exist and was replaced with one for Northern Ireland.

Constitution and Procedure of the General and Branch Councils

Schedule 1 to the Medical Act 1983 and rules made by the Council determine the proceedings of the General Medical Council and the branch councils and their officers.

Proceedings A quorum for a General Council meeting is 22, of whom not less than 12 shall be elected members (The General Medical Council (Quorum Rules) Order of Council 1979 SI 1979 No. 1358). Matters are to be decided by the votes of a majority of members present at any meeting and, in the case of equal votes, the person presiding shall have an additional casting vote. The validity of proceedings of the Council or councils are not to be affected by any defect in the election, appointment or nomination of any member or by any vacancy.

Officers The General Medical Council must elect a president from its members and may elect a chairman and treasurer, but their duration of office may not exceed the duration of their membership of the Council. The General Council must appoint a registrar and may appoint such deputies and assistants as the Council thinks fit.

Committees Section 1 of the 1983 Act confirms the existence of four committees of the General Council: the Education Committee, the Preliminary Proceedings Committee, the Professional Conduct Committee and the Health Committee, and these are referred to as the "Statutory Committees". The Preliminary Proceedings Committee has responsibility to investigate any case in the first instance in which it appears that a doctor may be liable to disciplinary proceedings or any case in which his fitness to practise may be questioned because of mental or physical illness. It may, if it finds there is a case to answer, refer any disciplinary case to the Professional Conduct Committee and any fitness to practise case to the Health Committee. The function of the Education Committee is to promote high standards in, and co-ordinate all stages of, medical education.

In addition to these specific committees, the General Council may form other committees, and these committees may co-opt non-Council members with the approval of the General Council. However, this does not apply to the Disciplinary or Health Committees. The General Council may delegate to any committee any function it thinks fit, and the Council also decides the quorum of such committees. At present, the Council maintains an executive committee, a finance and establishment committee, an overseas committee, a registration committee and a committee on standards of professional conduct and medical ethics.

Finance

The Council operates essentially as a self-financing body. Schedule 1 makes all registration fees payable to the Council and requires its expenses to be defrayed from this income and from the income received from the sale of registers. The various fees related to the registration process are contained in the General Medical Council (Registration (Fees) Regulations) Order of Council 1986 (SI 1986 No. 149) as amended by SI 1987 No. 102. Schedule 1 also requires the Council to keep proper accounts which must be audited by appropriately qualified auditors. The audited accounts must be published by the Council and a copy supplied to the Privy Council. The Privy Council must lay a copy before both Houses of Parliament.

Remuneration Schedule 1 to the 1983 Act empowers the General Council to pay to its members such fees, travelling, subsistence and other allowances as it permits.

Functions of the General Medical Council

The main functions of the General Medical Council under the Medical Act 1983 are:

Registration The Council is responsible for the registration of medical practitioners under Parts II, III and IV of the 1983 Act (sections 3–34).

Education The Council is responsible for determining the educational standards and experience to be obtained by persons seeking medical registration, and for approving training courses and examinations at universities and similar institutions (Part II of Medical Act 1983). The Education Committee of the General Council is responsible for promoting high standards of medical education.

Discipline The Council is responsible for professional discipline under Part V of the 1983 Act (sections 35–45).

Fitness to Practise Part V of the Act also empowers the General Medical Council to consider a doctor's fitness to practise in so far as it is influenced by his ill-health.

Professional Conduct Section 35 empowers the General Medical Coucil to provide advice for the medical profession on matters of professional conduct and medical ethics.

All of these functions are considered later in greater detail.

Control of the General Medical Council

Section 50 of the 1983 Medical Act empowers the Privy Council to intervene if it considers the General Medical Council to be in default. If it appears to the Privy Council that the General Medical Council or its Education Committee have failed to secure the prescribed standard of proficiency at examinations, or has otherwise failed to perform any duty imposed by the Medical Act, the Privy Council must inform the General Council or the Education Committee of its views. If the General Council or the Education Committee fail to comply with the Privy Council's views then it may act in their place.

The Registers: Registration

Two registers are kept under the Medical Act 1983. One is called "the register of medical practitioners" and the other is called "the register of medical practitioners with limited registration" (sections 2 and 30).

Register of Medical Practitioners

Section 30 of the 1983 Act divides this register into four lists:

The principal list consists of all fully or provisionally registered medical practitioners. This is the familiar "Medical Register" as published.

The overseas list consists of fully or provisionally registered medical practitioners who reside outside the United Kingdom, Republic of Ireland, Channel Islands, Isle of Man or other member states of the EEC.

The visiting overseas doctors list which includes doctors registered under section 27 of the 1983 Act (see below).

The visiting EEC practitioners list which lists doctors temporarily registered under the provisions of section 18.

Register of Medical Practitioners with Limited Registration
This is a register of doctors registered under the provisions of section 22 of the 1983 Act (see below).

The Specialist List
The Medical Qualifications (EEC Recognition) Order 1977 SI 1977 No. 827 also requires the Council to have a specialist list. Any national of a member state of the EEC who is registered as a medical practitioner may apply to have any recognised specialist qualification included on the list. The General Medical Council may publish the list but does not do so at present.

Keeping the Registers. The Registrar
Section 30 of the 1983 Act imposes a duty on the registrar of the General Council to keep the register in accordance with the provisions of the Medical Act and any regulations made by the General Medical Council. The registrar is empowered to enquire by letter if a registered person has changed his address and, if he receives no reply in six months, to erase that name. To help keep the register up to date, section 30(6) requires that where a registrar of births and deaths registers the death of a medical practitioner he shall send free of charge to the registrar of the General Medical Council a certified copy. Section 31 of the 1983 Act empowers the General Council to make regulations with respect to the form and keeping of the registers and the procedures for registration. The regulations are made in the form of statutory instruments and are not effective until approved by the Privy Council. The present regulations are the General Medical Council (Registration Regulations) Order of Council 1979 SI 1979 No. 844.

Publication of part of the registers is provided for by section 34 of the 1983 Act. The "Medical Register" is an annual publication by the General Council of all names on the principal list as at the first of January each year. In addition, the General Council may publish the "Overseas Medical Register", being a list of persons appearing on the overseas list. Section 34 provides that the presence of a name on a copy of one of these published registers is evidence that that person is registered; absence of a name is evidence that he is not registered. However, schedule 3 to the Act requires the registrar when he registers a qualification or a person under the Medical Act to issue to the applicant an appropriate certificate of registration. Section 34 provides that where a name does not appear on a published register then such a certificate is evidence of registration. In addition, a certified copy of an entry in the register issued under the hand of the registrar is also evidence of that entry.

Registration

Doctors Qualifying in England, Wales, Scotland or Northern Ireland
Section 3 of the 1983 Act provides that anyone who holds one or more primary United Kingdom medical qualifications, has passed a qualifying examination and has obtained the prescribed experience is entitled to be registered as a fully registered medical practitioner and to have his primary qualification registered.

Primary Qualifications Section 4 lists the primary qualifications as being the degrees of Bachelor of Medicine, Licence or Licentiate in Medicine, or degree of Bachelor of Surgery, granted by any university in England, Wales, Scotland or Northern Ireland, and a variety of other primary qualifications granted by the Society of Apothecaries of London and the various medical Royal Colleges.

Qualifying Examinations A qualifying examination is one held for the purpose of granting a registerable primary qualification. Such a qualification may be granted by certain United Kingdom universities (Oxford, Cambridge, London, Manchester, Birmingham, Liverpool, Leeds, Sheffield, Newcastle, Bristol, Nottingham, Southampton, Leicester, Wales, Glasgow, Aberdeen, Edinburgh, Dundee, Belfast) or by the various Royal Colleges (section 4). In addition, section 4 of the Medical Act permits universities and other bodies to enter into combination to grant such qualifications. Section 8(1) permits the addition of extra United Kingdom qualifying examinations to this list where it appears to the Education Committee that the standard of proficiency required of candidates conforms to the prescribed standard. Such university examinations are added by Orders in Council so as to amend section 4 of the Act.

Required Experience. Provisional Registration
Having qualified and in order to gain the experience required by section 10 of the Act for full registration, a doctor must have been engaged for the period prescribed by the General Medical Council's regulations in a resident medical capacity at one or more approved hospitals and must have obtained a certificate to that effect. The present regulations concerning experience are still the Medical Act 1950 (Period of Employment as House Officers) Regulations Approval Order of Council 1952 SI 1952 No. 2050.

"Resident" is defined in section 11(3) as meaning that the person employed is resident in the hospital, or is employed in and resides conveniently near to it and that the terms of his employment require him to be so resident. Hospitals are approved for this purpose by any of the universities or other bodies which may grant any registerable qualification. The present regulations require a doctor to be employed in a resident medical capacity at one or more approved hospitals for 12 months – six months in medicine and six months in surgery. Special provision is made (section 10 (4)) for a doctor who is unable to embark on a surgical job because of physical disability, to hold a second medical job instead.

Full registration carries with it certain privileges and in particular that of prescribing certain medicines and drugs. To enable a doctor to practise medicine fully while he is gaining experience he must first obtain provisional registration under the terms of section 15. Anyone who, but for lack of prescribed experience, would be entitled to be registered under section 3 is entitled to be provisionally registered on presentation to the registrar of evidence that he has obtained the necessary qualifications and has been selected for appropriate employment. A provisionally registered medical practitioner is deemed to be fully registered so far as this is necessary to enable him to engage in employment in a resident medical capacity but not further (section 15(3)).

Doctors Qualifying Overseas

Provisions for the registration of doctors qualifying overseas were modified in the late 1970's by three separate statutory provisions. These were: the Medical Act 1978 (sections 17–28) which replaced the provisions of Part III of the 1956 Act dealing with the registration of overseas qualified medical practitioners; the Irish Republic (Termination of 1927 Agreement) Order 1979 SI 1979 No. 289 which ended the agreement between the United Kingdom and the Irish Republic mutually recognising their respective medical qualifications and now putting Irish qualifications on the same footing as those of any other member state of the EEC; and the Medical Qualifications (EEC Recognition) Order 1977 SI 1977 No. 827 which deals with the registration of doctors who are nationals of other EEC member states. It should be noted that, although the previous agreement with Eire has been terminated, transitional provisions were made which continued the right to full and provisional registration on the award of a primary Irish qualification before 30th August 1985. The 1983 Act includes the provisions for registration of overseas and EEC doctors.

Registration of overseas qualified medical pratitioners may be divided under three headings: provisional and full registration by virtue of recognised overseas qualifications, limited registration, and provisions for visiting doctors.

Registration by Recognition of Overseas Qualifications

EEC Nationals Section 3 of the Medical Act 1983 entitles medical practitioners who are nationals of other EEC states and who hold certain specified European medical qualifications listed in the schedule 2 to the Act and SI 1986 No. 23 to apply for full registration, if the qualification was obtained after the date on which the particular country had implemented the Second Medical Directive (No. 75/363/EEC relating to co-ordination of activities of doctors). However, where it was obtained before this date, or if training began before this date, the applicant must satisy the registrar that the qualification complies with the standards laid down in the second Medical Directive or alternatively produce evidence he has been in lawful medical practice in an EEC country for at least three consecutive years of the five previous years (section 17). When recognition of EEC qualifications was first introduced, in addition to providing evidence of his qualifications to the registrar an EEC doctor applying for registration was also required to satisfy him that he had the necessary knowledge of the English language. The necessary knowledge was defined as that which in the interests of himself and his patients is necessary to the practice of medicine in the United Kingdom. However, this requirement for linguistic knowledge as a pre-requisite for registration was challenged by the EEC as being illegal under Community law in that it contravened the basic requirements of the Treaty of Rome for the free movement of labour. The requirement was therefore withdrawn by the British Government (European Communities (Medical, Dental and Nursing Professions) (Linguistic Knowledge) Order 1981 SI No. 432). However, the Government now requires all National Health Service employers or contracting authorities to make linguistic proficiency a condition of employment – a requirement that is considered not to offend EEC law.

Non-EEC Doctors Under the provisions of section 19 of the 1983 Act any doctor who can satisfy the registrar that he holds a recognised overseas qualification, has the necessary knowledge of the English language and is of good character may be registered if the General Council agree. If he can satisfy the Council that he has obtained such experience as is required by section 10 of the Act for United Kingdom doctors (see above) then he may apply for full registration. If, however, he cannot, he may apply for provisional registration under section 21 of the Act so that he can obtain the required experience. As with a United Kingdom doctor, provisional registration is equivalent to full registration only insofar as it is necessary for the doctor to be engaged in the prescribed period of resident medical employment.

The General Council will recognise an overseas qualification if it is satisfied that the qualification provides a sufficient guarantee of the possession of knowledge and skill confirmed by passing an examination of the required standard of proficiency (section 19(2)). The necessary knowledge of English is defined by section 55 as that which in the interests of the doctor and the patients is necessary for the practice of medicine in the United Kingdom. The General Council provides facilities to test an applicant's standard of English and thus, as far as language proficiency is concerned, non-EEC doctors are treated in a different way from EEC doctors.

Limited Registration

Before the 1978 Medical Act overseas doctors wishing to practise medicine in the United Kingdom or the Isle of Man for a limited period could apply for temporary registration even though they were not eligible for full or provisional registration. This was replaced by a similar system known as limited registration but existing temporarily registered doctors were protected by provisional arrangements. A doctor gaining limited registration has his name entered on the register of medical practitioners with limited registration and receives an appropriate certificate of limited registration. Like any other registered medical practitioner, one with limited registration is liable to have his name erased from the register as a disciplinary measure.

Sections 22–25 of the Medical Act deal with limited registration. In order to obtain limited registration an overseas medical practitioner must satisfy the registrar of the General Medical Council of the following:

1. He must have been selected for employment as a medical practitioner in a hospital or institution in the United Kingdom or the Isle of Man approved by the Council for this purpose.

2. He must hold, have held, or passed the examinations necessary to gain, some acceptable overseas qualification. Section 22(4) defines "acceptable overseas qualification" as one accepted by the General Council for the purposes of limited registration as furnishing a sufficient guarantee of the possession of that knowledge and skill required for the practice of medicine under the supervision of a fully registered medical practitioner.

3. He must have the necessary knowledge of English which is again defined by section 55 as that which in the interests of himself and his patients is necessary for the practice of medicine in the United Kingdom. The General Council provides facilities for English tests for applicants.

4. He is of good character.

5. He has the knowledge and skill, and has acquired the experience necessary, to practise as a medical practitioner with limited registration. The knowledge, skill and experience required depend upon the nature of the employment and the particular branch of medicine concerned and are to be determined by the General Council (section 23(2)). However, section 23(5) empowers the General Council, in specific cases, to exempt applicants from the requirements of knowledge and skill or experience or all three.

Nature of the Limitation
The precise limitation on an individual's registration is specified in that registration, but in broad terms they relate to time, place and supervision.

Time The registration will specify a time period, and section 22(3) provides that no-one may be so registered for a period in excess of five years or, if he has been previously so registered, an aggregate period of five years.

Place The registration is limited to the particular employment concerned. If the employment terminates before expiry of the specified period of time then registration also lapses.

Supervision Section 22(8) requires the practitioner with limited registration to work only under the supervision of a fully registered medical practitioner.

Effect of Limited Registration
Section 22(7) provides that a medical practitioner registered with limited registration is to be treated as a fully registered practitioner as far as anything done, or omitted to be done, in the course of the employment to which his registration applies and for the duration of that employment. This includes anything incidental to that work which may be lawfully done only by a fully registered medical practitioner. However, in all other aspects he is treated as not registered.

Procedure to Full Registration
Section 25 of the Medical Act provides for a medical practitioner with limited registration to obtain full registration under section 19. In order to do so he must show to the General Council that he is of good character and has the necessary knowledge and experience. If he does obtain full registration then he is entitled to have registered any acceptable overseas qualifications, any primary United Kingdom qualifications and any additional registerable qualifications.

Full Registration of Visiting Doctors
Section 27 of the Medical Act permits the General Council to give full registration to a visiting doctor for a period not exceeding 12 months and to issue an appropriate certificate to him. Before doing so the General Council must be satisfied that the doctor holds one or more recognised or acceptable overseas qualifications, has special knowledge and skills in a particular branch or branches of medicine and will provide medical services in that branch of medicine.

As far as visiting EEC doctors are concerned section 18 supplies a somewhat different procedure. A national of a member state of the Community who is lawfully established in medical practice in any state other than the United Kingdom may give medical services on a temporary basis here without first being registered under the Medical Act. He must supply to the registrar of the General Medical Council details of the services he intends to render and for how long. He must show he is in lawful medical practice and holds a medical qualification which member states recognise. The registrar, if satisfied, must then enter the doctor's name on the register of visiting EEC doctors. His status will lapse if he establishes his medical practice in the United Kingdom or, except in an emergency, renders any medical services outside his declaration.

Review Board for Overseas Qualified Practitioners

The 1978 Act established a body known as the Review Board for Overseas Qualified Practitioners, and section 28 of the 1983 Act continues its existence. The constitution and procedure of this Board are determined by the General Medical Council (Review Board for Overseas Qualified Practitioners Rules) Order of Council 1979 SI 1979 No. 29. The chairman and deputy chairman must not be members of the General Medical Council. They are appointed by the president of the General Medical Council on the advice of the Council for Post-graduate Medical Education in England and Wales, the Scottish Council for Post-Graduate Medical Education and the Northern Ireland Council for Post-graduate Medical Education. The Board also includes four elected members of the Council, two appointed members and one member who is, or has been, registered under the present or the previous arrangements for overseas practitioners.

The Board is responsible for reviewing a wide range of decisions made by the General Medical Council in respect to application for registration by overseas practitioners. The Board has the power to require the registrar to give written reasons for any such decision. If the Board thinks that any such decision should be reversed it will inform the Council of this conclusion and the Council must decide whether or not to act on that advice. The applicant for a review must also be informed of the Board's opinions.

Overseas Doctors and Immigration Controls

From the first of April 1985 doctors (and dentists) from abroad were made subject to the same immigration controls as other groups from abroad. They are not permitted to practise in the United Kingdom unless they are citizen of the EEC or have £150,000 to invest in a practice. Existing overseas doctors are not affected. This represents the end of a Governmental policy started in the 60s to attract overseas graduates to make up the shortfall in output from British medical schools.

Professional Conduct and Fitness to Practise

As with the other professional groups covered in this book registered medical practitioners are subject to prescribed disciplinary procedures. However, in addition, a medical practitioner's physical or mental ability to practise is also a matter for review and action. This latter procedure was first introduced by the Medical Act 1978. The issue of professional conduct and fitness to practise is dealt with by Part V of the 1983 Act (sections 35–45).

Disciplinary Offences and their Sanctions

Section 36 of the Medical Act 1983 provides that where the Professional Conduct Committee finds that a fully registered medical practitioner has been convicted of a criminal offence in the United Kingdom, the Channel Islands or the Isle of Man, or has been guilty of serious professional misconduct, it may erase his name from the register, suspend his registration for up to 12 months, or make his registration conditional upon such requirements as it thinks fit for up to three years. The criminal conviction or serious professional misconduct may have occurred while the practitioner was registered or unregistered. Moreover, practitioners registered with limited registration and provisionally registered doctors are also liable.

In addition to these offences, if a medical practitioner whose registration is subject to conditions fails to comply with them then the Professional Conduct Committee may erase his name or suspend his registration for up to 12 months. Furthermore, section 36(3) allows the Committee, where it has suspended a medical practitioner's registration, to extend the period of suspension (but not for more than 12 months at a time), erase his name, or make his registration conditional. Similarly, section 36(4) permits the Professional Conduct Committee, where it has issued a direction for conditional registration, to extend that period (but not beyond 12 months at a time) or revoke the direction or revoke or vary the conditions.

Where the Professional Conduct Committee gives a direction for erasure, suspension or conditional registration or varies the conditions then the registrar must serve notice of this upon the practitioner and also inform him of his rights of appeal.

The Professional Conduct Committee

The Professional Conduct Committee is a committee of the General Medical Council, established by the Medical Act 1978, and it replaced the earlier Disciplinary and Penal Cases Committee (section 1(3) 1983 Act).

The constitution of the Committee is determined by the General Medical Council (Constitution of Fitness to Practise Committee) Rules Order of Council 1986 SI 1986 No. 1390, made by the General Council under powers conferred by section 6 of the Medical Act 1978 (now in schedule 4 to the 1983 Act). To be effective, these rules must be approved by the Privy Council, and they are subject to annulment by resolution of either House of Parliament. The rules provide that the Professional Conduct Committee consists of a chairman, deputy chairman, 12 elected members of the Council, four appointed members and two lay members. The president of the Council may choose whether he wishes to be a member of the Committee and if he does so he automatically becomes chairman. If not, he appoints a chairman. In either case he appoints a deputy chairman. The members of the Professional Conduct Committee are elected by the General Council from their ranks by means of a single transferable vote, and elections, which are held annually, also cover the Health Committee and the Preliminary Proceedings Committee. No-one may be a member of more than one committee except the president who may sit concurrently on the Professional Conduct Committee and the Health Committee. No-one may be elected to the Professional Conduct Committee if in the previous year he was a member of the Preliminary Proceedings Committee.

A quorum of the Committee is at least five and not more than ten, invited so as to include the chairman, or deputy chairman, or both, six elected members, two appointed members and one lay member. As far as possible, invitations are in rotation.

Fraud in Relation to Registration

Section 39 of the Medical Act 1983 empowers the General Council itself to erase from the register any entry which it is satisfied has been fraudulently obtained or is incorrectly entered. In such a case the Registrar must serve notice of the General Council's direction on the doctor and also inform him of his right of appeal. The matter of fraudulent registration is dealt with, among other things, by the Registration Committee of the Council. The procedure for inquiring into an alleged fraudulent registration is laid down in the General Medical Council (Fraud or Error in Relation to Registration) Rules Order of Council 1980 SI 1980 No. 860. The inquiry is essentially a hearing of the allegation and the practitioner is entitled to be legally represented.

Fitness to Practise

Section 37 of the 1983 Act gives a committee of the General Council – the Health Committee – power to take action where it judges the fitness of a doctor (fully or provisionally registered or registered with limited registration) to practise to be seriously impaired by his physical or mental condition. In such a situation it may either suspend his registration for a period of up to 12 months or may make his registration conditional upon such requirements as the Committee imposes for a period of up to three years. It was decided in Compton v GMC (No. 2) (Lancet August 17th 1985 page 400) that the term 'mental condition' used in the Medical Act is different from the term 'mental disorder' used in the Mental Health Act 1983. This case was an unsuccessful appeal in which the doctor contended that because he did not suffer from a 'mental disorder' as defined by the Mental Health Act the GMC could not take action against him.

If a doctor whose registration is subject to conditions is judged by the Health Committee to have failed to comply with them, it is empowered to suspend his registration for a period not exceeding 12 months. Moreover, where the Health Committee has given a direction for conditional registration, it may extend that period, but not beyond 12 months at a time. Alternatively, it may revoke or vary any of the conditions imposed by the direction. Where the Health Committee has directed that a doctor's registration should be suspended it may extend that period, but not for more than 12 months at a time, or it may, on expiry of the suspension, make the registration conditional.

Where the Health Committee issues a direction for suspension or conditional registration the registrar must serve notice on the individual and also inform him of his right of appeal (section 37(6)).

The Health Committee

The Health Committee was first established as a committee of the General Council by the 1978 Medical Act and its existence is confirmed by section 1 of the 1983 Act. The Council is empowered to make rules concerning the Committee's constitution. Before becoming effective, however, the rules require approval by the Privy Council. They are also subject to annulment by resolution of either House of Parliament. The constitution of the Committee is embodied in the General Medical Council (Constitution of Fitness to Practise Committees) Rules Order of Council 1986 SI 1986 No. 1390. The Committee consists of a chairman, a deputy chairman, six elected Council members, three appointed Council members and one lay member. The president of the General Council may choose to sit as chairman, but, if he does not, he chooses the chairman. He also chooses a deputy chairman. A quorum of the Health Committee is five and members are elected annually by the Council by means of a single transferable vote. The result of the election is determined in the order: Preliminary Proceedings Committee first, Professional Conduct Committee next, and finally the Health Committee. Except for the chairman, no-one may sit on more than one committee at any time.

Procedure

Preliminary Proceedings Committee

The Preliminary Proceedings Committee was established by the 1978 Act. Its functions are dealt with by section 42 of the 1983 Act. The Committee has a duty to consider any case referred to it where it is alleged that a medical practitioner is liable to erasure, suspension or conditional registration for a disciplinary or health matter and to decide whether or not the case should be referred to the Professional Conduct Committee or the Health Committee. The Preliminary Proceedings Committee is constituted by rules made by the General Council, of which it is a committee. These rules require the approval of the Privy Council before becoming effective and may be annulled by resolution of either House of Parliament. The constitution is embodied in the General Medical Council (Constitution of Fitness to Practise Committees) Rules Order of Council 1986 SI 1986 No. 1390 (see also schedule 4 to the 1983 Act). The Committee consists of a chairman, six elected members of the Council, two appointed members and two lay members. A quorum of the Committee is five.

Initial Procedure

Before any case is referred to the Preliminary Proceedings Committee it must first be considered by the president of the Council or, if he proposes to sit on the Professional Conduct Committee or the Health Committee, by someone nominated by him for the purpose. The initial procedure, as well as that before the Preliminary Proceedings Committee and the Professional Conduct Committee, is dealt with by the General Medical Council Preliminary Proceedings Committee and Professional Conduct Committee (Procedure) Rules Order of Council 1980 SI 1980 No. 858 (see also schedule 4 to the 1983 Act). Where the registrar is notified of a conviction against a doctor which is not of a type exempted by the Preliminary Proceedings Committee from further consideration – for example, minor offences – he must notify the practitioner, informing him of the date of the next meeting of the Preliminary Proceedings Committee and asking him to make any observations he may have. This information is submitted to the president who must then refer the case to the Committee.

Where alleged professional misconduct is concerned a statutory declaration of the complaint must be obtained except where the complainant is acting in a public capacity. No case may proceed further until such a declaration has been obtained. The president, assisted by Council staff acting under standing instructions, must then decide whether, on the basis of the declaration, the matter should proceed further. If he does decide to go ahead the registrar must notify the doctor in writing of the nature of the complaint, sending him a copy of any declaration, informing him of the date of the next meeting of the Preliminary Proceedings Committee and asking him to submit any explanation he may have. On the basis of this information the president (or his nominee) decides whether to refer the case to the Committee or not. Acting in this way he is called the preliminary screener.

If in the case of a conviction or an alleged misconduct it appears to the president that the doctor's fitness to practise may be impaired by reason of physical or mental ill-health he may direct the registrar to inform the practitioner of his view and invite him to furnish medical evidence of his fitness to practise for submission to the Preliminary Proceedings Committee.

Procedure before the Preliminary Proceedings Committee

As has already been stated, the basic function of the Preliminary Proceedings Committee is to consider cases submitted to it and to decide whether to refer them to the Professional Conduct Committee or the Health Committee, or to take no further action (section 42). The Committee meets in private (rule 15). It may be able to reach a decision on the information supplied to it, but, if not, it may make such further investigations as it thinks fit. Before referring a case to the Health Committee it may ask the doctor to be medically examined. If the Committee decides that a case should go no futher the registrar must inform the practitioner and any complainant, but no-one – practitioner, complainant or informant – then has any right of access to the documents submitted to the Committee. Nor does the Committee have to state a reason for its decision (rule 16).

Rule 12, together with section 42 of the Act, empowers the Preliminary Proceedings Committee to make orders for interim suspension or interim conditional registration where it is satisfied that it is necessary for the protection of the public to act at once. It may suspend registration for a period of up to two months or make registration conditional on some requirement for up to the same period of time. In the latter event, it may act where it believes it is in the interest of the practitioner to do so. When it intends to make such an order it must give the doctor an opportunity to appear before it, and he may be represented.

A decision of the Preliminary Proceedings Committee to make interim orders or to refer a case to the Professional Conduct Committee or the Health Committee must be notified to the practitioner by the registrar.

Procedure before the Professional Conduct Committee

Correct procedure in relation to the hearing of a case before the Professional Conduct Committee is presented in great detail in the General Medical Council Preliminary Proceedings Committee and Professional Conduct Committee (Procedure) Rules Order of Council 1980 SI 1980 No. 858 (see also section 43 and schedule 4 to the Act). It should be noted that, under rule 9, whenever the registrar writes to a practitioner informing him that he may be liable to disciplinary proceedings then a copy of these rules must also be sent.

Once it has been decided to refer a case to the Committee, the Council's solicitor must send a "Notice of Inquiry" to the practitioner specifying the charges and stating the time and place of the inquiry which (except with the practitioner's agreement) must not be earlier than 28 days after posting the notice. A copy of the notice is also sent to any complainant. Parties to the inquiry may have access to all documents relating to the case except communications between the Council and its solicitors. The president has a variety of powers prior to the opening of a hearing before the Committee. He may postpone the inquiry to such later date as he thinks fit, and the parties must be notified. He may amend a charge prior to the hearing provided this would not cause any injustice; again the parties must be notified. He may even cancel an inquiry altogether after the Preliminary Proceedings Committee has referred it but before the hearing has begun. To do so he must have the support of a majority of members of the Preliminary Proceedings Committee. If they are equally divided they must find in favour of the practitioner, and the hearing is dropped. Again, notice of this decision must be given.

An inquiry before the Professional Conduct Committee must be held in the presence of all parties to the case. It is normally held in public. However, the Committee may exclude the public from part or all of the hearing if their presence might unduly prejudice the practitioner's case. However, the announcement of the Committee's decision must always be made in public. The Committee operates very much like a court of law and may receive oral, documentary or other evidence. Although it should normally follow the rules of evidence observed in a court, it may choose to do otherwise if it is in the interests of justice to do so and after consultation with the legal assessor (see below). The Committee reaches a decision by vote. In the case of equal voting the question is deemed to have been found in favour of the practitioner.

An inquiry begins with a reading of the charge, and the doctor is given an opportunity to object to the Notice of Inquiry. In the case of a conviction, evidence of that conviction is heard (or the doctor may admit to it) and pleas in mitigation by the doctor are heard. He will be invited to address the Committee which then proceeds to reach a decision. Where professional misconduct is alleged evidence of this is presented to the Committee. The practitioner may present evidence or argue that either the facts are not proved, or that if they are they do not amount to serious professional misconduct. If the Committee finds that the facts are proved, then pleas in mitigation are heard on behalf of the practitioner who is invited to address the Committee. The Committee then decides if the facts do indeed amount to serious professional misconduct.

If the Committee finds that a medical practitioner has been convicted or has been guilty of serious professional misconduct it must decide what action to take. Rule 34 directs it to consider possible actions in the following sequence: firstly, it must decide whether to admonish the doctor; if not, whether to postpone its decision; if not, whether to impose conditional registration; if not, whether to suspend his registration, and, if none of these, whether or not to erase his name from the register. Finally, it must announce its decision publicly.

Procedure before the Health Committee
Procedure before the Health Committee is determined by the rules contained in the General Medical Council Health Committee (Procedure) Rules Order of Council 1980 SI 1980 No. 859 (see also section 43 and schedule 4 to the Act). Cases coming before the Health Committee are referred to it by either the Preliminary Proceedings Committee or the Professional Conduct Committee or by the president.

Committee Referrals Where the Preliminary Proceedings Committee or the Professional Conduct Committee refers a case for consideration to the Health Committee, the president may, prior to the hearing, invite the practitioner to have a medical examination by at least two medical practitioners who are chosen by the president and submit their report to the Health Committee. The practitioner may also nominate another doctor to examine him at the Council's expense.

Referrals from the President Where the registrar receives information that a doctor may be unfit to practise through ill-health, he must refer the case to the president and, except where the information comes from someone acting in a public or quasi-public capacity, a statutory declaration must be obtained from the informant. At this stage the president directs the registrar to write to the doctor inviting him to agree within 14 days to undergo a medical examination by two doctors chosen by the president and to make any other observations he wishes. He is also told he may nominate an additional doctor of his own. If he agrees, he is examined and medical reports are sent to the president. The president must send copies of these reports to the doctor but he may exclude any material which is not relevant to the question of fitness to practise and which it would not be in the best interests of the practitioner to see. If the president is of the view that the reports do raise a question of fitness to practise, he will ask the doctor to say within 28 days whether he is willing voluntarily to accept the recommendations of the medical examiners concerning the management of his condition. If he does accept and the president is satisfied with his undertaking, he will postpone further action on the case. If, however, the doctor does not accept the recommendations or has refused to be examined, the president, after consultation with at least two other Council members appointed for this purpose, must refer the case to the Health Committee. If the president is of the view that urgent action is required, he may initially refer the case to the Preliminary Proceedings Committee for consideration of an order for interim suspension or interim conditional registration.

Where a case is to be referred to the Health Committee, a Notice of Referral is sent to the practitioner giving details of what condition is alleged to impair his fitness to practise, and giving the time and place of the inquiry, which must (except with the doctor's agreement) be more than 28 days after the posting of the notice. The Health Committee sits in private but the practitioner may attend, as may his representative and his medical adviser. One or more medical assessors appointed by the General Council must attend Health Committee meetings to advise on medical matters. These assessors are experts in their particular fields and are nominated by various specialist bodies, but they must not be Council members. The Health Committee considers the evidence about the practitioner's fitness to practise and at the conclusion the practitioner or his representative may address the Committee and bring any evidence in his support. The Committee may adjourn to obtain further medical reports but, if it does not, it must decide whether or not his fitness to practise is seriously impaired. If so, it then decides whether it should impose conditional registration or suspend the doctor.

Legal Assessors

The fourth schedule to the Medical Act 1983 requires there to be a legal assessor present at all meetings of the Preliminary Proceedings Committee, the Health Committee and the Professional Conduct Committee to advise on questions of law. The legal assessor must be a barrister, advocate or solicitor of at least ten years' standing. The Lord Chancellor (the Lord Advocate in Scotland) may make rules dealing with the functions of legal assessors, and the present rules are contained in the General Medical Council (Legal Assessors) Rules 1980 SI 1980 No. 941. Where any Committee does not accept the advice of a legal assessor, a record of this must be made and a copy given to every party to the proceedings.

Appeals

Section 40 of the Medical Act 1983 provides for appeals to be made to the Judicial Committee of the Privy Council within 28 days of a decision. The decisions on which appeals may be made are those of the Professional Conduct Committee under section 36 of the Act (conviction or misconduct); those of the Health Committee under section 37 (ill health), or those of the General Council under section 39 (fraud). However, decisions of the Health Committee may be subject to appeal only on points of law. It should be noted that there is no appeal available where a practitioner is found guilty of serious professional misconduct but is ony warned or admonished (section 11(4)). Erasure, suspension or conditional registration must have been imposed before an appeal is possible.

The appeals are heard by the Judicial Committee of the Privy Council, and the procedure for this is laid down in the Judicial Committee (Medical Rules) Order 1980 SI No. 873. The Judicial Committee may allow or dismiss an appeal, substitute its own decision or refer it back to the Committee with a direction for its determination. Whether or not the General Council appears as a respondent in an appeal, it is always deemed to be a party for the purposes of costs.

Restoration of Names

Where a medical practitioner's name has been erased from the register under section 36 because of a conviction or serious professional misconduct, the Professional Conduct Committee may, if it thinks fit, restore that name. The doctor concerned may not make application for restoration in less than ten months from the date of the erasure or the date of the last application. The procedure for restoration is contained in rule 52 of the General Medical Council Preliminary Proceedings and Professional Conduct Committee (Procedure) Rules Order of Council 1980 SI 1980 No. 858. The Committee first reviews the circumstances of the original erasure and the applicant may address the Committee and present evidence in his support. The Committee may adjourn or may ask the applicant to supply more evidence of his conduct and condition since the erasure.

Controls on Medical Practice

Compared to other professions dealt with in this book there are relatively few statutory restrictions placed on the practice of medicine and related areas, and no attempt to limit the treatment of human illness to registered doctors has ever been made. However, there are certain specific statutory requirements that do in effect limit the practice of medicine to a considerable extent to fully registered medical practitioners.

Use of Titles

Section 49 of the Medical Act makes it an offence for anyone wilfully and falsely to pretend to be, or take or use the titles of, a physician, doctor of medicine, licentiate in medicine and surgery, bachelor of medicine, surgeon, general practitioner or apothecary, or any other title, description or addition suggesting he is registered under the Medical Act. However, a visiting EEC practitioner is exempt provided he has first complied with the requirements of section 18 (see page 92 above). On summary conviction the penalty is a fine of up to £500.

Fees

Section 46 of the Act bars anyone who is not a fully registered medical practitioner from recovering in any court of law any fee or charge for any medical or surgical advice or attendance, or for the performance of any operation, or for any medicine he may have prescribed or supplied. The only exception to this rule is for a visiting EEC practitioner who although not fully registered has complied with the requirements of section 18 (see page 92 above).

Appointments

Certain appointments as a medical officer are limited to fully registered medical practitioners. The appointments are prescribed in section 47 of the Act as being in the armed services, in any mental hospital or other hospital or infirmary or dispensary not supported wholly by voluntary contributions, in any prison or any other public establishment, or to any society providing mutual relief in sickness, infirmity or old age. There is an exception to this requirement in section 47(2) which allows a person who is a non-Commonwealth citizen to be a resident doctor at any hospital establishment exclusively for the relief of foreigners in sickness provided he is entitled to practise medicine in his own country and does no other work in this country.

It should be noted that suspension of registration by direction of the Health Committee does not terminate a public appointment, but the suspended doctor may not, of course, perform any duties (but see page 58).

Certificates

Section 48 of the Act provides that, where any enactment requires a certificate to be provided by a medical practitioner, then that certificate is invalid unless the medical practitioner is fully registered.

Effect on Other Professions

Section 54 of the Act provides that nothing in the Act shall be construed to extend to, or affect or prejudice, the lawful occupation, trade or business of chemists and druggists and dentists, or the rights, privileges or employment of licensed apothecaries in Northern Ireland insofar as their business of selling, compounding or dispensing medicines is concerned.

Medical Education

The Education Committee

Before the 1978 Medical Act, the General Council itself was responsible for the control of medical education. The 1978 Act established a committee of the Council – the Education Committee – which is charged with the general function of promoting high standards of medical education and co-ordinating all stages of medical education (section 3 and 4 1983 Act). More specifically, section 5(2) requires that the Committee shall determine the level of knowledge and skill required to grant a primary United Kingdom qualification and ensure that the instruction given in universities achieves that level; determine the standard of proficiency required from candidates and secure the maintenance of that standard, and determine the experience required under section 10 of the Act for general clinical training.

The members of the Education Committee are chosen by the General Council from its members so that the number of appointed members exceeds the numbers of elected and nominated members. The Committee has power to co-opt members (see schedule 1 to the 1983 Act). However, certain educational functions imposed by the Act remain the responsibility of the General Council. These are the testing of the English language, relaxation of requirements in the case of a disabled doctor, alternative requirements as to experience, and the matter of payments to visitors or inspectors appointed under the Act.

The qualifications and experience required for full registration have been dealt with earlier in this chapter.

Visitors and Inspectors

To ensure that first-hand information is gathered about the process of medical education the Medical Act requires the appointment of certain visitors and inspectors. Section 7 of the Act permits the Education Committee to appoint people to visit places where instruction is given to medical students. The visitors must report to the Committee on the adequacy of any instruction being given, but they must not interfere with it in any way. On receiving a visit report, the Education Committee must send a copy to the medical school inspected and seek its views, if any. Once these views have been received, the report and the comments on it must be sent to the Privy Council.

Section 6 of the Act permits the Education Committee to appoint inspectors to attend the examinations held by any approved institution in order to determine the standard of proficiency required at that institution. The inspectors must not interfere in any way with the conduct of the examinations but must report their findings to the Education Committee. Copies of these reports must be sent to the bodies holding the examinations. They must also be sent to the Privy Council together with any comments there may have been.

Section 13 of the Act permits the Education Committee to appoint people to visit any hospital or other institution approved for the purpose of post-qualification experience. The visitors must report to the Education Committee on the extent to which the general clinical training given provides the experience required at this stage of medical education.

Sanctions

Where the Education Committee believes that either the course of instruction given at a medical school is inadequate or that the standard required in any examination fails to meet the standard of proficiency required, section 9 gives them certain powers.

Section 9 provides that, where the Education Committee considers that any course of study and examination is inadequate to secure the required knowledge and experience, it may make representations to the Privy Council. The Council, if it thinks fit, may determine that the qualification in such a case shall no longer be registerable under the Medical Act. Similarly, if the Education Committee believes the standard of proficiency in any examination is insufficient, it may make representations to the Privy Council, which may, after hearing any objections, deem that the examination is not a qualifying one for the purpose of the Act. Any orders of this sort may be revoked by the Privy Council if it is satisfied, after representation by the Education Committee or the university or both, that the defect has been rectified. However, such revocations do not have retrospective effect.

Chapter Eight

The Dental Profession

The Dentists Act 1984

Up to 1984 the profession of dentistry in the United Kingdom was regulated by three statutes – the Dentists Act 1957, the Dentists (Amendment) Act 1973 and the Dentists Act 1983. The Dentists Act 1983 extended the regulation of dentists by introducing a Health Committee (similar to that introduced in the medical profession by the Medical Act 1978) to control the registration of dentists whose fitness to practise was seriously impaired for health reasons. It also introduced the penalty of suspension of registration as an alternative to erasure in disciplinary cases (as did the 1978 Medical Act for doctors), increased the number of elected members of the General Dental Council and dealt with post-graduate dental education. The Dentists Act 1984 repealed these three earlier Acts and re-enacted them in a single consolidated statute. The Act extends to the whole of the United Kingdom.

The General Dental Council. The Controlling Body

The controlling body for the profession of dentistry is the General Dental Council, the existence of which is confirmed by section 1 of the Dentists Act 1984. Its constitution, powers and committees are laid down in section 1 and 2 of the Act and part 1 of the first schedule to the Act.

Composition

The Council consists of the president and 29 members together with members nominated by the dental authorities. Dental authorities are defined by section 3 (4) of the Act as any medical authority (for example, a university) which issues dental degrees, licences or other diplomas. Of the 29, 18 are registered dentists elected from among the profession, such that 14 are elected by dentists registered in England, the Isle of Man or the Channel Islands, one from Wales, two from Scotland and one from Northern Ireland. Four members are the individuals who for the time being are the chief dental officers to the DHSS, to the Welsh Office, to the DHSS for Northern Ireland and to the Secretary of State for Scotland. Six lay members (three for England and one each for Wales, Scotland and Northern Ireland) are nominated by Her Majesty on the advice of the Privy Council. One member is elected from among themselves by the Dental Auxiliaries Committee (see below). All other members must be registered dentists, the University of London nominating two and all the other dental authorities one each. The General Medical Council nominates three from its members but they may act and vote only in matters of dental education and examinations.

Members hold office for five years, and a casual vacancy of an elected member is to be filled by election if it occurs more than 12 months from the end of any five-year period. Nominated members are replaced whenever necessary. The Council elects one member who must be a registered dentist to be president, and he holds office until he retires from Council membership. If on his election he is an elected or nominated member he ceases to be so and the Council must take appropriate steps to fill this vacancy. The president holds office for such time as a nominated member replacing him would hold office. The Council may pay its members' fees for attendance at meetings in addition to travelling and subsistence expenses.

Section 14 of the Dentists Act requires the Council to appoint a registrar for such period and at such salary as the Council fix. The Council may also appoint an assistant registrar.

Functions and Committees

Section 1 of the Act provides that the general concern of the Council is to promote high professional and educational standards and conduct among dentists and perform the duties assigned to it by the Act. The main functions of the Council are:

Educational The Council through its Education Committee controls standards of dental education. It may appoint visitors to assess the adequacy of courses of dental training given at various institutions.

The Dental Register The General Dental Council is responsible for the form and keeping of the dental register, the fees payable in respect of it and admission to, and erasure from, it. It is also responsible for the publication of annual copies of the register.

Discipline The Council through its Professional Conduct Committee controls discipline in the profession. A Preliminary Proceedings Committee decides whether a disciplinary case should be brought and, if so, refers it to the Professional Conduct Committee for consideration (section 27).

Fitness to Practise Through its Health Committee – a committee initially set up by part III of the 1983 Act (repealed) – the Council is able to consider whether a dentist's fitness to practise is seriously impaired by reasons of physical or mental ill-health. In such a case the Committee has the power to suspend a dentist's registration or make it conditional on specified requirements.

Auxiliary Dental Workers Section 45 of the Act permits the Council by statutory instrument to establish classes of auxiliary workers and make regulations controlling their practice. Before the 1983 Act auxiliary dental workers were known as ancillary dental workers.

Registration

The Dental Register

Section 14 of the Dentists Act provides for the maintenance of the Dentists Register. A procedure has been introduced to permit the registration of EEC-qualified dentists, and they are registered under the provisions of section 15 of, and schedule 2 to, the Act.

The General Dental Council must appoint a registrar and establish his terms and conditions of service (section 14); it is the registrar who has custody of, and maintains, the register. The Council may appoint an assistant registrar. Section 14(5) states that the register is admissable as evidence of all matters recorded in it, while section 14(6) provides that a certificate issued by the registrar to the effect that at a certain time a dentist's name was, or was not, on the register is prima facie evidence in all courts of law of that fact. Section 22 requires the Council to publish, and make available for sale, correct copies of the register at least once a year. A copy is admissable as evidence in a court of law except that, where a dentist's honour or distinction is listed, these are held not to be part of the register (section 22(2)).

Section 19 permits the General Council to make regulations on the form and keeping of the register. It may prescribe a fee for both entry and retention of a name on the register. Regulations about fees must be approved by the Privy Council before they are effective (section 19(4)). These regulations are not published as statutory instruments, but copies are available for inspection at the offices of the General Dental Council.

Registration

United Kingdom Dentists Anyone who is a graduate or licentiate in dentistry from a dental authority is entitled to be registered (section 15(1)a). In effect, this means a graduate or licentiate in dental surgery from a university in the United Kingdom or the Republic of Ireland, or a licentiate in dental surgery from one of the Royal Colleges of Surgeons of England and Edinburgh, the Royal College of Physicians and Surgeons of Glasgow and the Royal College of Surgeons in Ireland. A degree or diploma in dental surgery is acquired by means of prescribed courses of training and examinations. As stated above, a dental authority is any medical authority which grants qualifications in dentistry, and a medical authority is any university or similar body which chooses appointed members of the General Medical Council. However, since the Irish Republic (Termination of 1927 Agreement) Order 1979 SI 1979 No. 289, Eire no longer chooses members, but the 1979 Order provides that, in terms of the Dentists Act, medical authorities continue to include those Irish bodies which were included before the termination order came into effect (on 30th April 1979). The general effect of the order is to terminate the agreement whereby Irish medical qualifications entitled doctors to registration and to rely on the new provision for registration of Irish doctors as EEC nationals (see Chapter Seven). However, it should be noted that, although the registration of EEC dentists in the United Kingdom register is now provided for, Irish dentists still have a direct right of registration in this country. However, section 49 of the 1984 Act provides for termination of the agreement of 1927 with the Irish Republic by Order in Council insofar as it relates to dentists.

The 1984 Act also requires that before registration under the Act of any graduate or licenciate in dentistry he must satisfy the registrar of his identity, that he is of good character and that he is in good physical and mental health.

EEC Dentists Section 15(1)b provides that anyone who is a national of a member state of the EEC and holds an appropriate European diploma in dentistry is entitled to be registered. Schedule 2 to the Act lists those diplomas in dentistry granted in Belgium, Denmark, France, Germany, Greece, the Republic of

Ireland, Italy, Luxembourg and the Netherlands which are "appropriate European diplomas". Spain and Portugal were added by SI 1986 No. 23. However, they are only a basis for registration under the Act where they are granted following a course of training begun after that country had implemented the EEC directive (No. 78/687/EEC) on the co-ordination of dental training. In other cases the holder must satisfy the registrar either that the diploma complies with the standards laid down in the EEC directive or furnish a certificate from a competent authority in that country that he has lawfully practised dentistry there for at least three consecutive years out of the last five. An EEC dentist disqualified in any member state may not be registered in this country.

Statutory Instrument 1980 No. 703 which originally introduced these provisions included a requirement for proficiency in the English language as a pre-requisite for registration, but this was considered contrary to the Treaty of Rome and was removed by the European Communities (Medical, Dental and Nursing Professions) (Linguistic Knowledge) Order 1981 SI 1981 No. 432. However, the Order modifies the National Health Service legislation to require those responsible for the provision of general dental services to satisfy themselves that an EEC practitioner has sufficient knowledge of English to be offered employment.

Overseas Dentists Section 15(1)c (4) and (5) of the Act provides that anyone who can show to the satisfaction of the registrar that he is of good character, holds a recognised overseas diploma in dentistry and has satisfied the General Dental Council that he has the pre-requisite knowledge and skill is entitled to be registered in the appropriate part of the register. The Council may determine his skill and knowledge by requiring him to sit examinations, and it has the power to make regulations – these need the approval of the Privy Council to be effective – controlling such examinations. However, if the overseas diploma is one that the Council recognises as providing evidence of the knowledge and skill required it may dispense with such examinations (section 16). The regulations relating to such examinations are not published as statutory instruments, but copies are obtainable from the offices of the General Dental Council.

Additionally, section 15 of the Act requires that before registration an overseas dentists must satisfy the registrar of his identity, that he has the necessary knowledge of English and that he is in good mental and physical health. The necessary knowledge of English is that which in his own interests and those of his patients is necessary for the practice of dentistry in the United Kingdom.

Temporary Registration Section 17 of the Act permits the General Dental Council to issue temporary registration to a holder of a recognised overseas diploma to permit that person to practise dentistry in a hospital or other institution for a specified period of time. Such a person may only practise dentistry lawfully within the said hospital. Except for this, such a person is not a registered dentist. The dentist must satisfy the registrar of his identity, that he is of good character and that he has the requisite knowledge and skill for the efficient practice of dentistry in the post in question. He must also have the necessary knowledge of the English language (as defined above) and be of good physical and mental health.

Another form of temporary registration, originally introduced by the Dental Qualifications (EEC Regulations) Order 1980 SI 1980 No. 703 and now covered by section 36 and schedule 4 to the Act, is for visiting EEC dentists. A visiting EEC dentist may provide dental services in the United Kingdom without first being registered, provided he supplies the registrar with a declaration of what services he intends to provide, and for how long, and also gives evidence that he is either lawfully in practice in a member state or holds a recognised European diploma in dentistry. The registrar must list such dentists' names on a list of visiting EEC practitioners. Such practitioners are subject to the disciplinary provisions of the Dentists Act and are treated as being fully registered for the purpose of practice within the scope of his declaration.

Removal from the Register

Section 23 of the Act requires the registrar to remove the name of a deceased dentist from the register. To facilitate this a registrar of births and deaths, on registering the death of a dentist, shall send without charge a copy of the death certificate to the Dental Council's registrar. Where a dentist has ceased to practise, his name may, with his consent, be removed from the register. The registrar may make enquiries through the post about whether a dentist is still in practice. If he receives no answer within six months he can erase his name. However, in such a case, a dentist's name may be restored to the register on payment of a fee.

Section 24 imposes a duty on the General Dental Council to remove from the register any name incorrectly or fraudulently entered. The Professional Conduct Committee is to determine whether an entry is fraudulent or not, and no name so removed may be restored except on application to the Council.

Regulations made under section 19 permit the registrar to erase from the register the name of a dentist who fails to pay a prescribed fee after the prescribed notice and warnings have been given.

Erasure from the register is the major disciplinary measure open to the Council. Section 27 of the Act provides that the name of any registered dentist who has been convicted of a criminal offence in the United Kingdom, or of an offence elsewhere amounting to a criminal offence in the United Kingdom, or has been guilty of serious professional misconduct, is liable to erasure or suspension. If the dental authority which issued the degree or diploma on which his registration is based cancels that degree or diploma, this does not automatically lead to erasure or suspension from the register. The decision to erase or suspend a name under Section 27 is made by the Professional Conduct Committee of the Council after the prescribed investigation.

Professional Discipline

Section 1 of the Dentists Act charges the General Dental Council with the promotion of high standards of professional conduct among dentists. The main sanctions available to the Council to enforce this disciplinary function are the removal or the suspension of a dentist's name from the register.

Section 27 of the Act provides that a registered dentist is liable to have his name erased from the register if, either before or after registration, he has been convicted of a criminal offence in the United Kingdom or any offence elsewhere amounting to a crime in this country or has been guilty of serious professional misconduct. Before the 1983 Act the phrase "infamous or disgraceful conduct in a professional matter" was used, but it is to be expected that the interpretation of what is serious misconduct will not significantly change. There is no definition of professional misconduct, and the note issued by the Council for guidance of dentists makes it clear that it may vary with the circumstances. It includes acts of immorality, indecency or dishonesty in respect of patients, making improper statements or certificates in respect of a professional manner, misuse of drink or drugs, and advertising and canvassing. In Clifford v Timms (1908) A C 12, H L, the issue of pamphlets derogatory of the profession was held to be infamous conduct. Where the misconduct relates to the keeping of records, the Privy Council has held that there must be some degree of moral turpitude, dishonesty or fraud; mere negligence will not suffice. In Felix v General Council (1960) 2 All ER 391, Lord Jenkins emphasised that "infamous and disgraceful conduct" meant "conduct deserving the strongest reprobation" and that it was much more than mere negligence. This view was re-confirmed by the Privy Council in the case of McEniff v General Dental Council (1980) 1 All E R461 which was an appeal against a decision of erasure. The dentist had permitted an unqualified assistant to insert fillings, and the appeal, which was rejected, related to the direction given by the legal assessor to the Disciplinary Committee as to the meaning of infamous or disgraceful conduct. Such previous cases are likely to apply to the new phrase "serious professional misconduct".

Preliminary Proceedings Committee

The existence of the Preliminary Proceedings Committee of the General Dental Council is confirmed by section 2 of the Act, and its composition is provided for by the first schedule (part II) to the Act. This Committee, which usually meets twice a year in March and September (but may meet as and when required), consists of the president of the Council and five other members, of whom one must not be a registered dentist. The president may appoint one or two extra members of the Council for the consideration of a particular case. The Council receives information about alleged professional misconduct from a variety of sources, including public authorities such as a Dental Services Committee, a university or academic body, or a member of the public. Complaints from the public must be supported by a statutory declaration. The dentist is informed about the situation, given a copy of any declaration and asked to comment.

The Committee considers these complaints and decides whether there is a case which should be referred to the Professional Conduct Committee for a public inquiry. It may decide there is no case and that no action should be taken; it may decide that no action should be taken on this occasion but warn the dentist that it may reconsider its decision if further information comes to its notice, or it may refer the case to the Professional Conduct Committee. In the latter case the dentist is sent a notice of inquiry at least four weeks before the disciplinary hearing.

Section 16 of the 1983 Act gave the Preliminary Proceedings Committee additional powers to order the interim suspension of a dentist's registration (now section 32 of the 1984 Act). They may do so where they have decided to refer a disciplinary case to the Professional Conduct Committee but are satisfied that it is necessary for the protection of the public to order an interim suspension. They may not make such an order unless the dentist has been given a chance to appear before this Committee to present his case, and he may be represented by counsel or a solicitor. The Committee must review each interim suspension at least every three months.

Professional Conduct Committee

What was previously known as the Disciplinary Committee was renamed the Professional Conduct Committee by the 1983 Act. The first schedule (part II) to the 1984 Act provides that it shall consist of the president and ten other members, of whom at least five shall be elected members and at least two neither elected nor registered dentists. Except for the president no-one shall be a member of the Preliminary Proceedings Committee and the Professional Conduct Committee at the same time. The president acts as chairman. The quorum is seven including at least two elected members and one non-dentist, and decisions are by a majority vote of the members present at a meeting.

Section 27 of the Act imposes a duty on the Professional Conduct Committee to hold an inquiry into any case referred to it. The only exceptions are where it considers further investigation to be necessary and refers the matter back to the Preliminary Proceedings Committee for that purpose, or it considers a matter of ill health is raised and refers the issue to the Health Committee. It must decide if the dentist is liable to erasure or suspension and, if so, must decide whether or not to erase or suspend his name. It may postpone its decision until a future meeting so that it can consider the dentist's conduct in the intervening period.

Proceedings before the Professional Conduct Committee

Schedule 3 to the Dentists Act requires the Council to make rules for procedure before the Professional Conduct Committee. Before making the rules the Council must consult those bodies representing dentists, and the rules do not come into force until approved by order of the Privy Council contained in a statutory instrument. The present rules are contained in the General Dental Council Professional Conduct Committee (Procedure) Rules Order of Council 1984 SI 1984 No. 1517.

Preliminaries

As soon as a case is referred to the Professional Conduct Committee its solicitor must send a notice of inquiry, together with a copy of the rules, to the respondent. Where there is a complainant, a copy of the notice and the rules must also be sent to him. The notice of inquiry states the matter alleged against the dentist and the time and place set for the inquiry. Except with the agreement of the respondent, the date must not be earlier than 28 days after the date of posting (rule 3). Any party to the inquiry may ask for copies of any documents or communications sent by any other party to the Council in relation to the inquiry.

Proceedings

Schedule 3 of the Act requires a legal assessor to be present at all proceedings before the Professional Conduct Committee, and the rules relating to the function of the assessors are contained in the General Dental Council Disciplinary Committee (Legal Assessor) Rules 1957 SI 1957 No. 1470. Such rules are made by the Lord Chancellor. The assessor is appointed by the General Dental Council and must be a barrister, advocate or solicitor of not less than ten years' standing. The assessor must advise the Committee on questions of law arising in an inquiry, point out any irregularities in the conduct of the proceedings and give such advice as he thinks fit to avoid a mistake of law being made. If the Committee fails to accept his advice, a record of this must be made and a copy given to every party to the proceedings.

A party to the proceedings may appear in person or be represented by counsel or a solicitor, by an officer or a member of an organisation of which he is a member, by a professional colleague, or by a member of his family (rule 7). Proceedings take place in public in the presence of all parties. However, the Committee has the power to deliberate in camera, and may, in the interests of justice or for some other special reason, exclude the public, but not from the announcement of the decision of the Committee. A shorthand note of all proceedings (except those for re-instatement of a name after penal erasure) is taken, and on the payment of the proper fee a transcript must be supplied to any party.

Evidence

Evidence may be heard under oath, which may be administered by the Committee. Parties to the proceedings may secure the presence of witnesses by sueing out writs of subpoena ad testificandum and duces tecum, but no-one may be compelled to produce documents he could not be compelled to produce in a court of law. Evidence may be oral or documentary, but the Committee may not receive evidence of a fact if that evidence would not be admissable in criminal proceedings, unless, after consultation with the legal assessor, the Committee is satisfied that in the interests of justice it is desirable to have it (rule 26).

Typical Procedure

Proceedings are opened with the charge being read out when the respondent may object in point of law to the charge, or part of it. If the objection is upheld the proceedings are terminated (rule 8). The case against the respondent is presented by the Council's solicitor who may call appropriate evidence. The respondent answers the case and also presents his evidence. In such a situation the solicitor or complainant may adduce evidence in rebuttal.

Special Cases

In cases relating to alleged fraudulent entry in the register the proceedings are fundamentally as for misconduct (rule 17). If the case is brought against a corporate body which is carrying on a business of dentistry the notice of inquiry must be sent to the registered office of that compnay; copies are also sent to anyone who appears to be a director of the company (rule 21). The company may appear through its clerk or other officer, or be represented by counsel or a solicitor. The sanction against a company is withdrawal of its rights to carry on the business of dentistry.

Determination

At the end of the proceedings the Committee must decide if the conviction or unprofessional conduct has been proved. If so, then the chairman announces that finding. The respondent or his representative may then present evidence of the circumstances of the case and point out past history of the respondent. The respondent may produce evidence and address the committee in mitigation. The Committee then announces whether the dentist's name is to be erased from the register or is to be suspended. However, where the Committee decides to suspend a dentist's name from the register, this may not be for a period in excess of 12 months. The effect of a suspension is that the dentist is considered not to be registered, notwithstanding that his name may still be on the register.

The question of whether the Professional Conduct Committee may take a dentist's previous convictions into account when deciding whether to erase a name arose in Ziderman v General Dental Council (1976) 1 WLR 330. The Privy Council decided in this case, which concerned shoplifting, that the Committee was correct to consider earlier convictions in determining whether the offence which was the subject of the disciplinary proceedings was sufficiently grave to justify erasure.

Appeals and Restorations

Appeals Where the Professional Conduct Committee has decided to erase or suspend a dentist's name from the register, the dentist may appeal within 28 days against the decision to the Judicial Committee of the Privy Council (section 29 of the Act). The procedure for appeal is laid down in the Judicial Committee (Dentists Rules) Order 1985 SI 1985 No. 172. The General Dental Council may appear as a respondent, but if it does not, it is nevertheless deemed to be a party for the purposes of costs. A decision by the Professional Conduct Committee to strike off a name is effective from dismissal of an appeal, from the withdrawal or striking out of an appeal or from the expiry of the time for appeal, as appropriate. However, section 30 of the Act empowers the Committee to order immediate suspension where it is necessary to protect the public or is in the best interests of the dentist. Such an interim suspension order remains in effect until any appeal has been heard or time has run out. The Act provides that any dentist subject to an interim suspension order may apply to the court for immediate termination of the order, and the court's decision is final. In Scotland the court is the Court of Session, in Northern Ireland the Norther Ireland High Court and in any other case the High Court of Justice in England.

Restoration to the Register

Section 34 of the Act provides that where a name has been erased from the register it may not be restored except by direction of the General Dental Council. No name may be restored within ten months of erasure or previous application. Applications for restorations are referred to the Professional Conduct Committee and procedure for hearing applications is laid down in rule 20 of SI 1984 No. 1517. It must give the applicant an opportunity to be heard and produce evidence.

Fitness to Practise

Part III of the 1983 Act made provision for the first time for action to be taken by the General Dental Council against a dentist whose fitness to practise is seriously impaired by reason of ill-health, be it mental or physical, and this is continued in the 1984 Act. Part III of the Act, and regulations made under it, came into effect on 1st January 1985 (The Dentists Act 1984 (Commencement) Order 1984 SI No. 1815.

The Health Committee

Section 2 of the 1984 Act establishes a new committee of the General Dental Council, called the Health Committee, the constitution of this committee to be the subject of rules made by the Council and approved by the Privy Council. The General Dental Council Health Committee (Constitution) Order 1984 (SI 1984 No. 1816) provides that the Health Committee shall consist of a chairman who must be a registered dentist, five elected members of Council, three nominated members (who must be registered dentists) and two members of Council who are not registered dentists. The president of the Council shall choose whether to be chairman, and if he decides not to be he must appoint a Council member as chairman.

Fitness to Practise Proceedings

The procedure to be followed in health cases is laid out in the General Dental Council Health Committee (Procedure) Rules Order of Council 1984 (SI 1984 No. 2010), to which reference should be made for details. Rule 5 requires that no case may be considered by the Health Committee unless it is referred by the president, by the Preliminary Proceedings, or by the Professional Conduct Committee.

Reference by the President If the registrar receives information suggesting a dentist may have a health problem he must refer the matter to the president (or someone else appointed for the purpose) to undertake an initial consideration of the case. If the president considers there is a case to investigate he will invite the dentist to agree within 14 days to examination by two medical examiners chosen by the president from a list maintained for this purpose (see rule 4 and the second schedule). The dentist may also nominate additional doctors to examine him and report on his case. If, on the basis of these medical reports, the president considers there is insufficient evidence of an impaired fitness to practise the dentist is so informed and the case goes no further. If, however, there appears evidence of impaired fitness the president must refer the case to the Health Committee.

Reference by the Preliminary Proceedings and Professional Conduct Committee
In such cases rule 9 provides that the president, if he thinks fit, may invite the dentist to be examined by two medical examiners as above and that he may nominate a further doctor to examine him and report on his case.

Hearing before the Health Committee
The registrar must inform the dentist of the time and place of the hearing, indicate to him the physical or mental condition by reason of which he is alleged to be unfit to practise and inform him that he may be represented if he wishes by an officer of his defence society or similar organisation, by counsel or a solicitor or any member of his family, and that he may be accompanied by his medical adviser (rules 10 and 16). The Committee sits in private and the president arranges for one or more medical assessors to attend. A legal assessor would also attend. The case against the dentist is presented by the General Council Solicitor and the dentist or his representative present the case arguing his fitness to practise. The Committee may adjourn the case for further medical reports (rule 20) or postpone its finding (rule 21). However, if it proceeds to a determination it must decide whether the dentist's fitness to practise is impaired. In the case of a dentist who has refused to submit to medical examination the Committee may take this refusal, together with the other information about him, as evidence of unfitness to practise. If it finds the dentist is unfit to practise the Committee must decide if it will be sufficient to make his registration conditional – usually on a course of appropriate treatment, for a period of up to three years. If it feels conditional registration would not be adequate it may suspend his registration for a period of up to 12 months.

Appeals and Immediate Suspension
Section 29 of the Act provides that a dentist may appeal to the Privy Council against a direction of the Health Committee. He must appeal within 28 days of service of notification of the Committee's decision. The rules relating to appeals are contained in the Judicial Committee (Dentists Rules) Order 1985 SI 1985 No. 172. The Privy Council may dismiss the appeal, allow the appeal and quash the Health Committee's decision, substitute its own decision or refer the issue back to the Committee with directions as to how it should deal with it. The Health Committee's decision does not take effect until the time for an appeal has run out and no appeal has been made, or when any appeal had been determined. However, section 30 of the Act provides that if the Health Committee is of the view that immediate action is required in the interests of protecting the public, or in the best interests of the dentist, then it may order immediate suspension of his registration. The dentist may appeal against an immediate suspension order to the High Court of Justice if he is in England or Wales, the Court of Session if he is in Scotland or the High Court in Northern Ireland. The court's decision is final.

Controls on the Practice of Dentistry

Definition of the Practice of Dentistry

Section 37 defines the practice of dentistry for the purposes of the Dentists Act. The practice of dentistry includes the performing of any operation or the giving of any such treatment, advice or attendance as is usually done or given by dentists. It also includes the giving of any treatment, advice or attendance preparatory to, for the purpose of, or in connection with, the fitting, insertion or fixing of dentures, artificial teeth or other dental appliances. However, section 37(2) exempts from the definition dental work done by a recognised student of dentistry or medicine as part of his course of study or examination or by student auxiliary dental workers in similar circumstances, provided (in both cases) it is under the direct personal supervision of a registered dentist.

The Practice of Dentistry is Limited to Registered Dentists or Medical Practitioners

Section 38(1) of the Act provides that no-one other than a registered dentist, medical practitioner or a visiting EEC practitioner shall practise, or hold himself out as practising, or being willing to practise, dentistry. To do so is an offence liable on summary conviction to a fine not exceeding £1,000 (Criminal Justice Act 1982). Proceedings may be commenced at any time within six months of evidence becoming available, but not more than two years after the offence. Two minor exceptions to the prohibition in section 38(1) used to exist under the 1957 Act. One permitted a registered pharmacist to extract a tooth in an emergency, provided he used no anaesthetic, and the other permitted minor supervised dental work done in any public dental service. Both exceptions were repealed by the 1983 Act.

The Use of Titles

Section 26 of the Act entitles a registered dentist to use the description "dentist", "dental surgeon" or "dental practitioner". However, the same section (section 26(2)) makes it an offence for a registered dentist to use any description in connection with himself or his premises that suggests he has any qualifications which, in fact, as indicated by his entry in the dental register, he does not have. On summary conviction an offender may be fined up to £200 (Criminal Justice Act 1982). The section also permits the Council by regulations to permit the use of a new title if a branch of dentistry becomes so distinctive as to merit a separate description and to list dentists entitled to such titles as an appendix to the dental register.

Section 39 of the Act makes it an offence for anyone who is not a registered dentist, medical practitioner or visiting EEC practitioner to use the titles "dentist", "dental surgeon" or "dental practitioner", or for anyone to use any title or description which implies he is a registered dentist if he is not so. Anyone contravening this provision is liable on summary conviction to a fine not exceeding £1,000. It should be noted that for the purposes of controls on dental practice someone on the list of visiting EEC practitioners is treated as a registered dentist provided he operates within the declaration he made to the registrar.

Dentistry Business

Definition Section 40 defines the business of dentistry for the purpose of the Act. Someone is carrying on the business of dentistry if he, or a partnership of which he is a member, receives payment for services rendered in the course of the practice of dentistry by him, by a partner, or by an employee of his or of a partner. However, section 40(2) excludes the following from the definition:

1. Payment received by an authority for National Health services.
2. Payment received by someone providing dental treatment for his employees without a view to profit.
3. Payment received by someone giving dental treatment without a view to profit under conditions approved by the Secretary of State or the Department of Health and Social Services for Northern Ireland.

Restriction of Dentistry Business

Broadly speaking, section 41 of the Act limits carrying on a dentistry business to registered dentists, registered medical practitioners or persons who were carrying on a dentistry business on 21st July 1955. Someone who carries on a business, and who is not one of these categories commits an offence and is liable to a fine of up to £1,000 on summary conviction. The section provides certain limited exceptions to the general rule in the case of death or bankruptcy of the person carrying on the business.

Death Section 41 of the Act provides that where a registered dentist or medical practitioner dies (after 3rd July 1956) and at his death he was carrying on a dentistry business, then his widow, any of his children, or trustees on behalf of his widow or children, may continue that business for three years from his death. Where a dentists died before 4th July 1956 and his widow or trustees on her behalf are carrying on the business, section 41(5) permits them to continue to do so for the rest of the widow's life.

Bankruptcy Section 41(6) provides that where a registered dentist or medical practitioner becomes bankrupt while carrying on a business of dentistry his trustee in bankruptcy (the official assignee in Northern Ireland) may continue that business for three years from the bankruptcy.

Effect of a Suspension Where a dentist's name is suspended for disciplinary or health reasons he may nonetheless continue to carry on a dentistry business (section 41(3)).

Position of Corporate Bodies

The general rule laid down by section 42(1) of the Act is that a corporation may not carry on a dentistry business, and a body contavening this section is liable to a fine of up to £200 on summary conviction. Where a corporate body is so convicted every director or manager is also guilty of the offence unless he can prove the offence was committed without his knowledge (section 42(3)). However, section 43(1) provides that a company which was carrying on a dentistry business at 21st July 1955, carries on no other businesss except one ancillary to dentistry, has a majority of its directors as registered dentists and all of whose operating staff are registered dentists or auxiliary dental workers, may carry on the business of dentistry. The exception does not apply to a corporate body which is registered under the Industrial and Provident Societies Act 1965 (or its Northern Ireland equivalent), or one that came into being on the reconstruction or amalgamation of a company carrying on a dentistry business on the said day. Further, should a corporate body cease to carry on a dentistry business, it loses the exemption permanently.

Control of Corporate Bodies

Section 43(4) requires every corporate body carrying on the business of dentistry to send to the Council's registrar a statement in prescribed form of the names and addresses of all persons who are directors or managers or who perform dental operations in connection with the business.

A corporate body carrying on a dentistry business may lose its privilege to do so if it is convicted of an offence under section 42, if a director's name is erased from the register under section 27, or if a director is convicted under section 38 and 41. In these cases section 44(1) provides that the Professional Conduct Committee may direct that the exception permitting the company to do business shall cease. In addition, if the name of one of the company's operating staff is erased from the register and it is the opinion of the Professional Conduct Committee that the grounds of the erasure were connived at, or instigated by, a director of that company, then the Committee may also withdraw the exemption from the company (section 44(2)).

Where the Committee withdraws the exception from a corporate body, the company may appeal within 28 days to the Privy Council if it considers the decision was unjust.

Control of Dental Education

The Education Committee

Section 13 of the Dentists Act 1984 requires the General Dental Council to refer any matter concerning dental examinations or education to its Education Committee, whose constitution is determined by part II of the first schedule to the Act. The Committee consists of the president and at least eight other members of the Council, who must be registered dentists, and the six members of the Council who are nominated by the General Medical Council. The chairman must be a registered dentist.

Qualifying Examinations

Section 15(1) of the Dentists Act entitles a graduate or licentiate of a dental authority to be registered under the Act. As stated earlier, a dental authority is a medical authority which grants diplomas in dentistry, and a medical authority is defined as any university or other body which chooses appointed members of the General Medical Council. Section 3(1) permits any medical authority which has the power to grant surgical degrees to hold examinations in dentistry and grant licences certifying the holder's fitness to practise. This power is given notwithstanding anything in any other Act, charter or other document. Section 5 confirms the right of the Royal College of Surgeons of England to hold examinations and grant licences in dentistry, in accordance with the College charter of 1859.

Section 4 provides that any dental authority may, for the purposes of examinations in dentistry, appoint a board of examiners to be called the Board of Examiners in Dental Surgery or in Dentistry. The Boards are to consist of not less than six members, at least half of whom must be registered dentists who may not be required to possess any other qualifications. The constitutions of these boards are to be determined by regulations or bye-laws made by the particular dental authority, and section 4(5) permits the charging of reasonable fees on the award of a degree or licence in dentistry. Section 6 requires a dental authority to admit to its examinations anyone who has complied with the education regulations in force laid down by the authority. A dental authority may not grant a degree or licence in dentistry to anyone under 21 years old.

Control by the General Dental Council

The General Dental Council has overall control over dental education through a variety of means.

Right to Demand Information Section 8 imposes an obligation on every dental authority to supply the General Dental Council on demand with information relating to courses of study and examinations and with any other information related to obtaining a degree or licence in dentistry.

Visitors Section 9 empowers the General Dental Council to appoint persons to visit dental schools and report on the sufficiency of the instruction given there. They may not, however, interfere with that instruction. On receipt of a visitors' report, the Council must send a copy to the dental authority or other body visited and it must be given an opportunity to make objections or other observations. The Council must then send a copy of the visitors' report, the dental school's comments and the Council's own views to the Privy Council. Section 10 empowers any member of the General Dental Council, or anyone appointed by them, to be present at examinations in dentistry. Section 16(3) empowers the Council to send visitors to report on the adequacy of examinations held in relation to recognised overseas diplomas.

Intervention by the General Dental Council For cases in which the General Dental Council comes to the view that the course of study and examination at a dental authority are not sufficient to secure the required knowledge and skill for the efficient practice of dentistry, section 11 empowers the Council to make representations to that effect to the Privy Council. The Privy Council may, if it thinks fit, order that the degree or licence is not, after a specified date, to confer a right to registration. When the Privy Council is of the view after discussions with the General Dental Council that the standard of training and examination has been restored to the required level it has the power to revoke such an order. However, this revocation does not have retrospective effect and anyone obtaining a qualification while the order was in force does not become registrable when the order is revoked.

If the General Dental Council is of the view that a dental authority has made the adoption or rejection of any particular theory of dentistry a test or condition of admission to the examination or to the granting of a degree or licence, then section 12 empowers the Council to make representations to that effect to the Privy Council. The Privy Council may direct the dental authority to desist from this practice. If the authority fails to do so the Privy Council can stop it granting degrees or licences as long as it continues to impose such restrictions.

Dental Auxiliaries

Before the 1983 Act dental auxiliaries were described as ancillary dental workers. Although the overall effect of the Dentists Act is to restrict the practice of dentistry to properly registered dentists, part V (section 45–48) of the Act permits the General Dental Council to establish by statutory instrument classes of dental auxiliaries who, subject to the regulations, may legally carry out various activities which amount to certain aspects of the practice of dentistry. The regulations are the Dental Auxiliaries Regulations 1986 SI 1986 No. 887. Section 45 empowers the Council to make such regulations. Section 46, however, provides that no regulations may permit any class of worker to extract teeth except deciduous teeth, or to fill teeth or extract deciduous teeth except in the course of the provision of National Health services, or to fit, insert or fix dentures or artificial teeth. The regulations have established two classes of dental auxiliary worker – dental hygienist and dental therapist. However, section 46 of the Act provides a mechanism whereby the categories may be altered by Order in Council.

Dental Hygienist

Dental hygienists may clean, polish and scale teeth and apply such prophylactic materials to teeth as the Council from time to time determines. They may act only under the directions of a registered dentist and only after that dentist has examined the patient and indicated what treatment the hygienist is to give.

Dental Therapist

A dental therapist may extract deciduous teeth under local infiltration anaesthetic, do simple dental fillings, clean and polish teeth, scale teeth, apply such prophylactic materials to the teeth as the Council determines, and give advice on any matter incidental to his approved functions. A dental therapist may do work only as part of the provision of National Health services and must work under the direction of a registered dentist who must first examine the patient.

Training and Registration

The regulations empower the General Dental Council to approve courses of instruction and examinations held by dental authorities and by other bodies the Council thinks fit for training of dental auxiliaries. However, section 45 directs the Council not to approve any such course if it would materially impair the facilities for training dental students. The Council may appoint visitors to satisfy themselves of the adequacy of the training and examinations.

Satisfactory completion of an approved course of training, passing the examination and obtaining the appropriate certificate confer on the holder a right to be enrolled in the appropriate class. The registrar keeps a roll for each of the two classes of dental worker and he must enrol anyone who has obtained a qualifying certificate, paid the fee, shown evidence of good character and generally complied with the regulations for enrolment.

Dental Auxiliaries Committee

Section 2 of the Dentists Act confirms the existence of a Dental Auxiliaries Committee to which all matters concerning ancillary dental services must be referred. The constitution of the Committee is provided by part II of the first schedule to the Act. The Committee consists of the president and eight to ten other Council members, together with nine non-Council members. Of these nine, three are appointed for three-year periods by the Secretaries of State responsible for health matters in England and Wales, in Scotland and in Northern Ireland. The other six are elected by enrolled dental auxiliaries, although it should be noted that until the 1983 Act there were no elected dental auxiliaries on this Committee.

The Committee has a disciplinary power over dental auxiliaries provided for by section 48, and the regulations deal with the detailed disciplinary procedure. An enrolled dental auxiliary is liable to disciplinary proceedings if before or after enrolment he has been convicted of any offence which, if committed in England, would be triable on indictment or if he is alleged to have been guilty of any misconduct. Where it is alleged that a dental auxiliary worker is liable to disciplinary proceedings, the registrar must gather together all relevant information and submit it to the chairman of the Committee. If, after consultation with the president, the chairman of the Committee thinks fit, he will bring the case before the Committee for hearing.

The respondent must be informed of the time and date of the hearing and invited to attend. He may be represented by a friend, counsel or a solicitor. The hearing proceeds with the evidence for both sides being presented. At the close of the hearing the respondent or his representative may address the Committee by way of mitigation. The Committee must then decide whether to erase the name or not. Up to the 1983 Act there was no statutory appeal provided for by the Act, but someone whose name has been erased was able to apply to the Committee for its restoration. However, section 48(3) of the 1984 Act provides that a dental auxiliary may appeal against a direction for erasure in the same way as a registered dentist in a similar situation could do.

Titles

The regulations permit an enrolled dental auxiliary to use the title appropriate to his class. Use of a title by anyone not so authorised is an offence liable on summary conviction to a fine not exceeding £200. It is also an offence for an enrolled dental auxiliary to use any title or description suggesting he has dentistry status or qualifications he does not have. The offence is liable on summary conviction to a fine not exceeding £200.

Chapter Nine

The Pharmaceutical Profession

The Pharmacy Act 1954

The profession of pharmaceutical chemist is regulated by the Pharmacy Act 1954 and bye-laws made by the Pharmaceutical Society of Great Britain under the powers in the Act. Certain aspects of the pharmacist's practice where it relates to medicinal products, controlled drugs or poisons are dealt with by the Medicines Act 1968, the Misuse of Drugs Act 1971 and the Poisons Act 1972 respectively. This chapter discusses the professional control exercised by the Pharmacy Act and the bye-laws made under it and, to a lesser extent, by the Medicines Act 1968. An introduction to the law on medicines and poisons is found in The Law on Poisons, Medicines and Related Substances, by P F C Bayliss, (Ravenswood Legal Publications, 2nd edition 1986). More detailed information is given in Pharmacy Law and Ethics, by J R Dale and G E Appelbe, (The Pharmaceutical Press, 3rd edition, 1983).

The Pharmaceutical Society of Great Britain

The Pharmaceutical Society of Great Britain was founded in 1841 and incorporated by Royal Charter in 1843. This was confirmed by statute in the Pharmacy Act 1852 (repealed). Except for the provisions of the 1843 charter which incorporated the Society, authorised its common seal and permitted it to sue and be sued, the 1843 charter and subsequent supplemental charters were replaced by a new charter of 1953.

The main objectives of the Society are to advance chemistry and pharmacy, to promote pharmaceutical education and knowledge, to maintain the honour, and safeguard the interests, of members in their professional capacity, and to provide relief to distressed members or their relatives or to students. The exercise of the Society's objectives has been the subject of at least two important legal decisions.

In Jenkins v Pharmaceutical Society of Great Britain (1921) 1 Ch 392, the High Court considered the Society's proposal to form an industrial council to regulate wages, hours and working conditions in the profession. The Court held that it was not within the Society's objectives to regulate its members' hours of business, wages or conditions of employment, or to regulate the prices its members sold at or to provide insurance for members. The objective in the 1843 charter, under which the Jenkins case was considered was the "protection of those who carry on the business of chemists and druggists". In the 1953 charter this became "to maintain the honour and safeguard and promote the interests of members in the exercise of the profession of pharmacy", and the scope of this came to be considered by the House of Lords in Pharmaceutical Society of Great Britain v Dickson (1968) 1 All ER 686. At a special general meeting the Society approved a motion that it should control the nature of premises in which all new pharmacies were to be situated. Mr Dickson, a member of the Society and a director of the Boots Pure Drug Co. Ltd., sought an injunction claiming that this was outside the scope of the Society's powers and would be in restraint of trade. The House of Lords held that the Society could not control selling activities which did not interfere with the performance of professional pharmacy duties, as the relevant part of the charter was to safeguard the interests of members in the exercise of their professional duties. The House of Lords also found that the move would be in restraint of trade. Section 66 of the Medicines Act 1968 permits regulations to be made which could control a very wide range of aspects of the physical design, structure and operation of pharmacy premises. However, at the time of writing, no such regulations have been made, although pressure exists within the profession for their enactment.

Membership

Every person whose name is registered on the register of pharmaceutical chemists in accordance with the provisions of the Pharmacy Act 1954 is a member of the Society and anyone who ceases to be registered ceases to be a member (section 14). In addition, the Society bye-laws permit the creation of honorary and student members, but these cannot attend or vote at general meetings of members.

The Council

The ruling body of the Pharmaceutical Society is the Council, whose powers and duties arise from both the 1953 charter and the 1954 Pharmacy Act. The Council consists of 24 members. Twenty-one are members of the Society who are elected by the members in accordance with the bye-laws of the Society. The other three, who need not be members, are appointed by the Privy Council under the provisions of section 14 of the Pharmacy Act 1954.

Statutory Powers and Duties

The Registrar Section 1 of the Pharmacy Act 1954 directs the Council to appoint a fit and proper person to be registrar for the purposes of the Act. The Council may also appoint a deputy registrar and such subordinate staff as it thinks fit. The Council pays their salaries and has the power to terminate their appointment.

Bye-laws Both the charter and the Act permit the Council to make bye-laws. The charter provides that bye-laws will be invalid if repugnant to the charter or to the general law, and at least 60 days' notice must be given to members as required by existing bye-laws. Section 16 of the Act provides that the Council may make bye-laws for the purposes of the Act but no bye-law made by virtue of the Act comes into operation until approved by the Privy Council. The present bye-laws were approved by the Privy Council on 27th February 1978. A copy of them may be seen at the Society's office, and they are reproduced in the Society's calendar.

The Statutory Committee Section 7 of the Pharmacy Act requires the Society to appoint a Statutory Committee, the constitution of which is determined by the first schedule to the Act. This Committee is the disciplinary body for the profession.

Benevolent Fund One objective in the Society's charter is the relief of distressed persons. Section 17 permits the Council to make provision out of the Society's property or from the benevolent fund for the relief of Society members, past members, widows, orphans and other dependants of deceased members or past members, or for students of pharmacy.

The Registration of Pharmaceutical Chemists

The Registrar and the Register

Section 1 of the Pharmacy Act 1954 directs the Council of the Pharmaceutical Society of Great Britain to appoint a fit and proper person as registrar, and it may also appoint subordinate registration staff. Section 2 imposes a duty on the registrar to maintain the register in accordance with the Act and the Society's bye-laws (section 2(1)(a)), and to prepare, in prescribed form, print, publish and sell an annual list of all names on the register on the first day of the preceding year (section 2 (1)(b)). This list is the Annual Register of Pharmaceutical Chemists. The register itself was first established by the Pharmacy Act 1852 and contains the names and addresses of all persons entitled to be registered.

Section 18 makes it an offence, liable to imprisonment for up to 12 months, for the registrar to falsify any matter relating to the register, or the annual publication, or any certficate he may issue concerning registration.

Procedure To have his name registered, an individual must satisfy the registrar that he is qualified and must pay the prescribed fee (section 2(2)). In addition, a retention fee is payable annually (section 2(3)).

Evidence of Registration Section 5 requires the Council, on demand, to issue to any registered pharmaceutical chemist a certificate of his registration, signed by the registrar and by the president or two Council members. The Council is obliged to issue only one such certificate (which is free of charge) except where the registrar is satisfied that the earlier certificate has been lost or destroyed and the applicant pays the prescribed fee. Section 6 provides that such a certificate is admissible in any legal proceedings as evidence that the individual named in it is a registered pharmaceutical chemist. In addition, section 6 provides that the current copy of the annual register is evidence that an individual is registered if it contains his name and, if his name is not included, is evidence that he is not registered.

Qualifications

Registration as a pharmaceutical chemist is achieved by obtaining a qualification in pharmacy which is recognised by the Society. Although the Act empowers the Society to hold qualifying examinations (section 3), the usual route to registration is by obtaining a degree in pharmacy at a university in England, Scotland or Wales (section 4). Provision is made for the registration of pharmacists who qualify in Northern Ireland or overseas. Fuller details are given later in this chapter.

Removal of Names from the Register

The registrar is required to remove the name of a pharmaceutical chemist from the register in a variety of situations. They are:

Disciplinary Cases Removal of a pharmacist's name from the register is an important professional disciplinary measure. The registrar must remove the name of the pharmacist if directed to do so by the Statutory Committee of the Society (section 8) or if there is an unsuccessful appeal to the High Court against a Committee decision (section 11).

Non-Payment of Fees Section 12 provides that where a registered pharmacist fails to pay his retention fee within two months of a demand the Council may direct the registrar to remove his name. However, if the fee is paid before the expiry of the year in which it is due the Council may allow the name to be restored, subject to the payment of a fee by way of penalty.

General Corrections Section 13 provides for a variety of corrections to the register to be made in specific circumstances. Where a pharmacist dies the registrar must remove his name, and any registrar of births and deaths, on registering the death of a pharmacist, must send a certified copy of the death certificate to the Society's registrar (section 13(3)). The registrar must remove from the register any entry which, in the opinion of the Council, was procured by fraud, and must correct any entry that the Council believes is incorrect. In either case the Council must give its directions to the registrar by order in writing. Finally, where the registrar, after enquiring by post of any pharmaceutical chemist whether he has ceased to practise or has changed his address, receives no answer within six months, and sends a second letter and receives no reply in three months, he must remove that chemist's name (section 13(2) and (4)).

Professional Discipline

The Statutory Committee

The Statutory Committee is the disciplinary body for the pharmaceutical profession. It is a committee of the Pharmaceutical Society of Great Britain and not of the Council, of which it is independent. It was created by the Pharmacy and Poisons Act 1933, and its existence is confirmed by section 7 of the Pharmacy Act 1954.

Constitution The Committee's constitution is determined by the first schedule to the Act. It consists of a chairman, appointed by the Privy Council, and five other members appointed by the Council of the Society. The chairman must be someone having practical legal experience and is usually an eminent member of the legal profession. Although there is no requirement that members must be a member of the Council or even of the Society (the chairman usually will not be), at least one member must be a pharmaceutical chemist resident in Scotland. In practice, the members appointed by the Council will be pharmacists. Members hold office for five years but are eligible for re-appointment thereafter. If the chairman becomes incapable through illness or incapacity of performing his duties the Privy Council may appoint someone to act in his place for a fixed period not exceeding six months. Members may resign by giving notice in writing, and a member may be removed from office by the body appointing him for inability to perform his duties or for misbehaviour.

Procedure and Expenses The first schedule to the 1954 Act provides that the Statutory Committee, in exercising its statutory powers and duties, has the power to make regulations concerning its procedure. Such regulations must be approved by the Privy Council and issued as a statutory instrument. This is subject to annulment in pursuance of a resolution of either House of Parliament. The present regulations are contained in the Pharmaceutical Society (Statutory Committee) Order of Council 1978 SI 1978 No. 20. A quorum of the Committee is three, of whom one must be the chairman. Decision is by a majority vote and the chairman has the casting vote. The Pharmaceutical Society pays the expenses of the Committee which are fixed by the Council and approved by the Privy Council.

Disciplinary Jurisdiction and Sanctions

Section 8 of the 1954 Act and the Statutory Committee Regulations (SI 1978 No. 20) determine the disciplinary jurisdiction of the Statutory Committee and the available sanctions. The following are the main disciplinary situations:

1. If someone who applies for registration has been convicted of any criminal offence or guilty of any misconduct which the Committee, after an inquiry, considers makes him unfit to have his name on the register, it may refuse to register him. Alternatively, it may determine to withhold registration until it decides otherwise.

2. If a registered person or anyone employed by him in a business is convicted of any criminal offence, or is guilty of misconduct which the Committee, after an inquiry considers makes him unfit to be registered, it may order his name to be removed from the register. Alternatively, it may caution or admonish the chemist.

3. If someone whose name has been removed from the register for non-payment of the annual retention fee (section 12) and that person or anyone employed by him in his business has either before or after the removal of the name been convicted of any criminal offence or is guilty of misconduct, the Committee may, after an inquiry, direct that his name is not to be restored to the register or, alternatively, not to be restored until the Committee directs otherwise.

4. Where a corporate body which carries on a retail pharmacy business is convicted of an offence under the Pharmacy Act 1954, the Medicines Act 1968 or the Misuse of Drugs Act 1971, the Committee may direct, after an inquiry, that the corporate body be disqualified for the purposes of the pharmacy provisions of the Medicines Act. The Committee may remove from the register of premises all premises occupied by the corporate body or just some of them. This area of the Committee's jurisdiction is provided for by section 80 of the Medicines Act 1968.

5. If any member of the Board of a corporate body which carries on a retail pharmacy business or any officer of, or a person employed by, that body is convicted of an offence or is guilty of misconduct, and the Committee is of the opinion that the offence or misconduct would, if he were a pharmacist, render him unfit to be registered, it may, after an inquiry, disqualify the corporate body and remove from the register of premises all or any of the premises it occupies. Again, this jurisdiction is found in section 80 of the Medicines Act 1968.

6. Where the representative of a pharmacist is carrying on the business and he or a person employed by him is convicted of a crime or is guilty of misconduct and the Committee is of the opinion that, were he a pharmacist, he would be unfit to remain registered, it may, after an inquiry, disqualify the representative for the purpose of the pharmacy provision of the Medicines Act. This power is found in section 80 of the Medicines Act.

Position of Employees

Where the Statutory Committee decides to remove the name of an employer from the register on the grounds of some default by an employee, section 9 of the Pharmacy Act lays down special requirements. In these circumtances the Statutory Committee must be satisfied of at least one of the following:

1. That the employee's default was instigated or connived at by the said person.

2. That the said person or employee was guilty of a similar default within 12 months before the said one and the said person knew or reasonably ought to have known of it.

3. That the default was a continuing one and the said person knew or reasonably ought to have known of it.

4. That if a criminal offence under the Pharmacy Act is concerned, the said person had not used sufficient diligence to prevent the execution of the acts which constituted the offence.

Nature of the Conviction or Misconduct

Section 8 requires the Statutory Committee to reach an opinion on whether a conviction or misconduct renders an individual unfit to have his name on the register. The Statutory Committee has pointed out that in the case of a conviction the individual has already been punished and it is not its function to give additional punishment but to detemine whether the public interest is served by removing the pharmacist's name from the register. This is equally true of misconduct. What conduct makes a pharmacist unfit to have his name on the register is a decision for the Statutory Committee alone, and it is not bound by its own previous decisions or by any professional codes of practice issued by the Pharmaceutical Society. However, the Council of the Pharmaceutical Society has issued the Statement upon Matters of Professional Conduct, which is updated periodically and, while not bound by this, it is an important guideline for the Statutory Committee and, of course, for the presentation of a complaint to the Committee. The statement contains guidelines on such issues as good pharmacy practice, advertising, promotion, relationships with other professions (especially the medical profession), and relationships with the general public.

Proceedings before the Statutory Committee

Proceedings before the Statutory Committee are controlled by the Pharmaceutical Society (Statutory Committee) Order of Council 1978 SI 1978 No. 20.

At least 28 days' notice of an inquiry must be given to the person involved. The hearing is opened in public and continues in public unless in the interests of justice the chairman decides otherwise. Irrespective of what he decides, the decision of the inquiry must be given in public. The hearing usually begins by the solicitor for the complainant presenting the case against the pharmacist who then replies to the charge either in person or through a solicitor or counsel. Evidence for both sides is presented, either orally or in written form, and witnesses may be examined and cross-examined. On conclusion of the hearing the Committee must deliberate in private. It must decide whether the conviction or misconduct is proved and, if so, whether it renders the individual unfit to practise. The standard of proof required for misconduct to be proved was considered in Bhandari v Advocates Committee (1958) 3 All ER 724 PC. It was held that where the misconduct amounted to moral turpitude or deceit then a high standard of proof was needed and not just a balance of probabilities. The Statutory Committee must decide what action to take, whether to remove the pharmacist's name or to issue a reprimand, and the decision may be postponed. The secretary to the Committee communicates the decision to the complainant and the pharmacist and to the registrar who is required to act on it.

Appeals

Section 10 of the Pharmacy Act 1954 permits any person to appeal to the High Court (the Divisional Court of the Queen's Bench Division) if he is aggrieved by a decision of the Statutory Committee to remove his name from the register, not to register his name or not to restore his name. The applicant must appeal within three months of the Committee's direction, and thus section 11(1) provides that a direction of the Committee to remove a name from the register is not to be effective until three months have passed. For the purposes of expenses, the Society is considered to be a party to the appeal, whether or not it appears at the hearing.

Restoration to the Register

Section 8(2) permits the Statutory Committee to restore to the register the name of a pharmacist struck off as a result of a conviction or misconduct. It may do so on its own motion or on the application of the party concerned. Application for restoration must be supported by a statutory declaration by the applicant and by at least two certificates of good character from two registered pharmacists or a pharmacist and a Justice of the Peace. If the action which led to removing the applicant's name resulted from a complaint, the complainant must be informed of the application and given an opportunity to oppose it. The applicant will then be asked for his observations on this. The Statutory Committee may consider the application in private or, if the chairman so directs, in public. If it decides to restore the applicant's name to the register in a case where there had been an unsuccessful appeal to the High Court, the approval of the Privy Council must be obtained to the restoration.

Controls on the Practice of Pharmacy

The Medicines Act 1968 part 4 (sections 69–84) controls the practice of pharmacy and, broadly speaking, restricts the practice of retail pharmacy to registered pharmacists.

The Practice of Retail Pharmacy

Section 132 of the Medicines Act 1968 defines a retail pharmacy business as a business which consists of, or includes, the retail sale of medicinal products (i.e. products controlled by the Medicines Act) other than medicinal products on the General Sale List which may be sold by other outlets. However, a retail pharmacy business does not include a professional practice carried on by a doctor, dentist, veterinary surgeon or veterinary practitioner. A retail pharmacy business may be carried on lawfully only by pharmacists or, in certain circumstances, by pharmacists' representatives or corporate bodies.

Pharmacists Section 69 of the Medicines Act provides that a pharmacist – someone registered in the register of pharmaceutical chemists kept under the Pharmacy Act 1954 in Great Britain or under the Pharmacy and Poisons Act (Northern Ireland) 1925 in the case of Northern Ireland – or a partnership of pharmacists (or, in Scotland, a partnership where one or more partners is a pharmacist) may lawfully carry on a retail pharmacy business. Section 70 requires that the business must be under the personal control of the person lawfully carrying it on or of another pharmacist and that his name and certificate of registration must be conspicuously displayed. Where a partnership is concerned, the business must be under the personal control of one or more of the partners or another pharmacist and the partners' registration certificate must be displayed.

Corporate Bodies Section 69 also permits a retail pharmacy business to be carried on by a corporate body but only if the keeping, preparing and dispensing of medicinal products (other than those on the General Sale List) are under the management of a superintendent who is a registered pharmacist (section 71). He must send to the registrar a signed statement of his name and whether or not he is a member of the board of directors. He must not act in a similar capacity for any other corporate body. The retail sale of medicinal products may be under the control of the superintendent or another pharmacist, and that person's name and certificate of registration must be conspicuously displayed at the premises.

Representatives of Pharmacists Where a pharmacist who carries on a retail pharmacy business dies or is adjudged bankrupt, or a receiver is appointed under the Mental Health Act 1983, then section 72 provides that his representative may lawfully carry on that business if the conditions specified in the section are fulfilled. The conditions are that the name and address of the representative and of the particular pharmacist have been notified to the registrar and that all premises where the business carries on the retail sale of medicinal products (other than those on the General Sale List) are under the personal control of a pharmacist whose name and certificate of registration are conspicuously displayed. Where a pharmacist has died his representative may carry on the business for a further five years or, in the case of bankruptcy, for three years. However, the Statutory Committee may agree to a longer period in particular circumstances.

Meaning of Personal Control

The Medicines Act 1968 requires the retail sale of medicinal products (except those on the General Sale List) to be under the personal control of a pharmacist at those premises. The meaning of personal control was considered in Hygienic Stores Ltd v Coombs 1937 1 All ER 63. In this case, a company had 16 chemist's shops but employed only three pharmacists, one of whom was part-time. It was held that personal control involved the allocation of one pharmacist to each shop, and that he must be present at all times so that the part-time pharmacist could not be considered in personal control of the shop he was allocated to. Precisely what amounts to personal control has been considered in several disciplinary cases. In one case, a pharmacist who arrived at his shop at 10 am each day, although it opened at 9 am, was held guilty of misconduct. In another case, a pharmacist who repeatedly took long absences from his premises was also found guilty of misconduct.

Use of Titles

Section 78 of the Medicines Act provides a variety of restrictions on the use of titles relating to pharmacy. Section 78(2) and (3) provides that no-one shall use the titles "chemist and druggist", "druggist", "dispensing chemist" or "dispensing druggist", or use the title "chemist" in connection with the retail sale of goods unless the individual is lawfully conducting a retail pharmacy business, and then he must not use them in respect of premises at which goods are sold retail unless they are a registered pharmacy.

Section 78(4) provides that no-one may use the term "pharmacy" in connection with a business carried on by him which involves the retail sale or supply of goods unless it is a registered pharmacy or the pharmaceutical department of a hospital or health centre.

Section 78(5) provides that only a pharmacist may use the title of "pharmaceutical chemist", "pharmacist" or "member or fellow of the Pharmaceutical Society". Moreover, no-one may use these titles in connection with a business consisting of the retail sale or supply of goods unless those premises are a registered pharmacy or a hospital or health centre.

Section 78(6) makes it an offence to use any title, description or emblem likely to suggest that, in connection with any business, he or his employees possess any qualifications in respect to the sale, manufacture or assembly of medicinal products that they do not in fact possess. In this connection, the use of the word "pharmacy" in relation to any business is taken to be likely to suggest that the person carrying on the business is a pharmacist.

Section 78(8) provides that a representative of a pharmacist lawfully conducting a retail pharmacy business may nevertheless use any title etc. in respect of that business which the pharmacist himself could have used. Section 84 provides that contravention of the requirements of section 78 is an offence liable on summary conviction to a fine not exceeding £100.

Pharmacy Education and Training

Section 3 and 4 of the Pharmacy Act 1954, together with the bye-laws made under the Act by the Pharmaceutical Society of Great Britain, deal with the topic of pharmaceutical education. There are various educational pathways which entitle an individual to be registered as a member of the Pharmaceutical Society, although some of these are not in active use.

United Kingdom University Qualifications in Pharmacy

Section 4 of the Pharmacy Act 1954 permits the Society to register anyone who has obtained a recognised degree in pharmacy awarded by a university in the United Kingdom or by the Council for National Academic Awards. In addition, they must satisfy the Society that they have completed the required one-year period of pre-registration experience in a general practice pharmacy, a hospital pharmacy, an industrial pharmacy concern or a school of pharmacy. At least 26 weeks must be in a general or hospital pharmacy. This route to registration is the normal one for pharmacy students in England, Wales and Scotland.

Recognised Overseas Qualifications

Section 4 also empowers the Society to make bye-laws recognising a diploma granted overseas in respect of a qualification to practise pharmacy, as a registrable qualification. Such arrangements have to be agreed by resolution of the Council and at present cover New Zealand, New South Wales, Queensland, South Australia, Victoria, Western Australia and Tasmania. It also covers South Africa in the case people qualified there before 31st March 1968.

Non-recognised Overseas Qualifications

Section 4 empowers the Society to consider the registration of an individual with a degree or diploma in pharmacy granted overseas where a reciprocal agreement is not in force. The applicant must satisfy an adjudicating committee of his knowledge and experience and, if English is not his language, he must show his knowledge of it. The committee may require that he takes certain examinations, and he will be required to complete a period of practical experience in Great Britain before his registration.

Northern Ireland

Section 4 also empowers the Society to make bye-laws which permit the registration without examination of a qualified military dispenser, a certified assistant to an apothecary under the Apothecaries Act 1815, or a pharmaceutical chemist registered in Northern Ireland. There is reciprocity of registration with Northern Ireland, but bye-laws have not been introduced to cover the first two possibilities.

Qualification by Society Examination

Section 3 of the Pharmacy Act 1954 requires the Society to appoint examiners, hold examinations and grant certificates of competence to practise as a pharmaceutical chemist. Appointments of examiners are not effective until approved by the Privy Council, and two boards of examiners are appointed annually, one for England and Wales and one for Scotland. The president and vice-president of the Society are ex-officio members of these boards. Council members or individuals who have been Council members within the past year may not be appointed examiners. The Society must permit anyone appointed for that purpose by the Privy Council to be present throughout any examination. A holder of a certificate of competence to practise as a pharmaceutical chemist, obtained under the provisions of section 3 and the relevant bye-laws, is entitled to be registered. However, this route to registration for United Kingdom students has been superseded by one entailing the acquisition of a university degree or diploma as described above.

European Qualification

As has been seen elsewhere in this book there is reciprocal recognition within the EEC of specified medical, dental and nursing qualifications. Such reciprocal recognition forms the basis for registration and hence practice in other member states. Such a scheme is to be introduced for pharmacy.

An EEC directive on pharmaceutical training (85/432/EEC) has been published. The directive enumerates the minimum contents of all pharmacy courses, and requires a period of training of at least 5 years. There must be at least six months practical training. However, there is a concession for England and Wales in that their pharmacy degree courses are recognised as equivalent to 5 year training.

Another EEC directive (85/433/EEC) lists those European qualifications that if obtained after the EEC training directive was adopted in any country gives a right to practise as a registered pharmacist in another member state. There are other interim provisions for qualifications which do not satisfy all the requirements of 85/432/EEC.

Member states must have introduced national legislation complying with these two directives on or before 1st October 1987 but at the time of writing no draft U.K. legislation has yet been published.*

*Draft published July 1987.

Chapter Ten

The Nursing and Midwifery Professions

Nurses, Midwives and Health Visitors Act 1979

Up to the end of the 1970s, there were seperate bodies of law controlling the nursing profession. One in England and Wales, one in Scotland and one in Northern Ireland. In England and Wales alone there were five main Acts of Parliament dealing with nurses. Each national legislation had its own controlling body, its own training schemes, its own registration of qualified nurses and its own disciplinary procedures. The Report of the Committee on Nursing, The Briggs Report, was published in 1972 and recommended a united nursing profession covering the whole of the United Kingdom with a common base of training for all nurses.

Although the majority of practising midwives qualify in nursing before specialising in midwifery, up to 1979 the profession was regulated by a body of legislation totally separate from that controlling nursing. As with nursing, different bodies of legislation existed in England and Wales, in Scotland and in Northern Ireland, although all were similar in principle. The Briggs Report also recommended that midwifery throughout the United Kingdom be included in consolidated nursing legislation.

Midwifery does, however, have some important historical differences from nursing. Midwives are traditionally independent practitioners, and they have always been subject to some form of local control. Their register has always been a "live" one – that is, it includes only midwives who are actually practising – and finally midwives were required to undergo refresher courses.

While it was recommended that midwifery should also come under the same legislation, it was agreed with the profession that there would be certain guarantees of autonomy. The "Briggs Bill" thus became the Nurses and Midwives Bill, and, because of demands for equality from the health visitors, that profession was then added to the proposed legislation, which became law in 1979 as the Nurses, Midwives and Health Visitors Act.

The Controlling Body

The Nurses, Midwives and Health Visitors Act 1979 established a United Kingdom Central Council for Nursing, Midwifery and Health Visiting (section 1(1)) and also four National Boards (section 5(1)). The general control of these three professions rests with the Council and the Boards. Those sections of the 1979 Act dealing with the Council and the Boards – all corporate bodies – were brought into effect from 1st November 1980 and 15th September 1980 respectively by the Nurses, Midwives and Health Visitors Act 1979 (Commencement No. 1) Order 1980 SI 1980 No. 893.

The Central Council for Nursing, Midwifery and Health Visiting

Membership The Secretary of State may fix the number of members by order at not more than 45, and has in fact set the number at 45 by the Nurses, Midwives and Health Visitors Act 1979 (Membership of Central Council) Order 1982 SI 1982 No. 961.

A majority of members of the Council are to be members of the National Boards (see below), nominated in equal numbers by those Boards (section 1(2) and (3)). The other members are to be appointed by the Secretary of State from nurses, midwives, health visitors, registered medical practitioners and others with such qualifications and experience as will be of value to the Council (section 1(4)). In nominating members of the Council, the National Boards must include at least two practising nurses, one practising midwife, one practising health visitor and one person engaged in teaching nursing, midwifery or health visiting (schedule 1 part 1). Statutory Instrument 1982 No. 961 sets the number to be nominated by the National Boards at 28 (seven each) and the number appointed by the Secretary of State at 17.

The Council is to have a chairman and deputy chairman appointed by the Council from among its numbers (section 1(6) and SI 1985 No. 789). Should that person cease to be a member of the Council, she will cease to be chairman or deputy chairman (schedule 1 part 2). Similarly, if a nominated Council member ceases to be a member of her National Board, she ceases to be a member of the

Council. If the chairman of the Council was appointed by the Secretary of State, she is disqualified from membership of the House of Commons (schedule 1 part 2 and the House of Commons Disqualification Act 1975). Part 2 of the first schedule to the Act provides for a variety of procedural and administrative aspects of the Council, including a quorum, formation of committees, appointment of non-Council people to such committees, remuneration, pensions and gratuities for employees, and payment to members of travelling and other expenses.

Functions Section 2 lays down the broad functions of the Council to be the establishment and improvement of standards of training and professional conduct for nurses, midwives and health visitors. In establishing training standards, the Council must ensure that any EEC requirements on the United Kingdom are met. The Council is to make rules for admission to training, for the standard of training to be required for registration and for possible further training for those already registered. The Council also has the power to provide advice to nurses, midwives and health visitors on standards of professional conduct.

Standing Committees Section 3 requires the Secretary of State to constitute by order a Midwifery Committee and a Finance Committee. Both are standing committees of the Council. He may constitute other standing committees to advise the Council on matters including training, clinical nursing standards, mental nursing and occupational health nursing. Where the Secretary of State constitutes a standing committee by order, he may provide for members who are not Council members, but he must provide for a majority of the Committee to have worked in the professional area it is primarily concerned with (section 3(4)). The Finance Committee must be consulted by the Council on all financial matters (section 3(2)). The Nurses, Midwives and Health Visitors (Finance Committee of Central Council) Order 1982 SI 1982 No. 1566 determines the constitution of this committee. It consists of between seven and 14 members, a majority of whom shall have worked in a field involving an element of financial management.

A standing committee – the Education Policy Advisory Committee – has been set up to advise the Council on all general matters relating to establishing and improving standards of education and training for nurses, midwives and health visitors (SI 1983 No. 726).

The Midwifery Committee The constitution of this Committee is laid down in the Nurses, Midwives and Health Visitors (Midwifery Committee of Central Council) Order 1982 SI. 1982 No. 1567. The majority of this Committee must be practising midwives, and the Council must consult the Committee on all matters relating to midwifery (section 4(1) and (2)). Section 15 requires the Council to make rules regulating the practice of midwifery, but section 4(3) requires the Council to refer any proposals to make, amend or revoke such rules to the Midwifery Committee. The Secretary of State may not approve any such rules relating to the practice of midwifery unless he is satisfied they are in accord with the recommendations of the Midwifery Committee. This arrangement in effect continues a high degree of independence for midwifery.

Council Rules Section 22 empowers the Central Council to make rules in order to give effect to the provisions of the Act, and those rules may differ in relation to England, Wales, Scotland and Northern Ireland. Before such rules are made, the Council must consult the representatives of any group of persons likely to be affected and also consult the National Boards for the parts of the United Kingdom to which the rules are to apply (section 22(3)). Rules come into force when approved by the Secretary of State by order. However, rules relating to section 12 – i.e. relating to the removal from, and the restoration to, the register – need approval by order of the Lord Chancellor and, if they extend to Scotland, by the Lord Advocate.

The National Boards

Section 5(1) provides that England, Wales, Scotland and Northern Ireland shall each have a National Board for Nursing, Midwifery and Health Visiting. The Boards are corporate bodies.

Membership The membership of the Boards is set by the Nurses, Midwives and Health Visitors Act 1979 (Membership of National Boards) Order 1982 (SI 1982 No. 962). A majority of each Board is elected while the rest are appointed by the Secretary of State. Statutory Instrument No. 962 sets the membership of the Board for England at 45 (30 elected and 15 appointed), for Scotland at 36 (24 elected and 12 appointed) and for Wales and for Northern Ireland each 35 (24 elected and 11 appointed). Members hold office for five years.

The elected members of the Boards are elected under a scheme prepared by the Central Council and approved by the Secretary of State (the United Kingdom Central Council for Nursing, Midwifery and Health Visiting (Electoral Scheme) Order 1982 SI 1982 No. 1104). Every qualified nurse, midwife and health visitor is entitled to vote. They vote for membership of the Board in whose territory they either work or live, and they may only vote for a candidate representing the profession they belong to. If an elector holds more than one qualification they may choose which candidate to vote for. The Electoral Scheme Order provides for a ratio of nurses to midwives to health visitors on all Boards to be 4:1:1. The electoral scheme uses the single transferable vote system, and an elector must apply to be put on a professional electoral roll. Candidates for election must be practising members of their profession, proposed, seconded and supported by eight other practising members of the same profession. The first elections were held in March 1983 for periods of office on the Boards to begin in September 1983 (SI 1983 No. 962).

As far as the members appointed by the Secretary of State are concerned, they must be nurses, midwives, health visitors, registered medical practitioners or people with such qualifications or experience in education or other fields as will, in his opinion, be of value to the Board (section 5). The Secretary of State must ensure an adequate representation of teaching experience on the Boards.

The Boards have a chairman and deputy chairman (section 5(7)). The chairman and the deputy chairman are appointed by the Board.

Part 2 of the second schedule to the Act makes provision for the tenure of office of Board members and chairman. If the chairman of any National Board is appointed by the Secretary of State she is disqualified from membership of the House of Commons under the House of Commons Disqualification Act 1975. The chairman of the National Board for Northern Ireland is disqualified from membership of the Northern Ireland Assembly under the Northern Ireland Assembly Disqualification Act 1975.

Part 2 of the second schedule also provides for such procedural matters as a quorum, transacting Board business in committee, the appointment to such committees of non-Board members, standing orders, and the payment of remuneration, pensions, allowances or gratuities to Board employees, or travelling and other expenses to the chairman and members of the Boards.

Functions Under Section 6, the broad functions of the Boards are to provide, directly or indirectly, courses of training for nurses, midwives and health visitors at institutions approved by the Board to permit people to become registered. The Boards must ensure that the training courses satisfy the requirements of the Central Council and must, directly or indirectly, hold examinations to allow people to obtain qualifications for registration. The Boards are also to investigate cases of alleged misconduct with a view to proceedings before the Council or a Committee of it for removal of a name from the register.

Standing committees Section 7 requires the Secretary of State to provide by order for two standing committees of each Board – a Midwifery Committee and a Finance Committee. It also empowers him to constitute other standing committees (section 7(6)). Each Board must consult with its Finance Committee on all financial matters and with its Midwifery Committee on all matters relating to midwifery. A majority of members of the Midwifery Committee must be practising midwives (section 7(2)), and, where the Central Council consults any Board about a midwifery matter, that Board must seek the views of its own Midwifery Committee (section 7(4)).

The constitutions of the Finance and Midwifery Committees of the Boards are contained in the Nurses, Midwives and Health Visitors (Midwifery and Finance Committees of National Boards) Order 1982 SI 1982 No. 1569 (in Northern Ireland SR 1982 No. 362).

Local Training Committees Section 9 empowers the Secretary of State to constitute by order Training Committees of the Boards for such geographical areas as the order specified. These local committees are to assist the Boards with the training function as set out in Section Six. For example, twelve such committees covering the whole of Scotland have been set up by the National Board for Nursing, Midwifery and Health Visiting for Scotland (Local Training Committees) Order 1983 SI 1983 No. 927 (S.73).

Joint Committees of the Central Council and the Boards

Health Visiting Joint Committee Section 8 requires the Secretary of State to constitute by order a joint committee of the Central Council and the National Boards, called the Health Visiting Joint Committee, of which a majority are to be practising health visitors. The Council or the Boards must consult this joint committee on all matters relating to health visiting. In establishing the joint committee, the Secretary of State may provide for matters of procedure etc. The constitution of this Joint Committee is laid down in the Nurses, Midwives and Health Visitors (Health Visiting Joint Committee) Order 1982 (SI 1982 No. 1568).

Other Joint Committees Section 8(4) empowers the Secretary of State to constitute other joint committees by order and to require the Council or the Boards to consult with them. In particular a District Nursing Joint Committee was envisaged in the Act (section 8(5)) and is constituted by the Nurses, Midwives and Health Visitors (District Nursing Joint Committee) Order 1983 SI 1983 No. 724.

Financial Aspects of the Council and the Boards

Finance Section 19 permits the Central Council and the National Boards to charge fees in respect of such matters as they, with the approval of the Secretary of State, determine, including the training, qualification, examination and certification of nurses, midwives and health visitors. The revenue raised by such fees is to be used to defray the expenses of the Council and the Boards. As a further source of income, section 19(3) permits the Secretary of State to make grants to the Council and the Boards towards expenses incurred in connection with the initial establishment of the Council and Boards, the promotion of improvements in the education and training of nurses, midwives and health visitors and the performance of the general duties of organising approved training courses for the professions. Where a Board, with the approval of the Central Council, incurs expenses which are not defrayed by fees received by the Board or funded by the Secretary of State, then the Council shall reimburse that Board (section 19(4)). Finance Committees have already been referred to.

Accounts and Reports The Council and the Boards must keep proper records of their accounts and prepare an annual statement of accounts (section 20(1)). These accounts are to be audited by an auditor qualified in accordance with the provisions of schedule 4 and are sent to the Comptroller and Auditor General for examination. The Comptroller may inspect the accounts of the Council and the Boards and any records relating to them. Each year the Council and the Boards shall prepare a report of the performance of their respective functions and the Secretary of State must lay the reports and the statements of accounts certified by the Comptroller before each House of Parliament, together with any comments he may make.

Registration

The Register

Before the 1979 Act, there were nine separate registers in the United Kingdom for nurses or midwives – three each for England and Wales, for Scotland and for Northern Ireland. Section 10(1) of the Nurses, Midwives and Health Visitors Act 1979 required the Central Council for Nursing, Midwifery and Health Visiting to prepare and maintain a single register of qualified nurses, midwives and health visitors for the whole of the United Kingdom.

The Nurses, Midwives and Health Visitors (Parts of the Register) Order 1983 SI 1983 No. 667 divides the new register into eleven parts and indicates into which part of the register the names of existing nurses, midwives and health visitors shall be transferred. The eleven parts are:

Part 1 – First-level nurses trained in general nursing.
Part 2 – Second-level nurses trained in general nursing (England and Wales).
Part 3 – First-level nurses trained in the nursing of persons suffering from mental illness.

Part 4 – Second-level nurses trained in the nursing of persons suffering from mental illness (England and Wales).
Part 5 – First-level nurses trained in the nursing of persons suffering from mental handicap.
Part 6 – Second-level nurses trained in the nursing of persons suffering from mental handicap (England and Wales).
Part 7 – Second-level nurses (Scotland and Northern Ireland).
Part 8 – Nurses trained in the nursing of sick children.
Part 9 – Nurses trained in the nursing of persons suffering from fever.
Part 10 – Midwives.
Part 11 – Health visitors.

Allocation to parts of the register of nurses, midwives and health visitors registered under previous Acts has been done as follows:

Registered Nurses Nurses registered in England or Wales under the Nurses Act 1957, in Scotland in the Nurses (Scotland) Act 1951 or in Northern Ireland under the Nurses and Midwives Act (Northern Ireland) 1970 are now transferred to parts 1, 3, 5, 8 or 9 of the new register depending upon whether they were registered as general nurses or nurses who had specialised in the nursing of mental illness (part 3), mental handicap (part 5), sick children (part 8), or infectious disease (part 9).

Enrolled Nurses The enrolled nurse was established originally by the Nurses Act 1943 which introduced the concept of assistant nurses. Nurses enrolled in England or Wales under the Nurses Act 1957, in Scotland under the Nurses (Scotland) Act 1957 or in Northern Ireland under the Nurses and Midwives Act (Northern Ireland) 1970 are now described as second-level nurses and transferred to part 2 (general nursing, England and Wales), part 4 (mental illness nursing, England and Wales), part 6 (mental handicap nursing, England and Wales), or part 7 (enrolled nurses, Scotland and Northern Ireland) as appropriate.

Midwives All enrolled midwives are transferred to part 10 irrespective of whether they were enrolled in England and Wales under the Midwives Act 1951, in Scotland under the Midwives (Scotland) Act 1951 or in Northern Ireland under the Nurses and Midwives Act (Northern Ireland) 1970.

Health Visitors The names of health visitors certified under the Health Visiting and Social Working Training Act 1962 are transferred to part 11.

The Central Council may make rules relating to the keeping of the register and in particular to such matters as evidence of qualification, fees, keeping of the register, obtaining of copies of extracts from it and for provisional registration (section 10(3)). Section 6 provides that a certificate issued and authenticated by the Council concerning registration status is valid evidence of that fact in a court of law. Section 10(7) provides that after the coming into force of the Act any reference to "registered" in relation to nurses, midwives or health visitors means registered in accordance with section 10.

Registration
To obtain registration, an individual must apply to the Central Council in accordance with its rules and, subject to payment of a fee, will be entitled to be registered if she is of good character and has the appropriate qualifications (section 11(1) and (2)). Section 11(3) defines three broad ways in which an individual may obtain the appropriate qualifications:

United Kingdom training The applicant has undergone the training and passed the examinations prescribed by the Central Council for admission to the appropriate part of the register (section 11(3)(a)). The training appropriate to admission to various parts of the register is stated in the Nurses, Midwives and Health Visitors Rules Approval Order 1983 SI 1983 No. 873, (as amended by SIs 1986 No. 786, 1897 and 2294, and 1987 No. 446.

EEC Qualification An EEC national may be registered if she has professional qualifications obtained in a member state (not the United Kingdom) which the Secretary of State has designated by order as having equivalence for registration purposes (section 11(3)(b)). The Nursing and Midwifery Qualification (EEC Recognition) Order 1983 SI 1983 No. 884 (which amends the 1979 Act) and the EEC Nursing and Midwifery Qualification Designation Order 1983 SI 1983 No. 921 deal with this issue. Both of these Orders are made under the European Communities Act 1972 (the Act which governs Britain's membership of the EEC), and they modify the 1979 Act in such a way as to achieve compliance with two EEC directives on the mutual recognition of nurses (Council Directives No. 77/452 EEC and No. 77/453 EEC) and two more on the mutual recognition of midwives (Council Directives No. 80/154 EEC and No. 80/155 EEC).

A nurse or midwife possessing the appropriate EEC qualifications listed in SI No. 921 (as amended by SI 1985 No. 1852) and who is a national of a member state is entitled to be registered in the appropriate part of the United Kingdom register provided she satisfies the Council of her good character. The Council must effect the registration within three months of receipt of the required documentation. Section 11(4) of the 1979 Act empowers the Central Council to make rules requiring proof of the necessary knowledge of the English language as a condition of EEC or overseas (see below) applicants. Earlier legislation on the recognition of EEC nurses included such a rule. However, this was repealed when challenged by the European Community as being contrary to the Treaty of Rome and the principle of freedom of movement in Europe.

However, before employment in the National Health Service, a European nurse must show competence in the English language.

Visiting EEC Nurses and Midwives

Statutory Instrument No. 884 also permits a European nurse or midwife to provide nursing services in the United Kingdom on a visiting basis without being registered in this country. She must, however, provide the Council with a declaration of what services are to be rendered and for what period. Certificates showing that the visiting nurse or midwife is qualified and in lawful practice in a member state of the EEC must be provided. A visiting nurse or midwife who has complied with these requirements is deemed to be a registered general nurse or midwife for the purposes of the United Kingdom legislation. She is liable to the same disciplinary code as any other registered nurse or midwife and may be subject to a prohibition if she renders services outside the scope of her original declaration.

Finally, SI 1983 No. 884 requires the Central Council to provide the necessary document to any United Kingdom nurse or midwife who wishes to practise in a member state of the EEC and requires such document.

Overseas Qualification

A nurse, midwife or health visitor who trained and qualified outside the United Kingdom or the EEC may be entitled to registration under the provisions of section 11 of the 1979 Act. This provides (section 11(3)) that if an applicant has successfully trained abroad in accordance with a scheme recognised by the Central Council as satisfactory for the purpose, and as long as the training was received at a recognised institution and she is of good character, she may, on application and the payment of any required fee, be registered in the appropriate part of the register. Section 11(3) provides that where a nurse, midwife or health visitor has trained abroad but cannot show to the Council that the training was in accordance with a scheme recognised by it or received at a recognised institution she may, nevertheless, be permitted registration after undergoing such further training and examination as the Council specifies. In either case, the Central Council may make possession of the necessary knowledge of English, or the obtaining of such knowledge in a specified period of time, a condition of registration.

Removal from and Restoration to, the Register

Section 12 of the 1979 Act requires the Central Council to make rules relating to the removal of a person from the register, the restoration of such people to the register, or the removal, alteration or restoration of any entry in the register. The Nurses, Midwives and Health Visitors (Professional Conduct) Rules 1983 Approval Order 1983 (SI 1983 No. 887) contains these rules. Broadly, the rules provide that a registered person may be removed from the register for misconduct or for reasons of ill-health. Section 13 of the Act provides that anyone aggrieved by a decision to remove her name may appeal within three months to the appropriate court, whose decision is final. In England and Wales the appropriate Court is the High Court, in Scotland the Court of Session and in Northern Ireland the High Court there.

Removal for misconduct

The Professional Conduct Rules (rule 1) define misconduct as "conduct unworthy of a nurse, midwife or health visitor as the case may be, and includes obtaining registration by fraud". Clearly, this is not a comprehensive statement of what misconduct may lead to removal of a name, but the Central Council has issued an advisory booklet on professional ethics (July 1983) which expands considerably on this definition. The misconduct may have been the subject of a conviction. Misconduct is not limited to the discharge of professional duties. Thus, in a midwifery case (Stock v Central Midwives Board (1915) 3KB 756 DC), the court held that misconduct was not limited to the discharge of midwifery duties per se but included any conduct which in the Board's opinion tends to make the woman unfit to discharge those duties. In Stock's case the issue was alleged immorality.

A two-stage process is adopted in the investigation of an alleged misconduct case.

Investigation by National Boards The National Board in whose territory the individual is ordinarily resident must carry out a preliminary investigation into any alleged misconduct case. The Board may set up a committee to carry out the investigation but, however it does it, it must ensure no Council member takes part (rule 4). It must also ensure proper representation of the particular profession.

The Board must seek the practitioner's comments on her alleged misconduct and may obtain what documentary evidence it requires from the complainants. The Board must then decide whether or not to refer the case to the Professional Conduct Committee, or if a question of ill-health is raised, be it physical or mental, to the Health Committee.

Determination by the Professional Conduct Committee The Professional Conduct Committee is a committee of the Central Council constituted by rule 5 of the Professional Conduct Rules 1983. Its function is to determine whether a practitioner (ie. a nurse, midwife or health visitor) shall be removed from the register or part of it, or whether any name should be restored or any entry altered.

There are ten members of the Committee, and a qurom is five. The composition at any particular hearing must have regard to the professional area the respondent works in. The chairman of the Council is chairman of the Committee.

The Professional Conduct Rules 1983 lay out in detail the procedure to be followed when a case is referred to the Committee. Notice must be sent to the respondent informing her of the time and place of the hearing and her right to be represented by a friend, counsel, a solicitor or an officer of her professional body or trade union. A copy of the rules must also be sent to her. Any complainant must also be informed of the hearing. The hearing starts with the charge being read out in public, and the respondent may object to the charge in point of law. Where a conviction is concerned, evidence of that conviction is presented; in other cases evidence of the misconduct is presented. The respondent may argue that the conviction or the facts presented do not amount to misconduct or even that the facts themselves are not proved. The respondent or her solicitor may cross-examine anyone giving evidence.

The committee must then determine whether they find the respondent guilty of misconduct. If they do they must decide whether to postpone judgment. If they do not they must determine there and then whether to order removal of the respondent's name from the register.

As stated earlier, section 13 of the 1979 Act permits a registered person to appeal within three months to the appropriate court against a decision of the Committee. The court may give such directions in the matter as it thinks proper, including directions as to costs, and its order is final.

Restoration in misconduct cases

Anyone whose name has been removed from the professional register for misconduct may apply to the Professional Conduct Committee for restoration. The applicant must forward two character references, confirm she has no convictions or is not the subject of any further conviction, and declare that she has not represented herself as a practitioner since her removal. The applicant must appear in person before the Committee, but may be represented by a friend, counsel, solicitor or officer of a professional organisation or trades union.

If the Committee agrees to the restoration it names a date from which it is to be effective, and a fee is payable for re-registration. If it refuses to restore a name, then the applicant has a right of appeal within three months against that decision to the appropriate court.

Proceedings of the Professional Conduct Committee

The Committee's proceedings are normally to be held in public in the presence of all the parties thereto. The Committee may deliberate in camera, and may in the interest of justice exclude the public on occasions from the hearing. However, its decision must be announced in public (rule 16). The Committee may receive oral, documentary or other evidence provided such evidence would be admissable in a court of law (rule 17). The Committee reaches its decisions by voting (rule 19).

Finally, at all proceedings before the Committee there must be present a legal assessor. Schedule 3 to the 1979 Act requires that legal assessors be barristers, advocates or solicitors of not less than ten years standing whose function is to advise the Council or the Committee on questions of law arising in proceedings under section 12 of the Act – removal of names from the register. The precise duties of these assessors are laid out in the United Kingdom Central Council for Nursing Midwifery and Health Visiting (Legal Assessors) Order 1983 SI 1983 No. 839. In particular, this Order provides that, should the Council or its Committee fail to follow an assessor's advice, a written note of the circumstances of this must be made and copies given to all parties to the proceedings.

Removal on health grounds

Section 12 of the 1979 Act provides that the Council may make rules relating to the removal of an individual's name from the register "for misconduct or otherwise". The Professional Conduct Rules (SI 1983 No. 887), under the "otherwise" term, have introduced new and important powers whereby a nurse, midwife or health visitor may be removed from the register if her fitness to practise is seriously impaired by reason of her physical or mental health.

As with misconduct cases, there is a two-phase approach to health cases. The first phase is investigatory in nature, aimed at gathering together medical information about the professional person. The second phase involves consideration and determination of the case by the Health Committee.

Preliminary procedure The precise preliminary procedure depends somewhat on the source of the information about the individual's ill-health. If the information is received by the Council – in effect its registrar – she must submit that information to the "professional screeners". Rule 23 of the Professional Conduct Rules 1983 requires the Council to establish a panel of at least 12 Council Members, including at least seven nurses, three midwives and two health visitors to be known as health screeners. For any individual case, a group of three of these screeners is selected having regard to the area the registered person is working in.

Having received information about a registered person's alleged ill health, the registrar must obtain the details from the complainant in the form of a statutory declaration. If the professional screeners consider this does not give reasonable support to the allegation they direct the registrar so to inform the complainant and, if they feel necessary, the practitioner, and the case goes no further. The professional screeners may seek advice of a selected medical examiner to assist them make this decision. The Second Schedule to the Professional Conduct Rules require the British Medical Association and the Royal College of Psychiatrists to nominate individuals to be medical examiners for the purpose of the Rules.

If the professional screeners consider that the matter needs further consideration they will direct the registrar to inform the practitioner of the situation and invite her to agree in 14 days to examination at the Council's expense by two medical examiners. She may nominate other medical practitioners to examine her at her own expense and to give a report to the Registrar on her fitness to practise, and she is invited to give her own observations on her situation. The professional screeners must consider whether the medical examiners' report supports the view that the registered person is unfit to practise and, if that is their conclusion, they will refer the case to the Health Committee.

The preliminary procedure is a little different where a case is referred by a National Board or by the Professional Conduct Committee to the Health Committee. Here, the Health Committee directs the registrar to invite the practitioner to submit to medical examination by two of the Council's medical examiners who must report to the Committee on her fitness to practise. Again, she may nominate another medical practitioner at her own expense.

The Health Committee Rule 22 provides that this Committee is to consist of any ten of 25 members selected for the purpose from among its number by the Council. A quorum of the Health Committee is five and the chairman is appointed by the Council. The Committee's remit is to determine whether a person's name is to be removed from the register for failure of health or, once having been removed, should be restored.

Removal of a name for health reasons Once a case is referred to the Health Committee for determination, the registered person must be informed of the fact and given the time and place of the hearing which must not be earlier than 28 days from posting the Notice of Referral. The practitioner may be represented at the hearing and may also bring along her own medical adviser. She must be sent a copy of any reports and other information to be presented to the Committee.

The Health Committee sits in private, and the practitioner is entitled to be present, represented by counsel, a solicitor, an officer of a professional organisation or trades union or a friend, and may be accompanied by her medical adviser. Evidence of the practitioner's fitness to practise is presented and she or her representative may address the Committee and adduce evidence in support of her fitness. The Committee may deliberate in camera at any time and may exclude the practitioner, her representative and her medical adviser if it so chooses. As with misconduct cases, a legal assessor (see above) must be present to advise the Committee on matters of law.

At the end of the hearing, the Committee first decides whether to adjourn the case to seek further medical reports. If not, except where it finds that the practitioner's fitness to practise is not seriously impaired, it must decide whether or not to postpone judgment. If not, and it has found that her fitness to practise is seriously impaired, it must direct the registrar to remove her name from the register or parts of it.

Hearing for restoration of a name A practitioner whose name has been removed from the register for health reasons may apply to the Health Committee to have it restored. She must state the grounds upon which the application is made and confirm she has not been, and is not, the subject of any criminal proceedings, declare she has not represented herself to be registered, and supply the name of a medical practitioner to whom the Council may apply for a report on her health.

Before the hearing, the Health Committee will invite the practitioner to be examined by two of the Council's medical examiners to be chosen by the professional screeners. The medical examiner must report to the Committee on her fitness to practise. The Health Committee will then meet in private to consider the reports and any other evidence and decide whether to restore the name.

Appeals in health cases As with misconduct cases, any person aggrieved by a decision to remove her from the register may appeal within three months of the decision to the appropriate court, whose decision is final. The appropriate court in England and Wales is the High Court, in Scotland the Court of Session and in Northern Ireland the High Court. In health cases, the court is most unlikely to interfere with medical opinions per se.

Controls on the Practice of Nursing

The practice of nursing the sick is not restricted by law to registered nurses. However, the fact that all senior nursing posts in the National Health Service are limited to qualified staff, and that under the Nurses Agencies Act 1957 agencies supplying nurses may (subject to certain exceptions) supply only registered staff, means that to embark on a realistic career in nursing requires an individual to be qualified.

What legal controls exist are designed to prevent unqualified people using the title "nurse" except in specified circumstances, and also to prevent individuals making false claims to be registered.

Offences under the 1979 Act

Section 14 of the Nurses, Midwives and Health Visitors Act 1979 establishes a variety of offences related to making false claims to be registered. The main offences are:

1 Falsely representing one is qualified in nursing, midwifery or health visiting with intent to deceive.

2 Falsely representing one is registered in the register or part of it with intent to deceive.

3 Causing or permitting another to make representations about one which, if made oneself with intent to deceive, would be an offence under (1) or (2).

4 Falsely representing about another anything that, if made by that person, would be an offence under (1) or (2).

These offences may be committed by word or in writing or by the use of any name, description, uniform or badge. A person guilty of any of these offences is liable on summary conviction to a fine of £500.

Controls on Professional Training

The Nurses, Midwives and Health Visitors Act 1979 charges the Central Council with an overall responsibility for the standard of training in all three professions (section 2). The Council must ensure that standards of training meet any EEC obligation on the United Kingdom. To carry out these functions, the Central Council is empowered to make rules with respect to the kind and standard of training required for registration and also for the further training of people already registered. Section 6 makes the National Boards responsible for providing courses of training and for holding examinations that satisfy the rules set by the Council.

As has already been noted above, an Educational Policy Advisory Committee of the Central Council has been established (SI 1983 No. 726). Moreover, section 9 of the Act provides for the establishment of local training committees of the National Boards, charged with assisting the Boards in the exercise of their training functions, and some have already been set up (SI 1983 No. 927). The present training requirements for different categories of registration are found in the Nurses, Midwives and Health Visitors Rules Approval Order 1983 SI 1983 No. 873 (as amended by SI 1986 No. 786 and 1897 and SI 1987 No. 446). However the Central Council has issued a consultation paper entitled "Project 2000" which makes some far reaching proposals. It suggests a single level of qualification removing the enrolled nurse in the future. However, existing SENs will not be affected and conversion courses to upgrade their registration are suggested. There is a proposal to establish colleges of nursing and midwifery to provide all levels of training.

Midwifery

As was stated at the beginning of this chapter, midwifery has important historical differences from nursing. Midwives have traditionally operated more as independent practitioners, although this has always been offset by some degree of local control. Their register only included midwives who were actually practising, and they were required to undergo periodic but regular refresher courses. The Briggs Report recommended that, while nursing and midwifery legislation should be consolidated into one statute, many of these features of midwifery should be maintained to ensure a continuing degree of independence for the profession.

The following provisions of the Nurses, Midwives and Health Visitors Act 1979 which help maintain the status quo ante of midwifery have already been described above.

1 **Central Council** When nominating members of the Council, National Boards must include at least one practising midwife. The Act requires there to be a Midwifery Committee of the Council, a majority of which must be practising midwives. The Council must consult with this Committee on all issues relating to midwifery, and the Secretary of State may not approve any rules made by the Council that relate to midwifery unless he is satisfied they are in accord with the recommendations of the Midwifery Committee.

2 **The National Boards** The scheme for electing Board members ensures that the ratio of nurses to midwives to health visitors is 4-1-1, and the scheme ensures that midwives represent midwives. The Act requires that each Board has a Midwifery Committee which it must consult on all matters relating to the profession. A majority of the Committee must be practising midwives.

3 **The Register** Although the 1979 Act has introduced a single register, midwives (and indeed other groups) continue to occupy a specific and exclusive part of it (Part 10).

4 **Disciplinary Procedure** Although the 1979 Act introduced a single disciplinary process for nurses, midwives and health visitors, the Professional Conduct Rules (SI 1983 No. 887) require that at both a preliminary investigation and at proceedings before the Professional Conduct Committee due regard must be paid to the professional area the respondent is working in when choosing members.

In addition to the above general provisions regarding midwives, the 1979 Act (section 15–18) makes a variety of specific provisions for midwifery. These cover rules as to midwifery practice (section 15), local supervision of midwives (section 16) and controls on the attendance of unqualified people at childbirth. These topics, together with a brief account of the function of men in midwifery, will now be considered.

Midwifery Practice Rules

Section 15 of the 1979 Act empowers the Council to make rules regulating the practice of midwifery. These rules must be approved by the Secretary of State by order before becoming effective (section 22). As has already been indicated, section 4(4) requires the Secretary of State to satisfy himself that the rules are in accordance with the recommendations of the Council's Midwifery Committee before approving them.

Section 15 provides that the rules should, among other things, deal with the circumstances in which a midwife may be suspended from practice, the requirement for midwives to notify their local supervising authority (see below) of their intention to practise and the requirement that midwives should attend courses of refresher training. The present rules are found in the Nursing, Midwives and Health Visitors (Midwives Amendment) Rules Approval Order 1986 SI 1986 No. 786. These rules apply to the whole of the United Kingdom.

Local Supervision of Midwives

Section 16 of the 1979 Act continues a system of local supervision of midwifery. The supervising bodies are, in England the Regional Health Authorities, in Wales the Area Health Authorities, in Scotland the Health Boards and in Northern Ireland the Health and Social Services Boards. It is the duty of the supervising authority to report any prima facie case of misconduct to the appropriate National Board, and it exercises the supervisory powers laid out in the Midwives Rules (SI 1986 No. 786).

The powers and duties of the local supervising authority include a power to suspend a midwife in order to prevent the spread of infection or where a case of misconduct is pending against her, a duty to maintain a record of all midwives who have notified their intention to practise, and to report this on a regular basis to the appropriate national board.

Section 16(3) requires that any person appointed by a supervising authority to exercise supervision over midwives in its area must be qualified in accordance with rules made by the Council. The present rules are in SI 1986 No. 786 and require the supervisor to be a midwife of at least 3 years experience who has undertaken within 12 months of appointment a specific course of training for supervisors.

Control on Midwifery Practice

Section 17 of the Act prohibits anyone other than a registered midwife or a registered medical practitioner from attending a woman in childbirth. Anyone contravening this is liable on summary conviction to a fine of up to £500. However, Section 17(3) makes two exceptions to this prohibition. One is where the attention given is a case of sudden or urgent necessity; the other concerns someone training to be a doctor or midwife, provided the attendance is part of a course of practical instruction in midwifery recognised by the General Medical Council or one of the National Boards. A case of a father being prosecuted for delivering his own child was referred to in Chapter 5 (Page 56).

The Position of Men in Midwifery

Today, men may train as midwives and practise as freely as if they were women. However, this situation only came about in 1984. Before 1975 the Midwives Act 1951 prohibited the training and practice of men in midwifery. The Act was amended by the Sex Discrimination Act 1975 (section 20(4) to permit men to train and become certified midwives. However, the course of training for a man had to be specifically approved by the Secretary of State. It was still lawful to discriminate against a man as far as midwifery training was concerned, and even if he became certified he could only practise in a place specially approved by the Secretary of State. The 1979 Act (section 17(2)) continued this state of affairs until a day appointed by the Secretary of State. That date was named as the 1st January 1984 by the Sex Discrimination (Midwifery)(Specified Date) Order 1983 SI 1983 No. 1841, since when men have been on an equal footing with women in this profession.

Chapter Eleven

The Opticians' Profession

The opticians' profession is governed by the Opticians Act 1958 as amended by the Health and Social Security Act 1984 (section 1–4 and schedules 1 and 2) and the various statutory instruments made under this legislation. The Act extends to the whole of the United Kingdom.

The General Optical Council

The General Optical Council, which is the professional body for opticians, was established by section 1 of the Opticians Act 1958. Paragraph 10 of the schedule to the Act provides that it is a body corporate with perpetual succession, a common seal and the power to hold land.

Constitution of the Council

Membership The constitution of the Council is dealt with by the schedule to the Opticians Act and by the General Optical Council (Membership) Orders of Council 1959 (SI 1959 No. 412), 1983 (SI 1983 No. 1842), 1985 (SI 1985 No. 664) and 1986 (SI 1986 No. 309). The Council consists of six persons nominated by the Privy Council, five elected to represent registered ophthalmic opticians (this number increased to seven on 1st January 1987 – SI 1983 No. 1842), two to represent registered dispensing opticians, six persons nominated by certain examining bodies and six registered medical practitioners. Of the members nominated by the Privy Council, one must be qualified to advise on educational matters generally; he may be a registered optician or medical practitioner but may not be in practice. Otherwise, none of the nominations of the Privy Council may be registered opticians, registered medical practitioners or directors of opticians' businesses. The seven members chosen to represent the practising opticians are elected by the profession. Of the medical members, four are ophthalmologists nominated by the Faculty of Ophthalmologists, one of whom is a Scottish representative. Of the other two, one must be engaged in the pre-clinical training of students and one must be representative of the medical profession. The examining bodies who nominate members of the Council are listed in SI 1983 No. 1842 and SI 1986 No. 309.

Appointment Members hold office for five years, but retirement is staggered so that about half retire one year and the rest two years later, and the next retirements are three years later. Retiring members are eligible for re-election. A member may resign at any time by written notice to the registrar, and casual vacancies in membership are filled as they arise. In such a case, the replacement holds office only for as long as the member whom he replaced would have done.

Chairman The chairman of the Council is selected by the Privy Council from the members it has nominated.

Functions of the Council

Section 1 of the Opticians Act places on the Council the function of promoting high standards of professional education and conduct among opticians and the additional functions specifically assigned to it by the Act.

Registration The Council is responsible for the registration of opticians and opticians' businesses. Section 2 requires the Council to establish and maintain registers of opticians. Section 4 requires it to maintain a list of corporate bodies carrying on the business of opticians. The Council must appoint a registrar (section 20) and must publish the registers and lists regularly (section 8). Section 7 empowers the General Optical Council to make rules with respect to the form and keeping of the registers and lists, including fees, and these are contained in the General Optical Council (Registration and Enrolment Rules) Order of Council 1977 SI 1977 Nos. 176, as amended by SI 1979 No. 1638, SI 1980 No. 1936, SI 1981 No. 1821, SI 1983 No. 1 and SI 1985 No. 2024.

Education Section 5 of the Opticians Act permits the Council to approve institutions for the training of opticians and also to approve any qualification as representing adequate knowledge and skill for professional practice. Section 3 limits registration to individuals who possess approved qualifications from an approved institution. Section 6 imposes a duty on the General Optical Council to keep itself aware of the nature of instruction given in approved institutions, and to do so it may appoint people to visit the institutions and attend the examinations. The visitors must report their findings to the Council and, if the Council is of the opinion that the training offered is not adequate to ensure that a student acquires the proper skill and knowledge to practise as an optician, it may withdraw its approval of the institution or qualification. An institution whose approval has been withdrawn may appeal against the Council's decision to the Privy Council. Section 17 requires the General Optical Council to set up an Education Committee to advise on matters of training and examination. The Council may make rules for the constitution of the Committee, and these are contained in the General Optical Council (Education Committee Rules) Order of Council 1975 (SI 1974 No. 149) (as amended by SI 1984 No. 1249).

Discipline The maintenance of professional conduct and discipline is the responsibility of the Council. In particular, section 9 requires the Council to set up an Investigating Committee to investigate whether cases of alleged misconduct referred to it should be heard by the Disciplinary Committee, another Committee set up by section 10.

FinanceThe constitution of the Council permits it to hold land. Section 27 gives the Council wide powers to use its money, whether raised from fees or otherwise, for any purpose related to its functions once it has paid its expenses. The Council must keep accounts which must be audited annually, published and laid before Parliament.

Rules The Opticians Act gives the General Optical council powers to make a wide variety of rules within the scope of the Act. These rules, which have the force of law, are made as statutory instruments and are not effective until approved by the Privy Council. In some instances specified below, the General Optical Council must observe further requirements before the rules become effective.

Investigating Committee Section 9(3) empowers the General Optical Council to make rules in respect to the constitution of the Investigating Committee. Rules made under this section are subject to annulment by resolution of either House of Parliament. The present constitution is contained in the General Optical Council (Investigating Committee Rules) Order of Council 1960 SI 1960 No. 1935, as ameneded by SI 1971 No. 1528, SI 1983 No. 545 and SI 1984 No. 1248.

Disciplinary Committee Section 10(2) empowers the General Optical Council to make rules in respect of the constitution of the Disciplinary Committee. These rules are subject to annulment by resolution of either House of Parliament and are contained in the General Optical Council (Disciplinary Committee Rules) Order of Council 1960 SI 1960 No. 1934, as amended by SI 1971 No. 1526 and SI 1984 No. 1250. The Council is also empowered by section 15(2) to make rules relating to procedure before the Disciplinary Committee. Before making such rules, the General Optical Council must consult such organisations representing the interests of opticians and opticians' businesses as appear requisite to the Council. The rules are contained in the General Optical Council (Disciplinary Committee) (Procedure) Rules Order of Council 1985, SI 1985 No. 1580.

Other Rules Section 17 requires the General Optical Council to make rules in respect of the constitution of the Education Committee, and these rules are contained in the General Optical Council (Education Committee Rules) Order of Council 1974 SI 1974 No. 149 as amended by SI 1984 No. 1249.

Section 18 requires the General Optical Council to establish rules for the constitution of the Companies Committee, and, before doing so, it must consult with bodies appearing to represent the interests of corporate bodies carrying on the business of opticians. The rules are contained in the General Optical Council (Companies Committee Rules) Order in Council 1959 SI 1959 No. 955, as amended by SI 1971 No. 1525. Section 20 permits the General Optical Council to make rules exempting trainee opticians from the restrictions on sight-testing imposed by that section. The rules are contained in the General Optical Council (Rules on the Testing of Sight by Persons Training as Ophthalmic Opticians) Order of Council 1974 SI No. 1329.

Section 25 gives the General Optical Council powers to make rules relating to a variety of items, including advertising by opticians, administration of drugs by opticians, the practice of orthoptics, and the prescription, supply and fitting of contact lenses. Such rules are subject to annulment by resolution of either House of Parliament.

Committees

Much of the work of the General Optical Council is done by various statutory committees. The Investigating Committee (section 9), the Disciplinary Committee (section 10) and the Education Committee (section 17) have already been mentioned. Section 18 requires the General Optical Council to set up a Companies Committee from which it seeks advice on all matters (other than those dealt with by the Investigating Committee or the Disciplinary Committee), relating to corporate bodies carrying on an ophthalmic or dispensing optician's business. As mentioned above, the Council, after consultation with appropriate company representatives, may make rules for the consititution of this Committee (SI 1959 No. 955 and 1971 No. 1525).

Section 19 gives the General Optical Council a general power to set up committees for any purpose of the Act, except that such committees may not make rules under the Act and may not deal with matters which the Act has allocated to another Committee. At least two-thirds of the membership of such committees must be Council members.

Supervision of the General Optical Council

Section 28 imposes on the Privy Council a general supervisory role over the General Optical Council. If it appears to the Privy Council that the General Optical Council has not discharged a function it ought to have, then it may direct the Optical Council to do so; if it fails to do so, the Privy Council may itself discharge the function. This supervisory role applies to all functions of the Council except for section 1 (general statement of functions), section 3 (qualifications for registration), sections 5 and 6 (approval and supervision of training institutions and qualifications), section 16 (legal assessors to the Disciplinary Committee) and section 27(1) (allocation of money once expenses have been paid).

The Opticians' Registers

The Opticians Act 1958 provides for a system of registration for opticians and their businesses.

The List and Registers

There are five main lists or registers, one of ophthalmic opticians engaged in the testing of sight and the supply of optical appliances (section 2(a)), one of ophthalmic opticians engaged only in the testing of sight (section 2(a)), one of dispensing opticians (ie people engaged in the fitting and supply of optical appliances (section 2(b) and section 30), one of corporate bodies carrying on business as ophthalmic opticians, and one of corporate bodies carrying on business as dispensing opticians (section 4(1)).

The registers of opticians must include their names, addresses, qualifications, registration number and date of registration. The lists of corporate bodies must include their names and their principal places of business.

The Keeping of the Registers and Lists

Section 25 establishes the post of registrar to the General Optical Council. The first registrar was appointed by the Privy Council, but his successors are appointed by the General Optical Council.

Section 7 permits the General Optical Council to make rules with respect to the form and keeping of the register and lists and the entries therein. The rules are set out in the schedule to the General Optical Council (Registration and Enrolment Rules) Order in Council 1977 SI 1977 No. 176, as amended by SI 1979 No. 1638, SI 1980 No. 1936, SI 1981 No. 1821, SI 1983 No. 1 and SI 1985 No. 2024. The rules include provision for application for registration, transfer from one register to another, notification of changes in particulars, fees to be paid on registration or for retention, and for the registrar to refuse to register or restore a name unless the appropriate fee has been paid.

Publication and Evidential Value

The General Optical Council was required by section 8 of the Opticians Act to print and publish the register and lists within three years of the establishment of the Council and thereafter as it thinks fit. However, where in any one year there is no publication, the Council must publish in that year a list of the alterations to the register and lists made since the last publication.

Section 8(3) provides that the published lists and registers, as amended, are evidence of registration and that the absence of a name or a company from the register or list is evidence of non-registration until the contrary is proved. However, where someone is registered and the name is not yet on the register or list, a certified copy under the hand of the registrar to the Council is evidence of the entry in the register.

Entitlement to Registration

Opticians Section 3(3) provides that, in order to be registered, an optician must satisfy the General Optical Council that he holds a qualification as either an ophthalmic optician or a dispensing optician which is approved by the Council under section 5 and obtained from an approved institution. He must also satisfy it that he has received adequate practical experience. For an ophthalmic optician this means, in effect, obtaining the fellowship diploma of either the British Optical Association (FBOA), the Worshipful Company of Spectacle Makers (FSMC) or the Scottish Association of Opticians (FSAO), and, for dispensing opticians, the fellowship of the Association of Dispensing Opticians (FADO) or the dispensing certificate of the British Optical Association (BOA (Disp)) or of the Worshipful Company of Spectacle Makers (SMC (Disp)). Study for these qualifications usually takes place at an approved university. Section 3(4) provides for the registration of an optician who has qualified outside the United Kingdom as long as the General Optical Council recognises the qualification and the optician has adequate practical experience and is of good character.

At the time of setting up the register, provisions of the Act (section 3(1) and (2)) permitted the registration of opticians who were either on one of the Health Service Ophthalmic Lists or held a qualification recognised by the Council, and who had adequate practical experience and were of good character.

Although an optician may be qualified to be on several registers, he may have his name on only one at any time.

Corporate Bodies Section 4(2) provides that a corporate body may be enrolled in the appropriate list in the following circumstances:

1 Where it satisfies the General Optical Council that a majority of its directors are registered opticians, or, if it only has one director, that he is a registered optician.

2 Where it satisfies the General Optical Council that, although the greater part of its business is not the testing of sight and the supply and fitting of optical appliances, such part as is, is carried out under the management of a registered ophthalmic or dispensing optician as the case may be.

3 Where the body is a society registered under the Industrial and Provident Societies Act 1965 and it can satisfy the General Optical Council that the testing of sight or the fitting of optical appliances is carried out under the management of an appropriately registered optician.

In addition, any optician's business named on one of the Health Service Lists immediately prior to the Act was also entitled to be enrolled.

Approval of Qualifications and Training Institutions

Registration is by means of obtaining an approved qualification following a period of training at an approved institution, and section 5 empowers the General Optical Council to approve such qualifications and institutions. Approval of an institution is given on the basis of the training there being such as to secure adequate knowledge and skill for professional practice (section 5(1)). Similarly, a qualification is approved if it appears to the Council that it is granted only to candidates who have reached such a standard of knowledge and skill. Approval may be in respect of training and qualifications for ophthalmic and/or dispensing opticians, and the General Optical Council publishes a list of approved training institutions and qualifications. Where the General Optical Council refuses to approve an institution or qualification, an appeal to the Privy Council can be lodged within one month of the refusal and the Privy Council may, after considering the case, order the General Optical Council to issue an approval.

Once the General Optical Council has approved an institution or qualification, section 6 imposes a duty on it to keep itself informed of the nature of the training and the examinations involved (section 6(1)). To do so, the General Optical Council appoints people to visit approved institutions and to attend examinations. The visitors, whose fees and expenses are paid by the Council, report back to the Council on the adequacy of the training and examinations and provide any other relevant information. Where an adverse report is received, the General Optical Council may inform the institution of its intention to withdraw its approval and give the institution at least one month in which to comment. If the Council decides to withdraw approval, it must issue notice in writing, and the organisation, if aggrieved, has one month in which to appeal to the Privy Council against the decision.

Removal from the Registers or Lists

Removal from the registers or lists is an important disciplinary measure discussed below, but it may also occur in other circumstances.

Non-payment of Fees The rules made under section 7 allow the name of an optician or business to be removed for non-payment of a retention fee, once the prescribed notices and warnings have been issued.

Death Where an optician dies, his name is to be removed from the register. To facilitate this, section 7(2) requires a registrar of births and deaths, on registering the death of an optician, to send a copy of the death certificate to the registrar to the Council. The cost of this is payable by the Council.

Fraud or Error In any case where the Disciplinary Committee is satisfied that any entry has been fraudulently or incorrectly made, it may direct that the entry shall be erased.

Discipline A registered optician is liable to have his name removed from the register by the Disciplinary Committee if he is guilty of a criminal offence or is adjudged guilty of infamous conduct in any professional respect (section 11). The name of a corporate body carrying on an optician's business may be removed from the lists by the Disciplinary Committee where it is convicted of an offence under the Act or of aiding, abetting, counselling or procuring such an offence, or where it can no longer satisfy the conditions for enrolment.

Professional Discipline

Section 1(1) of the Opticians Act 1958 provides that one of the functions of the General Optical Council is the promotion of high standards of professional conduct, and to this end it is vested with extensive disciplinary powers.

Grounds for Disciplinary Measures

Originally, the main disciplinary measure available against a registered optician or corporate body was the erasure of their name from the list or register. However, section 4 of, and schedule 2 to, the Health and Social Security Act 1984 amended the Opticians Act (by introducing sections 10A, 10B and 10C) by adding suspension and penalty orders as further sanctions. Under a suspension order an individual or a corporate body have their registration or enrolment suspended for a period specified in the order. A suspension order, may not exceed 12 months and has the effect of de-registering the individual or company for the specified period. A penalty order is a sanction that requires the individual or company to pay a fine not exceeding £1,000. However, the Privy Council may adjust this sum by Order to keep pace with inflation. A penalty order must specify the period of time within which it must be paid, and the General Optical Council must pay money received under such orders into the Consolidated Fund.

Erasure orders, suspension orders and penalty orders are jointly referred to as disciplinary orders.

Opticians and corporate bodies may be liable to disciplinary orders in the following circumstances. These are found in the substituted section 11 of the Opticians Act (see section 4 of, and schedule 2 to the 1984 Health and Social Security Act), as follows:

Registered Opticians

1 Where he is convicted in any court in the United Kingdom of any criminal offence (section 11(1)(a)).

2 Where he is judged by the Disciplinary Committee to have been guilty of serious professional misconduct (section 11(1)(b)). Before the 1984 amendment the term was "infamous conduct in a professional respect".

3 Where a corporate body is convicted of an offence under the Opticians Act and the offence was instigated or connived at by a responsible officer, or where a disciplinary order is made against a corporate body and the offence was instigated or connived at by a responsible officer, if he is a registered optician he is liable to a disciplinary order (section 11(7)).

Corporate Bodies

1 Where an enrolled corporate body is convicted of an offence under the Opticians Act or of aiding, abetting, counselling or procuring the commission of, or inciting another person to commit, such an offence (section 11(2)(a)).

2 Where one or more of the conditions under which the company was registered no longer applies (section 11(2)(b)). However, in the case of the death of a registered optician who is either a director or manager of that business there is a period of three months before the company is liable to erasure and in which it may appoint a replacement (section 11(3)).

3 Where a director of a corporate body is the subject of a disciplinary order or a responsible official is convicted of an offence under the Act, or a registered optician employed by the corporate body is the subject of a disciplinary order on grounds which were instigated or connived at by a director, in all of which cases the corporate body is liable to a disciplinary order (section 11(6)).

Registered Opticians or Corporate Bodies

1 Where a registered optician or corporate body has contravened or failed to comply with any rule made under section 25 (eg relating to publicity) or failed to pay in the specified time the sum specified in a penalty order (section 11(3)).

2 Where a registered optician or corporate body is engaged in the fitting and supply of optical appliances but does not make arrangements for this to be done under the supervision of an ophthalmic optician registered in the appropriate register (section 11(5)).

Disciplinary Procedure

There are two phases to the disciplinary procedure. Initially, all cases are considered in a preliminary fashion by the Investigating Committee to determine if they should be referred to the Disciplinary Committee. If a case is referred, the Disciplinary Committee carries out a full inquiry.

Investigating Committee Section 9 required the General Optical Council to establish the Investigating Committee. The function of this Committee is to consider any case where an individual or body is alleged to be liable to disciplinary measures and decide whether the case should be referred to the Disciplinary Committee. Section 9(3) and (4) empowers the General Optical Council to make rules as to the constitution of the Committee, and these are contained in the General Optical Council (Investigating Committee Rules) Order of Council 1960 SI 1960 No. 1935, as amended by SI 1971 No. 1528, SI 1983 No. 545 and SI 1984 No. 1248.

Disciplinary Committee Section 10 required the General Optical Council to set up a Disciplinary Committee, the function of which is to consider and determine all disciplinary cases referred to it by the Investigating Committee, and any other cases of which it has cognisance under the Act. Section 10 empowers the General Optical Council to make rules concerning the constitution of the Disciplinary Committee and, in particular, to require that, except for the chairman of the General Optical Council, no member of the Investigating Committee shall be a member of the Disciplinary Committee considering the same case. The present rules are contained in the General Optical Council (Disciplinary Committee Rules) Order of Council 1960 SI 1960 No. 1934, as amended by SI 1971 No. 1526 and SI 1984 No. 1250. Moreover, section 15 requires the General Optical Council to make rules of procedure and evidence for the Disciplinary Committee, and these are contained in the schedule to the General Optical Council (Disciplinary Committee) (Procedure) Rules Order of Council 1985 SI 1985 No. 1580.

Procedure for a Disciplinary Case Once a complaint has been received about an optician or corporate body, the Investigating Committee must consider the allegations and decide whether to refer the case to the Disciplinary Committee for consideration and determination.

Where a case is to be heard by the Disciplinary Committee, the individual or business concerned must be informed of the time and place of the hearing and is entitled to be represented by counsel or solicitor. Proceedings are usually held in public and are similar to those in a court of law. Section 15 permits the Committee to administer oaths, and any party to the proceedings may sue out writs of subpoena ad testificandum and duces tecum. However, no party may be compelled to produce any documents he could not be compelled to produce in a court of law. Section 16 requires that the General Optical Council must appoint a legal assessor to the Disciplinary Committee. His function is to advise on questions of law arising in cases before the Committee. The legal assessor may be a barrister, advocate or solicitor of not less than ten years standing. Rules as to the functions of the legal assessor are made by the Lord Chancellor (section 16(3)) and are at present contained in the General Optical Council Disciplinary Committee (Legal Assessor) Rules 1961 SI 1961 No. 1239.

Erasure for Fraud or Error The Disciplinary Committee also considers cases in which an entry on a list or register is alleged to have been made fraudulently or incorrectly. If this is proved to its satisfaction it may direct that the entry be erased.

Appeals

If the Disciplinary Committee determines that a disciplinary order be made against an optician or business it must serve notice on the party concerned. Section 14 provides that he then has 28 days in which to appeal to the Judicial Committee of the Privy Council. Appeals to the Privy Council are covered by the Judicial Committee (Opticians Rules) Order 1960 SI 1960 No. 1661. The General Optical Council may appear as a respondent in appeal cases, but it is deemed a party to the proceedings for the purposes of costs, even if it does not appear. If there is no appeal, or an appeal is thrown out for want of prosecution, the decision of the Disciplinary Committee becomes effective once the 28 days have expired.

Reinstatement

Where the Disciplinary Committtee has directed that the name of an optician or business be erased, section 12 provides that it may not be restored to the list or register unless, on application, the Disciplinary Committee so directs. However, application for restoration of a name may not be made in less than ten months from erasure or from the last application.

Where a name has been erased on the grounds of fraud under section 13, it may not be restored except on application to the Disciplinary Committee.

Controls on Opticians' Practice

Sight-Testing

Section 20(1) of the Opticians Act 1958 restricts the testing of sight to a registered medical practitioner or a registered ophthalmic optician. Section 20(5) provides that anyone who contravenes this provision is guilty of an offence and is liable on summary conviction to a fine of up to £500.

The Act provides two exceptions to the rules that only registered medical practitioners or registered ophthalmic opticians may test sight – both for students:

Medical Students Section 20(2) provides that a recognised medical student may, as part of his training or examinations by a recognised medical authority, test the sight of another.

Student Opticians Section 20(3) permits the General Optical Council to make rules permitting people training as ophthalmic opticians to test sight. These rules are contained in the General Optical Council (Rules on the Testing of Sight by Persons Training as Ophthalmic Opticians) Order of the Council 1974 SI 1974 No. 1329.

Selling Optical Appliances

Section 21(1) provides that no-one may sell an optical appliance unless the sale is effected by, or under the supervision of, a registered medical practitioner or a registered optician. Anyone contravening this provision is guilty of an offence, and section 21(5) provides for a fine of up to £500 on summary conviction.

The 1958 Act provided certain exceptions to this restriction, but the Health and Social Security Act 1984 (section 1) added an important new exemption (sub-section 3A–D) which in effect terminated the opticians' monopoly on selling spectacles (see page 6). The actual details of the exemption were introduced by the Sale of Optical Appliances Order of Council 1984 SI 1984 No. 1778. Under this order, optical appliances may be sold other than by an optician, provided the following conditions are fulfilled:

1 Contact lenses and low-vision aids may not be sold.

2 Appliances for children under 16 years old or people registered as blind or partially sighted may not be sold.

3 The appliance sold must comply with a prescription which is written by a registered opthalmic optician or a registered medical practitioner and which is not more than two years old.

4 A variety of technical requirements in the optical specification of the appliance, materials that may not be used in their construction and a requirement to comply with the relevant British Standards (see SI 1984 No. 1778 for details).

In addition to this major exception to the rule that only registered opticians may sell or supply optical appliances, the following other exceptions were introduced by the original 1958 Opticians Act.

1 Sale to a registered medical practitioner or registered optician or enrolled corporate body for the purpose of their practice or business (section 21(3)(a)).

2 Sale to a manufacturer or dealer in optical appliances for the purpose of his business (section 21(3)(b)).

3 Sale to an authority or individual carrying on a hospital, clinic, nursing home or other institution providing medical or surgical treatment (section 21(3)(c)).

4 Sale to a Minister of the Crown or Government department (section 21(3)(d)).

5 Sale for the purpose of export (section 21(3)(e)).

6 Sale as an antique or second-hand article by someone who did not know, and had no reason to believe, it was to be used to correct, remedy or relieve a defect of sight (section 21(4)).

Fitting contact lenses

The Health and Social Security Act 1984 (section 2) modified the Opticians Act by introducing a new section 20A which prohibits the fitting of contact lenses by anyone who is not a registered optician or a registered medical practitioner. However, section 20A makes an exception for a recognised medical student in training, and also permits the General Optical Council to make rules providing an exemption for recognised trainee opticians. These rules are to be found in the General Optical Council (Rules on the Fitting of Contact Lenses) Order of Council 1985 SI 1985 No. 856.

The Use of Titles

Section 22(1) as amended by section 3 of the Health and Social Security Act 1984 makes it an offence for anyone who is not appropriately registered to use the title "ophthalmic optician", "dispensing optician", "registered optician", "enrolled optician" or "optometrist". It is also an offence for anyone to use a name or title, addition or description which falsely implies that he is registered in any of the registers. Section 22(2) deals with the use of titles by corporate bodies and imposes the same prohibition as in section 22(1), unless that company is appropriately enrolled. These offences are liable to a fine of up to £500 on summary conviction.

Exceptions Section 23 provides exceptions to the limitations on the use of titles imposed by section 22 in the case of the personal representatives and the widow, children or their trustees of a deceased optician. In such a case, they may use any title the deceased optician was entitled to use at the time of his death for a period of up to three years (or longer where the General Optical Council so directs) (section 23(1)). A similar relaxation is also provided for the trustee of a bankrupt optician who is carrying on his business (section 23(2)).

The Health and Social Security Act 1984 amended the Opticians Act (at Section 22) to provide that someone who carries on the business of selling optical appliances may as a defence to using the word "optician" state that he took or used the title in circumstances where it would be unreasonable for people to believe he was registered. A similar defence is also provided for corporate bodies.

Liability of Company Officers

Section 24 provides that, where an offence under the Act has been committed by a corporate body with the consent or connivance of, or due to the neglect of, any director, manager, secretary or similar officer of the company, that person shall be guilty of the offence and is liable to be proceeded against.

Duty to Refer Eye Disease

Section 25 and the General Optical Council (Rules Relating to Injuries or Disease of the Eye) Order of Council 1960 SI 1960 No. 1936 impose a duty on a registered optician to refer to a registered medical practitioner anyone who appears to be suffering from an injury to, or disease of, the eye. In an emergency, the rules permit the optician to give whatever services appear appropriate before referral to a doctor.

Controls on Advertising

Section 25 empowers the General Optical Council to make rules prohibiting or regulating, among other things, advertising. The present regulations are the General Optical Council (Rules on Publicity) Order of Council 1985 SI 1985 No. 203. The 1985 Rules replaced the more restrictive 1981 Rules which in turn replaced the even more restrictive 1964 Rules. The rules require publicity to be legal, decent, honest and truthful and not likely to bring the profession into disrepute. Claims must be capable of substantiation and not include disparaging references to other practices or businesses.

Control of Optical Education

Section 1 of the Opticians Act 1958 imposes on the General Optical Council a variety of functions, including that of promoting high standards of professional education. Furthermore, section 17 requires the Council to establish and maintain an Education Committee to which it must refer for advice on all matters relating to optical training and examinations. The constitution of this committee is dealt with by the General Optical Council (Education Committee Rules) Order of Council 1974 SI 1974 No. 149 (as amended by SI 1984 No. 1249) and is designed to ensure a membership competent to advise on all educational issues.

The Opticians Act also empowers the Council to approve training courses, institutions and qualifications, and to exercise an overall supervisory function in respect to these institutions and examinations.

Approval of Training Institutions and Qualifications

Section 5 provides for the approval of training institutions and of qualifications. The Council may approve any institution where it appears to it that the instruction given to opticians in training is such as to give them adequate knowledge and skill for the practice of the profession (section 5(1)). Similarly, the Council may approve any qualification which appears to be granted to candidates who reach a standard of proficiency at a qualifying examination as to secure them adequate knowledge and skill for the practice of their profession (section 5(2)). A qualification may be approved for the training of a dispensing or ophthalmic optician, or both (section 5(3)). The General Optical Council must publish a list of approved institutions and qualifications.

If the Council refuses to approve an institution or qualification, the Privy Council may hear any representations made to it within one month and may instruct the Optical Council to issue an approval (section 5(4)).

Supervision of Institutions and Examinations

Section 6 imposes a duty on the Council to keep itself informed of the nature of the instruction given at training institutions and of the examinations upon which the grant of any approved qualification is based. To do so, it may appoint visitors to visit approved institutions and attend examinations. The visitors, who must not interfere with any training or examination, must report their findings to the Council.

If it appears to the Council, either as a result of a visitors' report or otherwise, that the standard of instruction or examination is inadequate, it has the power to withdraw its approval in part or in whole. Where it intends to do so, it must inform the institution, giving it copies of any reports upon which the intention is based. The institution must then be given at least one month to object to the Council's views. The Council must take such representations into account, but if it nevertheless resolves to withdraw its approval it must serve notice on the institution. The decision will not take effect for one month, during which time the institution may appeal to the Privy Council, in which case, withdrawal will not take effect before the appeal is finally dealt with.

Chapter Twelve

Hearing Aid Dispensers

Hearing Aid Council Act 1968

The Hearing Aid Council Act 1968, which was extended to apply to Northern Ireland by the Hearing Aid Council (Extension) Act 1975, controls the profession of hearing aid dispensing. Section 14 of the 1968 Act defines a dispenser of hearing aids as an individual who conducts, or seeks to conduct, oral negotiations with a view to the supply of a hearing aid (either by himself or another) to, or for the use of, a person with impaired hearing. The same section defines a hearing aid as an instrument for use by someone suffering from impaired hearing to assist him to hear better. However, it does not include instruments for connecting conductors of electricity to equipment or to anything involved with telephonic communication.

As with other professions, the Hearing Aid Council Act 1968 provides for a controlling body, for registration of professionals, for controls on their practice and for discipline.

The Controlling Body. The Hearing Aid Council

The Hearing Aid Council was established by section 1 of the Hearing Aid Council Act 1968 as a corporate body with perpetual succession and a common seal. The general function of the Council is to secure adequate standards of competence and conduct amongst hearing aid dispensers. It is required to keep under review the training facilities available for hearing aid dispensers and advise on methods of improvement (section 1(2)). The Council must define, and from time to time revise, standards of competence for dispensers and of codes of trade practice for dispensers and their employers. These standards and codes must be approved by the Department of Trade and may be published by the Council (section 1(3), (4) & (5)). The Council is empowered to receive complaints from the public and may investigate them. It also has a variety of other specific responsibilities imposed by the Act. These are considered below.

Constitution, Powers and Proceedings The constitution, powers and proceedings of the Council are dealt with by the schedule to the Act. The Council consists of a chairman and eleven other members appointed by the Secretary of State for Trade. Six members must be capable of representing the interests of people registered under the Act because they are registered themselves or are concerned with the management of a registered firm. Five members must be people not so registered but who have either specialised medical knowledge of deafness or are capable of representing the interests of people with impaired hearing. The chairman is appointed as someone who does not represent any of these interests. Members hold office for four years, and a quorum of the Council is seven. The Council must appoint a registrar and has the power to do anything which, in its opinion, is calculated to discharge its proper functions.

Expenses and Accounts The schedule to the Act permits the Council to appoint such officers and servants as it wishes and to pay members of the Council and its committees such attendance, travelling and subsistence fees as the Secretary of State for Trade approves. The Council determines the salary of its officers and servants and may pay them pensions and gratuities. Section 12 permits the Council, after paying expenses, to allocate any moneys, received by way of fees or otherwise, to purposes connected with education and research in the area of hearing aid dispensing. The Council must keep accounts of all sums received and paid, and these must be audited annually by a professional accountant (section 12). As soon as possible after audit, the accounts must be published by the Council.

Registration

The Registers Section 2 of the Hearing Aid Council Act 1968 requires that the registrar appointed by the Council establishes and keeps two registers, one of dispensers of hearing aids and one of their employers. The registrar must enter in the appropriate register names of people who are qualified to be registered and who have applied in the prescribed manner and paid the appropriate fee. There is also an annual retention fee. The register is kept at the Council's offices and is available for public inspection free of charge at all reasonable times. Section 4 empowers the Council to make rules covering the form and keeping of the registers, entries, alterations and corrections and the issue of certificates of registration. To be effective, these rules require the approval of the Secretary of State for Trade.

Registration Anyone, other than a disqualified person (see below), is qualified to be registered as a dispenser of hearing aids if he satisfies the standards of competence published by the Council, as required by section 1. Anyone who, during the two years before the commencement of the Act, had acted as a dispenser for at least six months is also qualified for registration (section 4(a) and (b)).

Anyone may be registered as an employer of hearing aid dispensers if he employs, or proposes to employ, any such dispensers. However, a disqualified person, or someone in partnership with a disqualified person, is not eligible. Nor is a corporate body which has a disqualified person as a director or manager or in which a disqualified person has a controlling interest.

If registration is refused, the applicant may appeal to the Disciplinary Committee (section 2(6)) (see below).

Controls on Practice

The dispensing of hearing aids is controlled by section 3 of the Act. This section makes it a criminal offence for any unregistered person to act as a hearing aid dispenser unless he is in full-time training under the supervision of a registered dispenser and his name has been notified to the Council. It is an offence for any person not on the register of employers to employ anyone to act as a dispenser of hearing aids. It is also an offence for a registered employer to employ any unregistered person except someone notified as in full-time training under the supervision of a registered dispenser. The offences are liable to a £100 fine on summary conviction.

Professional Conduct

Grounds for Disciplinary Action There is a variety of offences for which a registered person is liable to have his name erased from the register, and these are covered in section 7. The main circumstances are:

1 Where a registered dispenser has been convicted in the United Kingdom of any criminal offence which renders him unfit to have his name on the register.

2 Where a registered dispenser is judged by the Disciplinary Committee to have been guilty of serious misconduct in connection with the dispensing of hearing aids.

3 Where it appears to the Disciplinary Committee that a registered employer has not made such arrangements as are necessary to ensure that the dispensing of hearing aids is carried out by, or under the supervision of, a registered dispenser.

4 Where a director of a corporate body who is a registered employer is guilty of an offence under this Act.

5 Where the Disciplinary Committee is satisfied that a person whose name has been removed from the register is acting as a director or manager of, or has a controlling interest in, a corporate body.

6 Where any registered person (dispenser or employer) employs, or carries on a partnership with, a person whose name has been erased from either register.

It should be noted that in (4) and (5) above it is the name of the corporate body which is liable to be erased.

The Disciplinary Bodies There are two committees of the Council concerned with disciplinary matters – the Investigating Committee and the Disciplinary Committee.

The Investigating Committee was set up by section 5(1) of the Act and has the duty to carry out a preliminary investigation into cases where it is alleged that a registered person is liable to have his name erased on one of the grounds outlined above. The Investigating Committee must decide whether to refer the case to the Disciplinary Committee, and it has the power to make rules in respect to its constitution. The rules require the approval of the Lord Chancellor to be effective, and this is done by statutory instrument (section 13). The present rules are embodied in the Hearing Aid Council (Investigating and Disciplinary Committees) Rules 1971 which were approved by the Lord Chancellor by the Hearing Aid Council Disciplinary Committee (Procedure) Rules Approval Instrument 1971 SI 1971 No. 754.

The Disciplinary Committee was set up by section 6(1) of the Act. It has the function of considering and determining disciplinary cases referred to it by the Investigating Committee or hearing appeals from people for whom registration has been refused. The Council may make rules concerning the constitution of the Committee, and, to be effective, these rules must be approved by the Lord Chancellor by statutory instrument. The present rules are the Hearing Aid Council (Investigating and Disciplinary Committee) Rules 1971, approved by SI 1971 No. 754. Except for the chairman of the Council, no-one may be a member of the Disciplinary Committee in respect of a case for which he was a member of the Investigating Committee.

Procedure Before the Disciplinary Committee Procedure before the Disciplinary Committee is dealt with by section 10 of the Act. This permits the Council to make rules of procedure and evidence after consultation with interested parties. To be effective, the rules require the Lord Chancellor's approval by statutory instrument, and he has the power to modify them as he thinks fit before approval. The present rules are contained in the Hearing Aid Council Disciplinary Committee (Procedure) Rules 1971 and approved by SI 1971 No. 754, to which reference should be made for details. They cover matters such as notification of proceedings, attendance at hearings, representation by solicitors or counsel, proceedings to be held in public and recording the determination of the Committee. The Disciplinary Committee may administer oaths and any party to the proceedings may obtain writs of subpoena ad testificandum and duces tecum.

In all proceedings before the Disciplinary Committee, section 11(1) requires there to be present a legal assessor who must be a barrister, advocate or solicitor of at least ten years standing. He is appointed by the Council, but, if no appointed assessor is available to act at any proceedings, then the Committee may appoint one. The function of the assessor is to advise the Disciplinary Committee on all matters of law relating to evidence, procedure or the rules, and this advice must be given in the presence of all parties to the proceedings. Assessors' remuneration is at rates set by the Lord Chancellor, who is also empowered by the Act to make rules to cover their function. The present rules are contained in the Hearing Aid Council (Disciplinary Proceedings) Legal Assessors Rules 1971 SI 1971 No. 755.

Appeals and Restorations Where the Disciplinary Committee has determined after an inquiry that a name shall be erased from the register, the party affected has 28 days in which to appeal (section 9(1)). Appeal is to the High Court – in effect a Divisional Court of the Queen's Bench Division – or to the Court of Session in Scotland.

Where a name has been erased because of a disciplinary offence under section 7 or because of failure to pay the retention fee or provide some necessary information when requested (see section 4(e)), then that name may be restored to the register only by direction of the Disciplinary Committee (section 8). However, section 8(2) requires that no such application may be made within ten months of the date of erasure or the last application.

Chapter Thirteen

Professions Supplementary to Medicine

The professions dealt with so far have been governed by separate Acts of Parliament. The Professions Supplementary to Medicine Act 1960, by contrast, covered seven separate professions, namely chiropodists, dieticians, medical laboratory technicians, occupational therapists, physiotherapists, radiographers and remedial gymnasts. Section 10 of the Act permits its extension to cover additional professions by order of the Privy Council, and the Professions Supplementary to Medicine (Orthoptists Board) Order of Council 1966 SI 1966 No. 990 extended the provisions of the Act to an eighth group – orthoptists. Section 10 also permits removal of a profession, and the Professions Supplementary to Medicine (Winding up of Remedial Gymnastics Board) Order of Council 1986 SI 1986 No. 630 merges from the 1st of April 1986 the remedial gymnasts with the physiotherapists from which they had become indistinguishable.

Like other legislation in this field, the Act creates controlling bodies for the various professions, provides for a system of registration, controls professional education and training, and makes provision for disciplinary procedures.

The Controlling Bodies

The Council Section 1(1) of the Act establishes the Council for Professions Supplementary to Medicine to supervise the various Boards set up under this Act and to fulfil a variety of other specific functions. The constitution and procedure of the Council are dealt with in part 1 and part 3 of the first schedule to the Act. The Council, which is a body corporate with perpetual succession and a common seal, consists of 23 members. A proportion of members are appointed by the Privy Council and the Health Ministers. Eight are representative of the various Boards, while six are registered medical practitioners appointed by the General Medical Council (1), the Royal College of Physicians of London (1), the Royal College of Surgeons of England (1), the Royal College of Obstetricians and Gynaecologists (1), and the Royal College of Physicians of Edinburgh, the Royal College of Surgeons of Edinburgh and the Royal Faculty of Physicians and Surgeons of Glasgow (2 jointly). The procedure of the Council with respect to such items as forming committees, making standing orders, tenure of office of members, chairmen, officers, expenses and accounts is dealt with in detail in the first schedule to the Act.

Section 1(3) of the Act gives the Council wide powers in supervising the various Boards. The Council has power under section 2 to make rules relating to registration and is involved in the process of approval of training courses, qualifications and institutions (section 4 and 5). Section 10 empowers the Council to recommend to the Privy Council the extension of the Act to new professions (e.g. the orthoptists in 1966) or the restriction of the Act, either by cessation or by amalgamation (e.g. the remedial gymnasts in 1986). Section 11 gives the Privy Council the power to act when it considers the Council or a Board has failed in its duties.

The Boards Section 1(2) of the Act, as amended by SI 1966 No. 990 and SI 1986 No. 630 establishes a Board for each of the professions covered by the Act. The Boards have the general function of promoting high standards of professional education and professional conduct among members of the relevant professions and the additional functions assigned to them by the Act. The constitution of the Boards is dealt with in part 2 of the first schedule to the Act and procedure is dealt with by part 3 of the same schedule. Membership varies between 11 and 17. It includes representatives of the particular profession, registered medical practitioners and others with particular experience or qualifications, especially in professional education. Like the Council, the Boards are corporate bodies with perpetual succession and a common seal. Part 3 of the first schedule to the Act provides for matters such as tenure of office, members, chairmen, committees, standing orders, expenses and accounts, and staff. In particular, the Council must finance the Boards out of sums received from registration fees.

Registration

Section 3(1) provides that a person is entitled to be registered under the Act if he can satisfy the appropriate Board that he has attended a training course approved by the Board and held at an approved training institution, and has obtained an approved qualification. Section 3(2) further provides that an individual is also entitled to be registered in his profession if he can satisfy the appropriate Board of one of the following conditions:

1 He is qualified in his profession for the purposes of regulation 3 of the National Health Service (Medical Auxiliaries) Regulations 1965, or

2 he holds a qualification for the time being recognised by the Board, or

3 he has sufficient training and practical experience as are considered by the Board to enable him to practise his profession, or

4 he is competent to practise his profession because of his practical experience.

As far as overseas qualifications are concerned, section 3(4) provides that if an individual holds a qualification granted outside the United Kingdom, which is for the time being accepted by the Board, and the Board is satisfied he has sufficient practical experience in the said profession, he also is entitled to be registered.

The Registers Section 2(1) of the Act imposes a duty on each Board to prepare and maintain a register of everyone who is entitled under section 3 to be registered in the particular profession and who has applied to the said Board in the prescribed manner. By definition, an individual is registered if his name is on the particular register (section 2 (2)), and the presence or absence of a name on the appropriate register is evidence in a court of law that that person is or is not registered (section 2(5)). The Council is empowered by section 2(3) to make rules relating to the keeping of the registers and, in particular, to such matters as entries, alterations, corrections, applications and fees. The Council must consult with the Boards before drafting such rules, which do not come into force until approved by order of the Privy Council. The present rules are contained in the Professions Supplementary to Medicine (Registration Rules) Order of Council 1962 SI 1962 No. 1765, as amended by 1968 No. 1973, 1975 No. 1691, 1979 No. 365, 1981 No. 178, SI 1983 No. 1799 and SI 1986 No. 660.

The Act imposes a duty on the Boards to print, publish and sell to the public copies of the register, and prepare and sell annually either a corrected edition or a list of alterations (section 2(4)). The Boards must deposit a copy of the current register with the Council, which must keep it open to the public for inspection at all reasonable times.

Training and Education

As stated above, registration under the Act is based on attendance at an approved training course at an approved institution and on the acquisition of an approved qualification. Sections 4 and 5 of the Act deal in detail with this. Section 4(1) empowers the appropriate Board to approve the following:

1 Any training course which it considers confers sufficient skill and knowledge for professional practice.

2 Any qualifications obtained by examination, taken in conjunction with an approved training course, which indicate sufficient knowledge and skill to practise the profession.

3 Any institution the Board considers properly organised and equipped for undertaking the whole or part of an approved training course.

The power of approval includes approval of any training course or qualification run or organised by the Board itself.

Where the Board receives application for approval of a course or qualification, it must send its recommendation to the Council, which sends it on, with any comments of its own, to the Privy Council. It is the Privy Council which finally determines whether the approval is granted (section 4(2)). Before any application is refused by the Privy Council, the applicant must be given the opportunity to make representations to it. When a Board proposes to withdraw its approval for a course or qualification, a similar procedure is followed (section 4(3)). The Council also has the power to recommend that approval for a training course or a qualification be withdrawn in view of changing circumstances. When it does so, it seeks the observations of the appropriate Board and makes recommendations to the Privy Council. Before reaching a decision, the Privy Council must give the person or body affected an opportunity to comment. When a Board refuses or withdraws an application for an institution, that institution may, within one month, appeal to the Privy Council, which, after considering the Board's representations, must determine the appeal.

To ensure the supervision of professional education, section 5(1) imposes a duty on each Board to keep itself informed of the nature of instruction given at approved institutions on approved training courses and of the examinations. To do so, the Board may appoint and pay the expenses of visitors whose duty it is to report back to the Board. However, section 5(3) specifically requires the visitors not to interfere with the training or examinations being inspected.

Controls on Professional Practice

The use of the term "state registered" in respect to the professions covered by the Act is limited to people who are properly registered (section 6(1)), and it is a criminal offence for an unregistered person to use such a title. It is also an offence to use any name, title, description or addition which falsely implies registration. In either case, the penalty is a fine of up to £50 on first conviction and up to £100 on second and subsequent convictions.

Professional Discipline

The Disciplinary Bodies Each board is required to set up two committees – an Investigating Committee and a Disciplinary Committee (section 8(1)). The Investigating Committee has a duty to carry out a preliminary investigation where it is alleged that a registered person may be liable to have his name erased from the register, and to decide whether or not to refer the case to the Disciplinary Committee. The duty of the Disciplinary Committee is to consider, and reach a decision on, all disciplinary cases referred to it.

The constitution of the committees is dealt with by part 1 of the second schedule to the Act which requires the appropriate Board to make rules concerning committee membership, times and places of meetings, quorums etc. Such rules require the approval of the Privy Council to be effective. In particular, no-one may be a member of the Disciplinary Committee in a case in which he was a member of the Investigating Committee. The procedure to be followed at any Disciplinary Committee is covered by part 2 of the second schedule to the Act and by the Professions Supplementary to Medicine (Disciplinary Committees) (Procedure) Rules Order of Council 1964 SI 1964 No. 1203. Matters of procedure and rules of evidence are covered, and the general approach in the Investigating and Disciplinary Committees is like that of a court of law.

The Act requires that a legal assessor is appointed by the Council to advise any Disciplinary Committee. The legal assessor must be a barrister, advocate or solicitor of not less than ten years standing and must advise the Committee on matters of law. The Lord Chancellor may make rules dealing with the functions of the legal assessor, and the present rules are contained in the Professions Supplementary to Medicine (Disciplinary Proceedings) Legal Assessor Rules 1964 SI 1964 No. 951.

Disciplinary Offences A registered person is liable to have his or her name removed from the register in three situations (section 9(1)).

They are:

1 Where he or she is convicted in the United Kingdom of a criminal offence which, in the opinion of the Disciplinary Committee, renders that person unfit to be registered.

2 Where he or she is judged by the Disciplinary Committee to be guilty of infamous conduct in a professional respect.

3 Where the Disciplinary Committee is satisfied that the individual has obtained registration fraudulently.

Section 6 requires each Disciplinary Committee, in consultation with its Board, to prepare, and from time to time revise, a statement outlining the sort of conduct it considers infamous in a professional respect. This must be sent to all registered members of the particular profession. However, the fact that a particular matter is not covered by such a statement does not preclude the Disciplinary Committee from judging it to be infamous in a professional respect.

Appeals Where a Disciplinary Committee directs a person's name to be removed from the register it must serve notice on the individual, and he has 28 days in which to appeal. Appeal is to the Judicial Committee of the Privy Council – "Her Majesty in Council". The rules relating to such appeals are contained in the Judicial Committee (Professions Supplementary to Medicine Rules) Order 1964 SI 1964 No. 1001.

An erasure is effective either when an appeal is determined or thrown out or when the 28-day period has elapsed (section 9(4)). Someone whose name has been struck off may have it restored only on application to the Disciplinary Committee.

Chapter Fourteen

The Veterinary Profession

The Veterinary Surgeons Act 1966

The veterinary profession is controlled by the Veterinary Surgeons Act 1966 and the various statutory instruments made under it. The Act extends to the whole of the United Kingdom. In addition, various Royal charters govern the constitution of the Royal College of Veterinary Surgeons.

The Controlling Body

The controlling body for the veterinary profession is the Council of the Royal College of Veterinary Surgeons, the present constitution of which is determined by the Veterinary Surgeons Act 1966. However, the College itself was created by a Royal Charter of 1844 granted to the graduates of the veterinary schools of London and Edinburgh. The 1844 charter created the College as a body corporate and provided that it should govern the veterinary profession. Eleven further Royal charters were granted between 1876 and 1966. The 1966 charter in effect revoked and consolidated most of the previous supplemental charters.

The College consists of fellows, members and honorary associates. On becoming registered as a veterinary surgeon, an individual becomes a member of the College. A fellow is someone who is elected to that position or who has presented a thesis, passed an examination or made a meritorious contribution to learning. Honorary associates are elected to the position by members of the Council. The College has perpetual succession.

Constitution of the Council

Section 1 of the Veterinary Surgeons Act 1966 confirms the continuing existence of the Council of the Royal College of Veterinary Surgeons and provides for its membership. The Act provides that the Council shall consist of 24 members elected by members of the College resident outside the Republic of Ireland, four persons appointed by the Privy Council and two members appointed by each of the recognised veterinary schools. At least one of each school's pair of appointees must be a member of the College. In addition, there are three appointed and two elected members who sit on the Council as representatives of the Republic of Ireland. Section 1(4) provides that if the size of the Council increases by virtue of the recognition of new veterinary colleges then the Privy Council may, after consultation with the Council, alter the number of elected members to ensure they have an overall majority. The Privy Council may also make alterations to the terms of office of the elected members in consequence of any change made in their total number. Section 1(2) provides that there shall continue to be a president and two vice-presidents elected by the Council from their numbers. Section 1(3) and Schedule 1 to the Act details the tenure of office, election and appointment of the president, vice-presidents and members of the Council.

The term of office for a member of the Council is four years, but every year the six longest-serving members retire. The president and vice-presidents hold office for one year and normally retire at the Council meeting after the annual general meeting. A member of the Council may resign at any time, and any member who ceases to be a member of the College also ceases to be a member of the Council. If a recognition order for a veterinary school should be withdrawn then the members appointed by that school would cease to be members.

Functions of the Council

The overall function of the Council is the management of the affairs of the Royal College of Veterinary Surgeons (section 1) but the Veterinary Surgeons Act 1966 also imposes the following duties:

Advisory The Council must advise the Privy Council on various matters prior to it (the Privy Council) exercising certain statutory powers – for example, alteration in the number of members of the Council under section 1(4) or the issue of a recognition order to a university veterinary school under section 3.

Education Section 5 places a duty on the Council to ensure that the courses of veterinary education and the standards of proficiency reached are such that a person who has been registered will have acquired the knowledge and skill needed for the efficient practice of veterinary surgery. To do this, the Council may appoint people to visit universities to report on the courses of study and also to attend examinations. Section 4 permits the Privy Council to direct the College to hold examinations in veterinary surgery in certain instances.

Registration of Veterinary Surgeons and Practitioners The registration of veterinarians is controlled by the Council, which, among other things, appoints the registrar and publishes the register. Section 11 empowers the Council to make regulations relating to the form of the register and its keeping and for payment of fees in respect of registration. However, section 25 provides that no such regulations shall have effect until approved by the Privy Council.

Discipline Professional discipline is the responsibility of the Council. Section 14 requires the Council to set up a Preliminary Investigation Committee and a Disciplinary Committee. Under section 14 the Council has a duty to refer to the Disciplinary Committee any case where it appears that an entry in the register is fraudulent, and, if it is found to be so, to remove that entry.

Rules The Council has the power to make rules and regulations related to the operation of the 1966 Act. However, section 25 provides that such rules do not have effect until approved by order of the Privy Council by statutory instrument. Such statutory instruments are subject to annulment by resolution of either House of Parliament.

Control of the Council by the Privy Council
Section 22 gives the Privy Council an overall supervisory role over the Council of the College. It provides that if the Council fails to fulfil any function under the Act the Privy Council may require it to do so, and, if that does not succeed, may itself discharge that function.

Registration

With certain limited exceptions, section 19 of the Veterinary Surgeons Act 1966 restricts the practice of veterinary surgery to people registered in either the register of veterinary surgeons or the supplementary veterinary register.

The Register

The existence of the veterinary surgeons register, which was established by previous statute, is confirmed by section 2 of the Veterinary Surgeons Act 1966. The section provides that the register shall be in four parts: the general list (consisting of United Kingdom graduates), the foreign list, the Commonwealth list and the temporary list.

Section 9 charges the registrar of the Royal College of Veterinary Surgeons with the keeping of the register, and the Council must appoint the registrar. The Council must have the register printed and published as often as it thinks fit, but, if any year it is not published, the Council must publish any alterations made to it since its last publication (section 9(3) and (4)). The register is evidence in a court of law of an individual's registration. Section 9(5) provides that the presence of a name on a copy of the register (as amended by published alterations) is evidence of registration, and absence of a name is evidence that that person is not registered. However, where a person's name is not on a copy of the register, section 9(6) provides that a certified copy of an entry under the hand of the registrar is evidence of registration. The registrar is required to insert in the register any changes in name or address of registered persons that come to his knowledge.

Section 11 permits the Council to make regulations concerning the form and keeping of the register and in respect of entries and their removal. In particular, the Council may make regulations prescribing fees for registration, or retention of registration, and may authorise the registrar to remove from the register the name of anyone failing to pay a prescribed fee. Section 25 provides that no such regulations are to be effective until approved by order of the Privy Council. The present regulations are contained in the Veterinary Surgeons and Veterinary Practitioners (Registration Regulations) Order of Council 1967 SI 1967 No. 395, as amended by SI 1975 Nos. 70, 2112, SI 1978 No. 1809, SI 1980 No. 2004 and SI 1984 No. 2009.

The Supplementary Register

Besides the main register, kept under the provisions of section 2, there is also a supplementary register of veterinary practitioners provided for by section 8 which is described below.

Registration

The General List Section 3 of the Veterinary Surgeons Act 1966 provides that a graduate of a university veterinary school in the United Kingdom which is recognised under the Act is entitled, on proper application (section 10) and payment of any prescribed fee (section 11), to be registered in the General List.

On being registered, an individual becomes a member of the Royal College of Veterinary Surgeons. To be recognised, a veterinary school must satisfy the Privy Council, through the Council of the College, that it provides courses of study and examinations leading to a veterinary degree which are sufficient to guarantee the necessary skill and knowledge needed for the efficient practice of veterinary surgery (section 3(1)). If the Privy Council is satisfied that this is the case it will issue a recognition order. The veterinary schools of the universities of Bristol, Cambridge, Edinburgh, Glasgow, Liverpool and London are all recognised under section 3. Section 3 permits the Privy Council to suspend or revoke a recognition order if it appears to the Council that the standard of study or examination at a particular school no longer reaches the required level. Section 4 permits the Privy Council, after consultation with the Council of the College, to direct the College to hold examinations in veterinary surgery for students of United Kingdom veterinary schools for which no recognition order is in force.

To confirm that the educational standards at a recognised veterinary school are maintained section 5 permits the Council to appoint people to visit universities to report on the courses of study and examinations.

Commonwealth and Foreign List Admission to either the Commonwealth list or foreign list is covered by section 6. Where someone can show to the satisfaction of the registrar that he is of good character, holds a Commonwealth or foreign qualification in veterinary surgery and has satisfied the Council that he has the requisite knowledge and skill to practise veterinary surgery in the United Kingdom he may be registered and become a member of the College. The Council may set examinations for a foreign or Commonwealth graduate to satisfy itself of his knowledge and skill; alternatively, it may accept the Commonwealth or foreign degree as satisfactory evidence. The regulations with respect to such examinations, including the fees payable to the College, are found in the Veterinary Surgeons (Examinations of Foreign and Commonwealth Candidates) Regulations 1967 SI 1967 No. 599 (as amended by SI 1971 No. 744, SI 1976 No. 1168 and SI 1980 No. 999 and SI 1984 No. 1072). The Council recognises certain veterinary degrees from some universities in Australia, Canada, New Zealand and South Africa.

Irish Graduates Section 21 empowers the Privy Council to give effect to a variety of agreements with the Republic of Ireland in respect to veterinary surgeons. In particular, section 21(1)(b)(i) empowers the Privy Council, on the recommendation of the Council of the College, to admit holders of Irish veterinary diplomas to the register. The present agreement with Ireland was made in 1972 (Cmnd 5238) and was brought into effect by the Veterinary Surgeons (Agreement with Republic of Ireland) Order 1972 SI 1972 No. 1991. Under this agreement, the degrees of the University of Dublin and the National University of Ireland have been recognised for registration in the United Kingdom (Veterinary Surgeons (Republic of Ireland University Degrees) (Dublin) Order of Council 1973 SI 1973 No. 1419 and Veterinary Surgeons (Republic of Ireland University Degrees) (National University) Order of Council 1973 SI 1973 No. 1420).

EEC Practitioners The Veterinary Surgeons Qualifications (EEC Recognition) Order 1980 SI 1980 No. 1951 introduced, from 21st December 1980, a system permitting veterinarians who qualified in the EEC to obtain full registration in the United Kingdom. The order was made under a power in the European Communities Act 1972 and in essence amends the Veterinary Surgeons Act 1966. Any national of a member state of the EEC who holds a recognised European qualification in veterinary surgery, as defined in the Order, is entitled to be fully registered in the United Kingdom and become a member of the Royal College of Veterinary Surgeons. Anyone who is subject to a disqualifying decision in a member state in which he practises may not be registered in this country so long as the disqualification continues. If an EEC national is refused registration because of a pre-existing disqualifying decision he may appeal to a special committee of the Council of the College. Greek veterinary qualifications were added to the 1980 Order by SI 1981 No. 205, and Spanish and Portuguese qualifications by SI 1987 No. 447.

Temporary Registration Section 7 permits temporary registration to be given to people who have passed the degree examinations of a recognised United Kingdom veterinary school but who have not yet received their degree, or to holders of a foreign or Commonwealth veterinary qualification. Although the registration permits them to practise they may do so only within the limitations placed by the registrar. Such limitations may include the period of practice and the place or circumstances of practice. Failure to observe these restrictions may lead to removal from the register.

Besides permitting the full registration of EEC-qualified veterinarians, the 1980 Order (SI No. 1951) provides a right for EEC practitioners to render veterinary services in the United Kingdom on a temporary basis. A veterinarian who is a national of a member state of the EEC may render services in the United Kingdom without first being registered under the 1966 Act provided he gives the registrar a declaration of what services he intends to provide and for how long, and also evidence that he is qualified and lawfully in practice in an EEC state.

The registrar must keep a part of the register as a list of such people – the list of visiting the EEC veterinary surgeons – and he must provide a limitation on duration. No fee may be charged. Registration ceases if the practitioner becomes established in practice in the United Kingdom or does anything (except in an emergency) outside the declaration he provides to the registrar.

Supplementary Register
The supplementary veterinary register is a list of people known as veterinary practitioners who, by and large, have no academic qualifications but practise by experience. Section 8 confirms the continuation of the register, but in effect no new names may be added to it. People on the register were on the supplementary register immediately before the 1966 Act, or had been previously registered and had their names restored to the register, or were licencees for seven years before the 1966 Act under section 7 of the Veterinary Surgeons Act 1948 as employees of certain societies providing free treatment for animals. This last group may only practise subject to the limitations imposed on them (usually, that they may practise only as an employee of one of the societies). Failure to comply with any such restrictions may lead to erasure of a name. No new names could be added to the supplementary register after six months from the commencement of the 1966 Act (section 10).

Procedure for Removal of a Name
The name of a registered veterinary surgeon may be removed from the register for a variety of reasons. They are:

Non-payment of Fees Section 11(2) permits regulations to be made authorising the registrar to remove from the register the name of a veterinarian who, after prescribed notice and warnings, fails to pay any prescribed retention fee. However, section 11(3) provides for the restoration of a name on payment of an extra fee.

Other Cases Section 13 requires the registrar to remove from the register the name of any deceased veterinarian. To facilitate this, a registrar of births and deaths must inform the registrar of the death of any practitioner which he deals with (section 13(11)). The name of a veterinarian who has ceased to practise may be removed from the register only at his request or with his consent (section 13(2)). However, where the registrar enquires by post of a practitioner if he has ceased to practise or moved his residence and does not receive a reply in six months, he may remove the name from the register (section 13(3)). However, a name removed under section 13(2) or (3) may be restored on application.

Section 14 requires the Council to remove from the register any entry which has been made incorrectly, and, in the case of an entry that appears fraudulent, to refer the matter to the Disciplinary Committee.

Removal for Disciplinary Reasons Erasure of a veterinarian's name from the register is the major disciplinary measure in the profession. Section 16 provides that the Disciplinary Committee may direct a name to be removed from the register, including the supplementary register, if he is convicted in the United Kingdom or elsewhere of a criminal offence which, in the Committee's view, renders him unfit to practise, or if he is judged by the Committee to have been guilty of disgraceful conduct in a professional respect, or if the Committee is satisfied that a name has been fraudulently entered in the register. Alternatively, the Committee may direct that, rather than erasure, the practitioner's name should be suspended.

Where a name has been erased for disciplinary reasons, that name may not be restored to the register unless, on application, the Disciplinary Committee so directs. Applications to the Committee for restoration of a name or removal of a suspension may not be made in less than ten months following the erasure, suspension or previous application.

Professional Discipline

The Council of the Royal College of Veterinary Surgeons is responsible for discipline in the veterinary profession. Section 16(1) of the Veterinary Surgeons Act provides that the removal or suspension of a veterinarian's name from the register, including the supplementary register, is a disciplinary sanction available to the Council.

Ground for Disciplinary Action

Section 16(1) provides that action may be taken against a registered person, including a person on the supplementary register, in three circumstances:

1. Where that person is convicted of a criminal offence in the United Kingdom or elsewhere which in the opinion of the Disciplinary Committee makes him unfit to practise veterinary surgery.
2. Where that person is judged by the Disciplinary Committee to have been guilty of disgraceful conduct in any professional matter. This conduct must be such as to bring the profession into disgrace and is not limited to moral turpitude.
3. Where the Disciplinary Committee is satisfied that a name has been fraudulently entered on the register.

In the first two instances, the sanction may be erasure or suspension; in the third case, only erasure is possible.

Disciplinary Procedure

Preliminary Investigation Committee Section 15(1) of the Veterinary Surgeons Act requires the Council to set up a Preliminary Investigation Committee whose duty it is to hold a preliminary investigation into every alleged disciplinary case and to decide whether to refer it to the Disciplinary Committee. The constitution of the Preliminary Investigation Committee is determined by part 1 of the second schedule to the Act. It consists of the president and vice-president of the College and three other Council members elected among themselves by the Council. Their term of office is determined by the Council, and a quorum for a meeting is three, of whom at least one must be the president or a vice-president of the College.

Disciplinary Committee Section 15(2) confirms the continuation of the Disciplinary Committee, set up under a previous Act. The function of the Committee is to consider and determine any disciplinary case referred to it by the Preliminary Proceedings Committee, and also applications for the restoration of a name to the register or the removal of a suspension. The constitution of this Committee is determined by part 1 of the second schedule to the Act. The Committee consists of a chairman and eleven members, all being members of the Council elected from among themselves. At least six members must be elected Council members and at least one member appointed to the Council by the Privy Council. Members of the Preliminary Investigation Committee may not be members of the Disciplinary Committee for one and the same case. Where the Disciplinary Committee is considering a case relating to someone on the supplementary register, four persons, appointed by the Ministers, who are in that register are to be added to the Disciplinary Committee. The 'Ministers' are the Minister of Agriculture, Fisheries and Food, the Secretary of State for Scotland, the Secretary of State for Wales and the Minister of Agriculture for Northern Ireland, acting jointly. A quorum is five, at least one of whom must be an elected member of the Council, but, in the case of a supplementary register case, the quorum is seven, of whom at least one must be an elected Council member with two people registered on the supplementary register.

Proceedings for Removal or Suspension

Procedure before the Disciplinary Committee is similar to that in a court of law with evidence being presented, on one hand against the registered person and, on the other, in his defence. Part 2 of the second schedule to the Veterinary Surgeons Act and the Veterinary Surgeons and Veterinary Practitioners (Disciplinary Committee) (Procedure and Evidence) Rules Order of Council 1967 (SI 1967 No. 659) determine the procedure before the Committee. The

Committee may administer oaths, and any party to the proceedings may sue out writs of subpoena ad testificandum and duces tecum in order to ensure the appearance of a witness or presentation of a document. Proceedings are held in public and any party may be represented by counsel or a solicitor.

At all disciplinary cases there must be a legal assessor present to advise the Committee on matters of law. The assessor, who is a barrister or solicitor of not less than ten years' standing, is appointed by the Council, and his duties are determined by the Veterinary Surgeons (Disciplinary Proceedings) Legal Assessor Rules 1967 (SI 1967 No. 684). These rules are made by the Lord Chancellor.

Appeals

Where the Disciplinary Committee directs that a name is to be erased or suspended, section 16(2) requires that notice of this action is served on the veterinary surgeon concerned. Section 17(3) provides that such a notice takes effect at the end of the time available for appeal or, if an appeal is made, when that appeal is withdrawn, struck out or dismissed. Section 17 permits a registered veterinarian to appeal against an erasure or suspension notice within 28 days of the date of service of the notice. Appeal is to the Privy Council. Procedure is determined by the Judicial Committee (Veterinary Surgeons Rules) Order 1967 (SI 1967 No. 1150) and the Council of the College may appear as a respondent. Whether it does so or not it is deemed to be a party to the proceedings for the purpose of costs (section 17(2)).

Restoration to the Register

Section 18(1) and (2) provides that where a practitioner's name has been erased or suspended that name may not be restored except on the direction of the Disciplinary Committee. Application for restoration to the register may not be made within ten months of the date of removal or suspension or within ten months of the last application.

Controls on the Practice of Veterinary Surgery

Restriction of the Practice of Veterinary Surgery

Section 19 of the 1966 Act limits the practice of veterinary surgery to individuals registered in the register of veterinary surgery or the supplementary veterinary register. It is an offence, liable on summary conviction to a fine not exceeding £100 or on indictment to any fine, for an unregistered person to practise, hold himself out as practising, or being prepared to practise, veterinary surgery. Summary proceedings for such an offence may be commenced at any time within one year from the offence (section 19(2)).

Exceptions
To satisfy a variety of situations in which it is considered expedient to permit an unregistered person to practise veterinary surgery (albeit to a limited extent), section 19 and the third schedule to the Act provide a variety of exceptions. These are:

Students Section 19(3) permits the council of the Royal College of Veterinary Surgeons to make regulations permitting students to carry out those veterinary tasks, treatments or operations prescribed by the regulations, subject to the prescribed conditions. The present regulations are in the Veterinary Surgeons (Practice by Students) Regulations Order of Council 1981 SI 1981 No. 988.

Animal Experimentation Section 19(4)(a) provides that, if they are authorised under the Animals (Scientific Procedures) Act 1986 animal experiments may be carried out by unregistered individuals.

Schedule 3 Exceptions Section 19(4)(b) provides that those veterinary procedures specified in part I of the third schedule to the Act and not excluded by part II of the same schedule may be carried out by unregistered individuals to the extent specified. The main exceptions in part I of schedule 3 are: treatment given to an animal by its owner or a member of the owner's household or someone in his employment; anything, except a laparotomy, done to an agricultural animal (as defined in the Agriculture Act 1947) otherwise than for reward by its owner or someone employed for the purpose; emergency first-aid to save life or relieve pain; the performing by a person over 18 of castration or caponising, tailing of lamb, docking of a dog's tail before its eyes are open or amputation of the dew claws of a dog before its eyes are open. However, a person of 17 undergoing training in animal husbandry may perform these operations if under instruction by a registered veterinarian or at a recognised institution.

Notwithstanding part I of the third schedule, part II (which is found in the Veterinary Surgeons Act 1966 (schedule 3 Amendment) Order 1982 No. 1885) provides that unqualified persons may not castrate any horse, pony, ass or mule, a bull, boar or goat which has reached two months, a ram of three months, or a cat or dog of six months. Nor may unqualified persons remove (except in an emergency) any part of a deer's antlers while in velvet, desnood a turkey of 21 days, decomb any poultry of 72 hours, cut the toes of domestic fowl or turkey of 72 hours, vasectomise or carry out electro-ejaculation on any animal or bird kept for the production of food, wool, skin or fur, remove supernumary teats in a calf of three months, or de-horn or disbud a sheep or goat (except trimming the insensitive lip of an ingrowing horn to prevent pain or distress).

Medical Practitioners A registered medical practitioner may operate on an animal to remove an organ or tissue for the treatment of human beings (section 19(4)(c)) or may carry out any treatment, test or operation at the request of someone registered in the register of veterinary surgeons or the supplementary register (section 19(4)(d)). Section 19(4)(d) also applies to a registered dentist.

Ministerial Order Section 19(4)(e) permits the Ministers, after consultation with the Council of the College, to make an order allowing the performance of specified minor tests, treatments or operations. Such orders have been made to permit, for example, the taking of blood from cattle to diagnose brucellosis (see, for instance, the Veterinary Surgeons (Blood Sampling) SI 1983 Order 1983 No. 6).

Prohibition of Descriptions Implying Veterinary Qualification

Section 20 creates three broad offences in connection with implying that an unregistered person is in fact qualified. Section 20(1) makes it an offence for an unregistered person to use the title "veterinary surgeon" or any name, title etc. implying that he is registered. Section 20(2) makes it an offence for someone not registered in the register or the supplementary register to style himself "veterinary practitioner" or by any name etc. imply he is a practitioner or qualified to practise veterinary surgery. Section 20(3) makes it an offence in connection with a business carried on by him to use a description implying that he or any person acting for that business has veterinary qualifications which he does not have. All of these offences are liable on summary conviction to a fine not exceeding £100 or on indictment to any fine. Where proceedings are brought against a corporate body they may also be brought against any director, manager, secretary or similar officer who has consented or connived at the offence. Summary proceedings may be begun at any time within one year of the offence.

Jury Service

Section 24 exempts from jury service people registered in the register of veterinary surgeons or the supplementary register and who are actually practising veterinary surgery.

Control of Veterinary Education

Recognition of United Kingdom Universities

Section 3 of the Veterinary Surgeons Act 1966 empowers the Privy Council, in consultation with the Council of the Royal College of Veterinary Surgeons, to issue a recognition order in respect of courses of training and examinations at United Kingdom universities. Before recognising them, the Privy Council must be satisfied, after consultation with the Council of the College, that a university's courses of study and its examinations are such as to guarantee that the holder of the degree will have acquired the knowledge and skills needed for the efficient practice of veterinary surgery. Veterinary degrees of the following universities are recognised: Cambridge (SI 1953 No. 404), London (SI 1952 No. 959), Edinburgh (SI 1952 No. 1602), Glasgow (SI 1951 No. 571), Bristol (SI 1950 No. 1301) and Liverpool (SI 1950 No. 1110).

To control the standards of these universities, section 3(4) gives the Privy Council the power to revoke or suspend (also by Order in Council) a recognition order. If at any time it appears to the Council of the College that the course of study and examination at a recognised university no longer justifies continuance of the order it may make representations to that effect to the Privy Council (section 3(2)). The Privy Council must inform the university of the concern to allow it to object or make whatever observations it wishes. The Privy Council must allow at least two months for the university to comment and must then decide whether to revoke or suspend the recognition order. Section 3(5) gives the Privy Council the power to revoke a suspension order.

Examination by the College
Section 4 empowers the Privy Council, after consultation with the Council of the College, to direct the College to hold examinations in veterinary surgery for students who have attended a course of training at a United Kingdom university for which there is no recognition order in force. Students passing such examinations are entitled to be registered and so become a member of the College (section 4(1)). However, if a recognition order comes into force for that university this arrangement will cease to have effect, and it may also be revoked by the Privy Council after consultation with the College and the university.

Supervision of Training
Section 5 gives the Council of the College various powers designed to ensure that courses of training and the standard of proficiency met are sufficient to guarantee the acquisition of that knowledge and skill needed for the efficient practice of veterinary surgery. It also imposes on the Council a duty to use these powers for this purpose (section 5(1)). Three broad powers are given to the Council: to visit universities, to review examinations and to demand information.

Visitors The Council may appoint people to visit universities for which a recognition order exists or is proposed or which trains students who take the College examinations. The visitors are to report on the courses of study, staffing, accommodation, equipment available and other arrangements and facilities for training.

Examinations
The Council may appoint people to attend examinations in any aspects of veterinary surgery at any university where a recognition order exists or is proposed. They must report on the sufficiency of the examinations.

Information The Council may request any university for which a recognition order exists or which trains students for College examination to supply information about courses of study or, where appropriate, examinations.

Copies of the reports of visitors or attendees at examinations must be sent by the Council to the university concerned. The university has two months to make what comments or objections it wishes. As soon as practicable, the Council must send to the Privy Council a copy of the report and the university's comments.

Bibliography and Further Reading

Medicine

Barbers and Barber Surgeons of London
Dobson, J.
Blackwell Scientific Publications. Oxford 1979

A History of Medicine
Guthrie, D.
Thomas Nelson and Son Ltd. London

Dentistry

A Short History of Dentistry
Lindsay, L.
London 1933

A History of Dentistry
Lufkin, A. W.
London 1948

Pharmacy

Laws and Ethics for the Practising Pharmacist
Stevens, C. C.
Leonard Hill. London 1969

The Pharmaceutical Society of Great Britain Calendar 1983-84
London 1984

Pharmacy Law and Ethics
Dale, J. R. and Appelbe, G. E.
The Pharmaceutical Press. London 3rd Edition 1983

Nursing

A History of the Nursing Profession
Abel-Smith, B.
London 1960

A Short History of Nursing
Bett, W. R.
London 1960

A General History of Nursing
Seymer, L. R.
London 1954

General

Chambers Encyclopaedia
ILSC Ltd. London 1973

British Qualifications
Ed. Priestly, B.
Kogan Page. 10th Edition London 1979

Laws on Poisons, Medicines and Related Substances
Bayliss, P. F. C.
Ravenswood Publications Ltd., Beckenham. 2nd Edition 1986

Law Relating to Hospitals and Kindred Institutions
Speller, S. R.
K. K. Lewis. London 1978

Dictionary of Medical Ethics
Ed. Duncan, A. S., G. R. and Welbourn, R. B.
Darton, Longman and Todd. London 1981

A Short History of Medicine
Singer. Underwood

The English Legal System
Cross, G. and Hall, G. D. G.
Butterworths. London 1964

Historical Foundations of the Common Law
Milsom, S. F. C.
Butterworths. London 1969

Constitutional Law
Wade, E. C. S. and Bradley, A. W.
Longmans. London 1968

Health Services Law
Finch, John D.
Sweet and Maxwell 1981

Aspects of Law affecting the Paramedical Professions
Finch, John D.
Faber and Faber 1984

Index

INVICTA